New Deal Radio

New Deal Radio

The Educational Radio Project

DAVID GOODMAN AND JOY ELIZABETH HAYES

Rutgers University Press

New Brunswick, Camden, and Newark, New Jersey, and London

Library of Congress Cataloging-in-Publication Data

Names: Goodman, David, 1957– author. | Hayes, Joy Elizabeth, 1966– author.
Title: New Deal radio : the educational radio project / David Goodman,
    Joy Elizabeth Hayes.
Description: First Edition. | New Brunswick, NJ : Rutgers University Press, [2022] |
    Includes bibliographical references and index.
Identifiers: LCCN 2021035461 | ISBN 9781978817463 (Paperback : acid-free paper) |
    ISBN 9781978817470 (Cloth : acid-free paper) | ISBN 9781978817487 (ePub) |
    ISBN 9781978817494 (mobi) | ISBN 9781978817500 (PDF)
Subjects: LCSH: Radio in education—United States—History. |
    Educational broadcasting—United States—History. |
    Public broadcasting—Political aspects—United States—History. |
    New Deal, 1933–1939.
Classification: LCC LB1044.5 .G66 2022 | DDC 371.33/31—dc23/eng/20220106
LC record available at https://lccn.loc.gov/2021035461

A British Cataloging-in-Publication record for this book is available from the British Library.

References to internet websites (URLs) were accurate at the time of writing. Neither the author
nor Rutgers University Press is responsible for URLs that may have expired or changed since
the manuscript was prepared.

♾ The paper used in this publication meets the requirements of the American National
Standard for Information Sciences—Permanence of Paper for Printed Library Materials,
ANSI Z39.48-1992.

www.rutgersuniversitypress.org

Manufactured in the United States of America

Contents

Illustrations

Figures

Tables

New Deal Radio

Introduction

A *Washington Post* reporter in early 1937 enthused over watching government radio being made: "To watch the Government program builders at work is to see master craftsmen engaged in an extremely complicated technique. They labor, yet they labor with a sparkle of inspiration and public pride in their eyes."[1] But who now remembers American government radio? This is a book about it and about a New Deal cultural program that has not had the attention it deserves. Much has been written about the historical and cultural programs of the Works Progress Administration (WPA)—the Federal Theatre Project, the Federal Music Project, the Federal Art Project, the WPA Guides series, and so on—but the U.S. Office of Education's Educational Radio Project is less known. Although some of its individual radio series have been remembered and studied, the Project as a whole has not yet found its biographer. That seemed to us a pity. The Project made some fascinating radio shows. It illustrated the possibilities of a mode of production combining public service broadcasting values and show business professionalism, and—importantly to us as historians— the whole thing was well documented, in correspondence and scripts and memos, and neatly boxed up at the National Archives in College Park, Maryland. There was also something about the form that intrigued us—a curious mix of documentary and drama (even melodrama). The earnest messages about citizenship and democracy, the extraordinarily fluent traversing of American history and relating of past to present grabbed our attention—but how to situate and explain these radio shows as creative cultural artifacts of their turbulent time? We found out a lot about the creators—men and women with diverse backgrounds and experiences—and became intrigued with some of the personal backstories. We discussed what to say about the politics of these shows—to emphasize the many ways they fall short of twenty-first-century standards of inclusivity and pluralism, or to wonder that government-sponsored mass media shows promoting tolerance, active citizenship, and friendship with Latin America and Latin Americans were made at all. Finally, we were taken by the fact that the Project represented a really important path not taken in American media history. What if such a hybrid model of educational broadcasting over commercial networks had been institutionalized during this formative period in U.S. broadcasting?

The fact that the United States did not develop a national public broadcaster in the interwar period, when most other Western nations did, has remained a central problem of U.S. broadcasting history. Many answers have been proffered. Was it because of greater general distrust of state involvement in broadcasting? Or a disbelief specifically in the distinction between a state broadcaster and an "independent" public broadcaster? Was it due to the strength of corporate broadcasting interests? Or the divisions between reformers? Historians have addressed these questions in a variety of ways.[2] But here we take another tack. Rather than ponder what might have been, we look at an aspect of what did happen. There *was* in fact a great deal of government involvement in broadcasting in the United States before 1945; local, state, and federal governments were each in different ways active in broadcasting. The "Why no American BBC?" (British Broadcasting Corporation) debate has had the unintended effect of shifting attention away from the government broadcasting that did occur in the United States and from the innovative public-private partnerships upon which it often rested.

In this book we set aside the rich traditions of state and municipal broadcasting to examine just one phase of the federal government's involvement in broadcasting during the New Deal period and the broadcasting of just one federal agency—the U.S. Office of Education's Educational Radio Project. Federal government broadcasting, mostly over commercial stations, was more extensive than is often remembered. Jeanette Sayre counted twenty-seven government agencies that were active broadcasters in 1936 and forty-two in 1940. Among the federal agencies on the air were the Department of Agriculture (most prominently through *The National Farm and Home Hour* [1928–1958] on National Broadcasting Company [NBC] stations) the National Park Service, the Commerce department, the WPA and the Federal Theatre Project (the Radio Division of which aired over fifty radio series and at its peak employed 190 people).[3] The Department of the Interior opened a radio studio in its Washington building in 1938 that was (publicity insisted) just for rehearsals: "to provide a sort of laboratory for preparation, rehearsal, and delivery to commercial networks of educational and informational programs."[4]

The Educational Radio Project involved cooperation between the federal government and the two big commercial radio networks: NBC and the

Columbia Broadcasting System (CBS). Its high-profile programs soon made it one of the most public and successful faces of government radio production in these years.[5] Some employees were based in the New York City production center; over the life of the Project they produced over a dozen radio series for national network broadcast.[6] Because most of the Project's funding came from the WPA relief program, it had to maintain a high ratio of relief workers on its staff—in 1936 there were eighty-five relief workers to nine nonrelief workers and six supervisors; by 1940 the ratio was nineteen to one.[7] The rotation of staff that entailed (there was an eighteen-month limit on WPA employment) complicated the work—nonetheless, at its peak the Project was producing three network broadcasts a day and boasting that it had received a million letters from listeners, fewer than 250 of which were critical.[8]

The Project represented then a significant government incursion into commercial broadcasting, but of a distinctively American kind. The shows *sounded* like commercial network shows—excited announcers, dramatic music, frequent use of dramatization, choruses of speaking or singing voices. The model was to cooperate with the commercial broadcasters, not to compete with them. The networks gave their staff, studios, and airtime, which was a considerable contribution—the Project estimated in 1940 that it had been given about $3.5 million worth of commercial airtime from radio networks (over $65 million in 2021 dollars).[9] Project organizers, in turn, aimed to produce content that met the needs of commercial broadcasters as well as educators.

Some series were recorded directly to electrical transcription disks for circulation to radio stations and educational institutions. Electrical transcriptions were high-quality recordings made on large acetate disks that were distributed for broadcast to local stations through independent marketers and network transcription services.[10] In chapter 6 we discuss, as one example, *Pleasantdale Folks*, a transcription series produced for the Social Security Board to increase understanding of the Social Security and welfare system. There were others—*Jobs for America* also for the Social Security Board, *Uncle Sam Calling* for the U.S. Census, and *Help Yourself to Health* for the U.S. Public Health Service.[11] In 1937 the Project opened a Script Exchange to circulate good educational radio scripts nationally—some written by Project staff, but also many submitted by other groups. Hundreds of scripts could be borrowed to be broadcast on local radio stations or played over loudspeaker systems within schools or acted out in classrooms or community organizations.[12] Project staff also ran Radio Workshops for teachers and directors of educational broadcasting, in Washington, D.C., and later at New York University, that covered everything from script writing to sound effects.

While New Deal supporters viewed these Project activities as innovative tools for promoting civic engagement among the nation's far-flung citizens, hostile critics perceived them simply as propaganda. We know that the New

Deal was immensely popular but that it also provoked fierce resistance. On one side, Project programs were seen to exemplify modern modes of citizenship education; on the other, they were perceived as particularly insidious examples of publicity for the kind of enlarged and enhanced government that conservatives abhorred.[13] A sympathetic journalist observed in 1936: "Broadcasting is one of Uncle Sam's specialties," allowing "hundreds of thousands of Americans—citizens who sit before loudspeakers to get official counsel on the solution of the thousand and one vicissitudes which beset daily living."[14] Less sympathetically, *Variety* complained, "Government use of radio is mounting to the point where the broadcast industry earmarks large chunk of its time for Federal programs. Bureaus having no money set aside for purchase of radio time, still manage to broadcast by calling programs educational."[15] The networks played along to show that they took their public service responsibilities seriously and to fend off a more serious federal intervention, perhaps even an American BBC. By 1940, however, a conservative campaign in Congress— *Variety* called it a "partisan rampage"—gained enough momentum to eliminate most funding for New Deal radio projects.[16]

Knowledge of this large-scale venture in government-industry cooperation is valuable for understanding the history of radio in the 1930s, but it is also important for making sense of the longer story of public broadcasting in the United States. The Educational Radio Project was a direct product of the struggle over the Federal Communication Act of 1934, and it became both an institutional scaffolding for public broadcasting and a testing ground for educational radio content. Only recently have historians begun to investigate the genealogy of public broadcasting in the United States beyond the more proximate origins of National Public Radio (NPR) and the Public Broadcasting Service (PBS). The story of the Educational Radio Project offers a direct line of connection—and indeed something of a missing link—between the efforts of educational broadcasters to shape radio in the late 1920s and early 1930s and the establishment of station set-asides in FM radio and television that formed the infrastructure for later public broadcasting.[17]

U.S. commissioner of education John Studebaker, who chaired the Federal Communications Commission's (FCC's) Federal Radio Education Commission (FREC) and oversaw the Educational Radio Project, was an advocate of public use of the airwaves. Reflecting on the Radio Project forty years on, its former director William Dow Boutwell recalled that Studebaker used examples of successful Project programs—such as the long-running *The World Is Yours* developed with the Smithsonian Institution—to argue in favor of public broadcasting before the FCC. "His testimony certainly influenced the decision to reserve 10 percent of FM frequencies for non-profit public institutions," Boutwell remembered, and "that precedent carried over to the later allocation of television frequencies for public use."[18] We leave the detailed institutional exploration of the genealogy of public radio to others—our aim here is to investigate the nature of cooperation between the Radio Project and commercial networks, evaluate the kinds of educational programs this partnership produced, and assess the experiments it undertook. We examine Radio Project programs to learn how educational goals (in the broadest sense) were encoded into broadcasting practices and genres at this formative moment in the development of American broadcasting. We also (where possible) evaluate listener responses to these programs and what they indicate about a latent audience for the kinds of educational and cultural content that, decades later, would be provided by public broadcasting.

The Educational Radio Project on the Air

To date there has been no scholarly attempt to examine the Educational Radio Project as a whole, although a few Project radio series have been written about individually.[19] Yet contextualizing the different series as part of a unified project about radio, democracy, and citizenship is crucial to understanding them. Over the five-year life of the Project, there was a shift from shorter, informational, and anthological programs to longer, more ambitious, and more thematically unified series. The series that went on the air between 1934 and 1936 contained shows that covered a potpourri of topics and included dramatized anthology, news, quiz, and club-style programs (table 1). Most of these early series had fifteen-minute programs, with the exception of *The World Is Yours*, episodes of which ran for thirty minutes.

Although these early programs deserve closer investigation, we focus in this book on some of the thematic series broadcast between 1937 and 1940, including both dramatized documentaries and fictional series (table 2). These programs used radio not only to popularize particular New Deal policies or promote educational innovations but also, we argue in this book, to *explain* and *dramatize the idea of government itself* as a positive and protective presence in the lives of the American people. "Dramatization of the real" was at the heart of early twentieth-century documentary, and this concept aptly describes those Radio Project programs that relied on in-studio reenactments, sound effects, narration, and strong musical elements to dramatize historical, cultural, and current events.[20] Before the late 1940s, most radio documentaries did not incorporate recorded actuality (sounds from the field). This was due in part to technological constraints and limits on recorded programming but also crucially, we argue, because radio producers believed that dramatization was the *best* way to hold an audience's attention, the essential prerequisite for education by radio.[21]

As we explore in the next chapter, while broadcasting genres were in formation and in flux during the 1930s, and neither *documentary* nor *dramatized*

Table 1
Educational Radio Project Early Programs: Dramatized Anthology, News, Quiz, and Club Shows

Radio Project program	Years & episodes	Network & participants	Description
Education in the News	1934–1938 154 episodes	Invited by NBC (started prior to Radio Project)	Dramatizations of educational news.
Answer Me This	1936–1937 47 episodes	NBC	Social science question and answer with dramatizations.
Have You Heard	1936–1937 73 episodes	CBS	Natural science question and answer with dramatizations.
Safety Musketeers	1936 25 episodes	CBS	"Child club" approach to safety education.
The World Is Yours	1936–1941 303 episodes	NBC Smithsonian	Dramatizations based on Smithsonian exhibits.
Treasures Next Door	1936–1937 25 episodes	CBS	Famous literature dramatized up to the climax; listener must read the book to learn the outcome.

SOURCE: Adapted from Sayre, *Radiobroadcasting Activities of Federal Agencies*, 81–83, and Sobers, "Preserving the World Is Yours."

documentary was used consistently to describe radio formats, American radio had already developed commercially successful models of dramatized documentary upon which the Project creatives could draw. Only relatively recently have radio historians begun to recognize that programs claiming to dramatize real events—such as dramatized news and true crime dramas—were staples of U.S. network radio.[22] Looking ahead in time, Radio Project series shared similarities with, but also differed significantly from, the sustained feature-length "docudramas" made for television from the 1960s. Their use of dramatized documentary technique was often fleeting and episodic—but consistent enough that we think that dramatized documentary needs to be recognized and analyzed as one of the core innovations of the Project. It was, after all, a technique in many ways perfectly suited to bridging the worlds of education and entertainment, which was the core mission of the Project.

Examining the later programs produced by the Project, it is possible to trace an evolution in program style from dramatic plays introduced and concluded with interpretive narration to more complex combinations of drama, narration, speech, and music. Jeanette Sayre put it well: "The techniques employed by the Project became increasingly complex, with the last few programs being melanges

Table 2
Educational Radio Project Later Programs: Dramatized Documentary, Sitcom, and Soap Opera

Radio Project program	Years & episodes	Network & participants	Description
Let Freedom Ring!	1937 13 episodes	CBS	Dramatizations of constitutional history.
Brave New World	1937–1938 26 episodes	CBS Pan American Union	Dramatizations of Latin American history and U.S.–Latin American relations.
Americans All, Immigrants All	1938–1939 26 episodes	CBS Service Bureau for Intercultural Education	Dramatizations of ethnic group contributions to American society.
Wings for the Martins	1938–1939 26 episodes	NBC National Association of Parents & Teachers	Situation comedy; benefits of modern educational practices for families and children.
Democracy in Action	1939–1940 38 episodes	CBS	Dramatizations of government efforts to address social problems.
Pleasantdale Folks	1939–1940 13 episodes	Transcription NBC Social Security Board	Soap opera; family and community benefits of social security and welfare.
Gallant American Women	1939–1940 18 episodes	NBC	Dramatizations of famous American women in history.
Freedom's People	1941–1942 9 episodes	NBC (produced after Radio Project defunded)	Dramatizations of achievements of Black Americans.

SOURCE: Adapted from Sayre, *Radiobroadcasting Activities of Federal Agencies*, 81–83.

of narrative, drama, choral and orchestral music, the use of many voices to weave the program together."[23] *Let Freedom Ring!*, airing in 1937, presented a dramatized history of the Constitution in thirty-minute episodes as part of the celebration of the sesquicentennial of the Bill of Rights. The program was made up of a series of plays that brought political leaders and constitutional debates to life for the listener. Similarly, each episode of *Brave New World* (1937–1938) presented a play dramatizing real events in Latin American history and U.S.–Latin American relations. In *Brave New World*, however, documentary plays were often accompanied by fictional sketches designed to engage the listener and highlight the contemporary lessons to be learned from the past. *Americans All, Immigrants All* (1938–1939) used lively music and narration to weave together shorter dramatic vignettes that presented the contributions of different ethnic groups to American history and life. The narrator served as an entertaining interpreter and guide, as the listener moved through an audio panorama of historical dramatizations. Finally, *Democracy in Action* (1939–1940) combined historical dramatizations with fictional (often polemical) sketches to bring to life dynamic and contrasting views of the role of government in American life. Such complex interweavings of dramatized documentary and fiction could also be heard in other late Project shows such as *Gallant American Women* (1939–1940) and *Freedom's People* (1941–1942), which we do not examine in detail here.

In addition to the dramatized documentary programs, we examine two fictional shows: *Wings for the Martins*, a situation comedy dealing with parent education, and *Pleasantdale Folks*, a soap opera produced for the Social Security Board to popularize and explain Social Security and welfare expansion. These programs provide important points of contrast with dramatized documentary in terms of their modes of communicating New Deal policies and their strategies for engaging audiences. Whereas dramatized documentaries often approached citizenship education as a national project of promoting public roles and values, the Project's fictional series focused on more private practices of citizenship as learning and socialization within families and communities. These fictional series also offer insights into the development of commercial program genres, most of which were still in formation during the 1930s. In the case of the emerging sitcom genre, we argue that the model of the family represented by *Wings for the Martins*, and the parent education movement more broadly, anticipated the rise of the nuclear-family-centered domestic sitcom. *Pleasantdale Folks* provides a different perspective on the white nuclear family encoded into New Deal social security and welfare provisions. It also shows how New Deal innovations were presented as being supportive of, and continuous with, long-standing American traditions of family and community.

The People of the Educational Radio Project

Throughout its life from 1936 to 1940, the Project was staffed by many energetic individuals at several different career stages, including an unusually large contingent from the Midwest—a productive hub of enthusiasm for both education and radio. Middle-aged men of European descent at the height of their careers held most of the senior positions at the Project. Younger men—many just out of college—held leadership roles in radio production or worked as writers, researchers, or staff.[24] We also encountered significant numbers of women involved in the Project's creative and investigative work and realized the need to consider first-wave feminism and its aftermath as an essential context of the Project. This is true thematically—Emily Westkaemper has told the story of the late Project series *Gallant American Women* and how its "feminist narratives" were shaped by consultant Mary Beard, program supervisor Eva von Baur Hansl, and scriptwriter Jane Ashman.[25] But it was true in a broader sense too, as part of the reason that so many women were actively involved in the creative work behind Project shows. Our somewhat late realization of the active and important role of women at the Project is ironic given that the ground we were exploring had already been staked out by a contemporary of these women, Jeanette Sayre (Smith), the 1935 Wellesley graduate who wrote the comprehensive 1941 study of the flowering of government broadcasting under the New Deal, *An Analysis of the Radiobroadcasting Activities of Federal Agencies*. Sayre worked with major figures in the emerging field of communication studies—Hadley Cantril at Princeton in the 1930s, Carl J. Friedrich at Harvard in the 1940s, and Paul Lazarsfeld at Columbia in the 1950s—and yet she is not well remembered in the history of communication research.[26] While we describe the men who directed and shaped the Educational Radio Project and its output, we also thus draw attention to the unsung women who labored at every level of the agency and influenced its educational goals and practices.

We begin, however, with the leaders of the Office and Project. Born in 1887 near McGregor, Iowa, on the western bank of the Mississippi River, U.S. commissioner of education John Ward Studebaker was one of five men who guided the Project. The 1900 census found his family in Toledo, Iowa, in the center of the state, where his father was a farmer. John lost his right eye in an accident at age twelve; he paid his way through Leander Clark College in Toledo by working as a bricklayer. In 1914 he became assistant superintendent of schools in Des Moines, Iowa; after earning a master's degree at Columbia University in 1920, he was promoted to schools superintendent in Des Moines. In 1933 the Carnegie Corporation awarded $120,000 (over $2.4 million in 2021 dollars) to Des Moines for a five-year adult education experiment with discussion forums. Studebaker was appointed U.S. commissioner of education the following year and always foregrounded his belief that the maintenance and indeed improvement of democracy had to be a central goal of American education. He took the idea of a forum program for adults to Washington and inaugurated the Federal Forum Project in 1936. Studebaker was a New Dealer, and his private correspondence with Franklin Roosevelt shows the extent of his devotion to the cause—"Thank God that you live and lead!" he wrote to Roosevelt in response to the president's September 1938 letter to Hitler seeking a peaceful outcome of the Czech crisis.[27] The Educational Radio Project reflected Studebaker's belief that education of the American people for and about democracy was an urgent task and an essential tool for fighting dictatorship.[28]

Director William Dow "Bill" Boutwell was born in 1900 in Waukegan, Illinois. His father was a traveling salesperson and the family home was, coincidentally, just a third of a mile from the house where future radio star Jack Benny, six years older than Boutwell, was growing up. Boutwell studied at the University of Illinois in Urbana, majoring in journalism. After graduation he worked as an editor in Washington, D.C.—with the Post Office Department, then with the National Geographic Society. In 1930 he was appointed editor in chief at the U.S. Office of Education, responsible for its monthly journal, *School Life*, and also from April 1933 for the NBC radio series *Education in the News*.[29] By the time the Educational Radio Project began in 1936, Boutwell was an experienced educational administrator and editor and also closely attuned to the practices of commercial broadcasting. Appointed during the Hoover administration, he sometimes had more pragmatic, less idealistic views than the subsequent New Deal appointees to the Project but he clearly believed in the core philosophy of the Project—that effective use of mass media for education required applying the "techniques of commercial radio to the problem of education on the air," combining the knowledge and goals of educators with the showmanship and audiences of the big broadcasters.[30]

Chester S. Williams was born in 1907 in Minneapolis, Minnesota, where his father was a carpenter. The family moved to Los Angeles when Chester was a child, and he went on to study at the University of California, Los Angeles (UCLA), where he developed strong internationalist interests. In 1928 he was chosen in a national competition of college students to attend a World's Peace conference in the Netherlands. He worked in fourteen countries between 1928 and 1929 as representative of the international Convention des Etudiants organization, including almost a year in China. He was executive secretary for the National Student Federation of America (NSFA) in 1930–1931. Williams met Edward R. Murrow at Stanford in 1929 and by his own account "had a hand" in getting Murrow elected as president of NSFA.[31] As a UCLA student, Williams was active in student journalism on free speech issues, concerned, for example, about communists being banned from speaking on campus; he was a Norman Thomas socialist in these years. In 1934, after Murrow recommended him to Studebaker, he was appointed assistant to the U.S. commissioner of education, working on the Federal Forum Project and also on the Educational Radio Project.

Philip H. Cohen (figure 1) was born in 1911 in Honolulu. His father was a career army officer. Cohen grew up in several military posts, including Panama and Sandy Hook, New Jersey; he graduated from Harvard in 1932, having excelled at debate. He worked as educational adviser at a Civilian Conservation Corps (CCC) camp in Sheffield, Pennsylvania. From 1936, at only twenty-five years of age, he became a crucial figure at the Educational Radio Project, producing national network shows and leading student productions at the Radio Workshops.

Rudolf R. Schramm was a composer, conductor, and arranger who wrote original musical scores for almost all Radio Project shows. Born in 1902 in

FIGURE 1 Educational Radio Project producer Philip H. Cohen (seated left) looks over scripts with other production staff at NBC Studios in New York. (National Archives photo no. 12-E-32-948. "Radio Division," Radio Project-WPA Photographs, 12-E-32, Box 39, RG 12 Office of Education, Still Picture Branch, National Archives, College Park, Maryland.)

Germany, he studied at the universities of Leipzig and Breslau, then migrated to the United States in 1922. He had a reputation for hard work, continuing to play piano accordion at a local restaurant each noon and at a nightclub some evenings and to teach sixteen pupils in piano accordion, while working to tight deadlines at the Project.[32] Over his career, Schramm was music director for more than 15,000 network radio programs and composed eighty-six film scores. His film work included the score for the 1947 release of Robert J. Flaherty's 1922 documentary classic, *Nanook of the North*.[33] Music was very important in all the Project series, and we examine the distinctive use of instrumental and choral music in particular programs.

Many women—all of European descent, from poor, rural backgrounds as well as upper-middle-class urban families—also played significant roles at the

Project. They used expanded access to education, hard work, and exceptional achievement as paths to public and professional success. In some cases, they may have been drawn to Washington, D.C., to participate in the somewhat-enhanced public life for women during the New Deal.[34] While we discuss these women in the chapters that follow, here we offer a brief overview of the group.

There were many women among the WPA relief workers who contributed to the Project as singers, musicians, actors, and office workers. The women who worked directly for the Project were primarily educators, advisers, or writers. Although men dominated the creative production process, from directing to producing and working directly with the commercial networks, women made significant writing contributions. Most of the women writers—including Jane Ashman, Pauline Gibson (Gilsdorf), and Selma Goldstone (Hirsh)—were recent college graduates in their twenties.[35] Laura Vitray, in contrast, was a woman in her forties who had had a successful career as a journalist, editor, and author before joining the Project, including becoming the first woman in the United States to hold a city editorship of a major metropolitan daily newspaper.[36] On the whole, however, the women writers tended to be younger and from the New York and New Jersey area (with the exception of Ashman, who was from Illinois). While some young male college graduates moved into management positions on the Project, the women remained researchers, writers, and fact checkers.

Women were also well represented on the special advisory committees that supervised program production. Most of these women had doctorates or master's degrees, and many were born in the Midwest and West, perhaps reflecting the stronger traditions of gender equality in those regions. Many shared first-wave feminist values of gender, racial and ethnic equality, and internationalism and pacifism, and these values found their way into Radio Project productions such as *Brave New World*, *Gallant American Women*, and *Americans All, Immigrants All*. Many of these women fought actively for women's rights and found their careers limited by sexism. Compared to the writers, they tended to be at the height of their careers and ranged in age from their thirties through their sixties. Perhaps the best known is Rachel Davis DuBois, a specialist in intercultural education, who came up with the concept for *Americans All, Immigrants All*, supervised the research, and acted as an adviser. DuBois, who lived to be 101 years old, contributed to the development of multicultural education and was an innovator in community conversation.[37] Other advisers included historians Mary Wilhelmine Williams and Mary Ritter Beard, feminist writer Eva vom Baur Hansl, immigration activist Edith Terry Bremer, political scientist Catheryn Seckler-Hudson, and international specialist Esther Delia Caukin Brunauer. Williams and Seckler-Hudson were education inno-

FIGURE 2 Assistant Commissioner of Education Bess Goodykoontz (left) edits Educational Radio Project scripts with fellow committee members in Washington, D.C. (National Archives photo no. 12-E-32-530. "Radio Checking Department," Radio Project-WPA Photographs, 12-E-32, Box 39, RG 12 Office of Education, Still Picture Branch, National Archives, College Park, Maryland.)

vators who published well-received studies of Latin American history and U.S. government, respectively. Williams's course, "History of the Woman Movement in the US," was one of the first college classes on women's history in the United States.[38] Brunauer worked for the American Association of University Women and joined the State Department in 1944. She was credited with outstanding service in helping organize United Nations Educational, Scientific and Cultural Organization (UNESCO) and became one of the first women appointed to minister rank at the State Department. Her stellar career was, however, cut short in 1951 when she was accused by Senator Joseph McCarthy of being a communist.[39]

Finally, the Office of Education staff included several women educational specialists who played a significant role in a number of Radio Project productions. These educators included Assistant Commissioner of Education Bess Goodykoontz (figure 2) and education specialists Effie Geneva Bathurst, Elise H. Martens, Helen K. Macintosh, and Mary Dabney Davis. Most of these women hailed from the West and Midwest, especially from the education-focused state of Iowa; starting as teachers, they slowly worked their way up to administrative positions from which they were able to gain college training and advanced degrees. By the time they entered government service in the 1920s and 1930s, they were often in their thirties or older. The majority of the women educators were in their forties and fifties when they worked on the Project. As we explore in more depth in chapter 4, these educators published extensively, organized national and international conferences, and generally worked tirelessly on educational policy, yet found their opportunities for advancement at the Office of Education to be limited. Although Director Boutwell's treatment of female staff members seemed fair and judicious in available interoffice correspondence, he privately commented to NBC's Franklin Dunham that he had been battling with the "crafty old cats" to produce commercial-quality radio productions and had made himself quite unpopular with the "old maid circle."[40]

Overall, our study offers insights into the experiences of a range of women who made educational, creative, and supervisory contributions to the Project. Women contributed in important ways not only to the flowering of the Radio Project but also to the New Deal experiment more broadly. Many of the social and cultural programs of the New Deal were influenced or directed by women, including Eleanor Roosevelt, Secretary of Labor Frances Perkins, WPA Administrator Ellen Woodward, and Federal Theatre Project Director Hallie Flanagan. According to Kate Dossett, women made up almost half of the WPA workforce and "the WPA served as a symbol of the New Deal's potential to challenge gender hierarchies."[41] Our examination of Project women offers new information on women's contributions to the New Deal and the limitations they faced.

The Educational Radio Project in Transnational Context

We contextualize the Educational Radio Project in relation to other nations that were experimenting with government-commercial cooperation in broadcasting. In countries with commercial broadcasting systems, or mixed commercial and public broadcasting systems, governments often worked with commercial broadcasters to produce educational and other government programming for national distribution. In the case of Argentina, Brazil, Mexico, and other Latin American nations, for example, commercial broadcasters were required to cooperate with the state in airing government programs. In the 1930s–1950s, this meant the same kind of direct cooperation between government agencies and commercial networks as is found in the activities of the Educational Radio Project. We take a brief look at the Mexican and Argentine cases in chapter 1.[42] In Latin America, scholars have argued that these cooperative arrangements were a quid pro quo for the development of oligopolistic commercial broadcasting networks.[43] This claim applies equally well to New Deal radio, although government activism was short-lived in the United States, whereas it continued throughout the twentieth century in much of Latin America.

We examine Radio Project dramatized documentaries as part of an international movement interested in documentary both as a way of representing reality using modern media and as a tool for authenticating, domesticating, and promoting state authority.[44] Documentaries in this mode relied on the authority of "real events" and "facts," while engaging listeners with dramatic narratives of national unity and purpose. Scholars have focused on documentary in the North Atlantic countries of the United States, the United Kingdom, and Canada, and research on the development of documentary broadcasting in other parts of the world (including Europe, Asia, Australasia, and Latin America) is still emerging. Thus, in chapter 1, we contextualize our study mainly within current research on the history of documentary in the North Atlantic world—particularly in relation to parallel developments in Britain, whose broadcasting practices stood in close but contrasting relationship to those of the United States.

Our study offers a detailed look at the American expression of this international movement in which education itself was being "reimagined as a universal institution" and government agencies came to view documentaries as essential tools for reinvigorating and directing mass democracies.[45] Zoë Druick argues that "the British documentary movement . . . was specifically organized to appropriate realism's more radical potential and apply the form to the liberal nation-building project" and that this spirit infused the Canadian National Film Board, which sought to use documentary "for education, nation building, and the governmental project of an administered welfare state."[46] Similarly, Radio Project series aimed to teach Americans about the New Deal governmental project, while working to reshape them as citizens in ways that made them more informed, open to the world, appreciative of and knowledgeable about the work of government, and available for continuing education and reeducation.

By situating the Radio Project within the international documentary movement, we show that the American system had more in common with public service broadcasting elsewhere than is normally recognized.[47] U.S. networks not only took the production of public-interest programming seriously but also operated as quasi-public broadcasters by donating hundreds of millions of dollars' worth of airtime to government agencies.[48] More than that, the BBC model and U.S. network broadcasting were "two sides of the same coin," argues Michele Hilmes, and "neither could have developed without the constant presence of the other." The Project was arguably part of the "constant circuit of influence and adaptation" that she identifies—for example, British ideas of documentary refracted through American understandings of entertainment and dramatization of the real.[49] As we will show, intellectual and personnel exchanges between the BBC and the Educational Radio Project were a part of this story.

Historical Background of the Educational Radio Project

The Office of Education gained a radio section from 1929 and a senior specialist in radio from 1930. This section's task was to investigate the use of radio in education, not to produce programs. The shift to the Office making programs happened only after the election of Franklin Roosevelt as president in 1932, the appointment of John Studebaker as commissioner of education in 1934, and the availability of federal funding through the WPA. The Educational Radio Project was announced, with four other Office of Education emergency projects, in December 1935. The Project was authorized to "present high-grade radio programs over radio facilities offered free to the Office of Education by commercial radio corporations for public service programs . . . using talent—actors, singers, directors and playwrights in the ranks of those on relief." The Office of Education received $75,000 (about $1.4 million in 2021 dollars) of emergency funds for the first half year of the Radio Project. In subsequent years, annual funding was $113,000 ($2.1 million) for 1936–1937 and 1937–1938, and $200,000 ($3.6 million) for 1938–1939, by which time there were 200 employees.[50]

The Radio Project was the result of a political compromise and hence always a second best for some of the more ardent radio reformers. It was neither a national public broadcaster nor the station set aside for noncommercial broadcasting that reformers had fought for in the late 1920s and early 1930s. The 1934 Wagner-Hatfield amendment to the Communications Act had unsuccessfully proposed a 25 percent set-aside of frequencies for educational and nonprofit broadcasters. Section 307c of the 1934 Communications Act as it finally passed required merely that the new FCC *study* the question of set-asides. After holding extensive hearings, the FCC recommended against set-asides and instead approved the formation of the FREC to "promote actual cooperative arrangements between educators and broadcasters on national, regional and local bases."[51] To battle-weary radio reformers, the 1935 formation of the FREC, dedicated only to studying educational broadcasting and fostering cooperation between existing broadcasters and educators, was both a meaningless sop and an insult to their accumulated wisdom and experience. Many of the radio and education reformers who thought they knew what was needed—a change to the rules that would mandate a certain proportion of educational content or stations on air—persisted in that belief after 1934. Others decided to work with the commercial broadcasters and go along with, or even embrace, the doctrine of "cooperation" between them. Thus, the reform movement split even further.

The FREC, however, led directly to the U.S. Office of Education's Educational Radio Project. John Studebaker claimed afterward that some of his personal stimulus for creating the Radio Project came from a six-week period in 1934 when, confined to the hospital, he listened to many educational radio broadcasts and became frustrated at educators' evident lack of experience in or aptitude for broadcasting.[52] The core idea of cooperation was that broadcasters and educators had much to learn from each other—educators needed the show business sensibility and large audiences of the commercial broadcasters, while the broadcasters needed the pedagogical guidance and factual knowledge of the educators. Broadcast historian Erik Barnouw observed that to some reformers it seemed that "educators had skillfully been shunted into busy-work." But he added: "This was true but not the whole truth. In winning their victory, networks and stations had made promises that were hostages. The very completeness of their victory put them glaringly in the spotlight."[53] They had to be seen to be active in educational and public service broadcasting: the Educational Radio Project was one result.

Revisionist radio historians painted a bleaker picture of cooperation in general, and the FREC in particular, than had Barnouw. Robert McChesney quoted Barnouw on busy-work, but not his qualification that this was "not the whole truth." The FREC, McChesney wrote, "never accomplished its mandate." He referred to its "seeming impotence" and concluded that "the late 1930s and early 1940s were far from halcyon days to many educators concerned with broadcasting."[54] Eugene Leach observed that in the long run, most cooperative partnerships "satisfied neither party and most disintegrated." Worse, while educational broadcasters were thus preoccupied with cooperative projects, "commercial operators were tightening their grip on the medium." He also concluded that cooperation served mainly to "delay the commitment of decent resources to non-commercial stations."[55]

A cautiously postrevisionist account of the FREC would note its productivity, not just its failings. While Leach argues that the doctrine of cooperation was in part a cloak for broadcaster self-interest, in that it "crucially undercut support for educational stations during the formative years of the industry," he nonetheless also observes that cooperation produced "some of the most adventurous public affairs and dramatic shows available to American listeners before World War II."[56] Both perspectives are important—playing along with cooperation was clearly in the networks' interest, in that it staved off more radical reform of broadcasting or the creation of a national public broadcaster. As John Studebaker pointed out in a 1936 speech, although the broadcasters were in business, the radio frequencies were "public property"—a reminder to the broadcasters that they had public obligations and were not free simply to maximize profits from the sale of airtime for commercial purposes.[57] But arguably, even in such compromised and compromising circumstances, creativity flourished and the best of the products of cooperation displayed the fruits of the marriage of effective presentation and educational content.

The activities of the Radio Education Project must also be situated within the context of larger, ongoing debates over the role of the federal government in education. A federal Department of Education was created in 1867, and the original act mandated its role as "collecting such statistics and facts as shall show the condition of education in the several States and Territories." When President Hoover renamed the agency the Office of Education in 1929, the *Kansas City Star* applauded the move: it thought the Office should restrict itself to "research and fact finding" because "there is widespread distrust of paternalism in the shape of federal school aid, and possible bureaucratic regulation with local school systems."[58] There was debate about federal subsidies for school education, stemming from a federal intervention to pay teachers in school districts unable to do so from 1933 to 1934.[59] University of Chicago president Robert Maynard Hutchins observed that "many intelligent and public-spirited" citizens "regard with horror" the possibility that the federal government might in some way participate in education. Yet without federal involvement, he warned, the United States risked becoming "not a nation, but an aggregation of communities."[60] Bills for the federal funding of local education, supported by the National Education Association, were introduced to Congress in 1936 and 1937, but they failed to pass.[61] The 1938 report of the President's Advisory Committee on Education stated that "unless the Federal Government participates in the support of the schools and related services, several millions of children in the United States will continue to be largely denied the educational opportunities that should be regarded as their birthright." The committee called for annual federal education grants to the states, rising to $200 million over five years and stipulating that, in states with segregated education, the money was to be shared equally between systems.[62]

Studebaker always maintained that federal subsidies need not mean full federal control, a possibility acknowledged by at least some southern newspaper editorial writers. But federal aid legislation again failed to pass through Congress in 1938 and 1939; by 1940 "federal aid to education was virtually dead."[63] The stated reason was fiscal restraint and budget trimming. But there remained an environment of overheated rhetoric about the dangers to democracy of federal involvement. Morse Cartwright, director of the Carnegie-funded American Association for Adult Education, warned that federal funding was bound to lead to federal control and that this posed particular dangers in adult education because the capacity to reach 27 million adults might become "a perfect support for any sorely tried political party in power seeking to perpetuate itself."[64] Major General Amos A. Fries's anti-communist Friends of the Public Schools of America claimed that federal aid to education was "the first step toward a dictator of education" and that the dictator would be the commissioner of education.[65] In the South, federal involvement in education always carried an implied threat to segregated education. Senator Josiah Bailey, from North Carolina, warned a constituent that federal funding would come with constitutional obligations to "provide equally for all groups, classes and individuals." On the other side, the National Association for the Advancement of

Colored People warned that the federal funding bill would need amendment to prevent southern states from spending all the federal money on white schools.[66]

We rehearse this background to make clear how contested the federal role was in education. Educational Radio Project staff members were always conscious of this political context. Their concern not to overstep the bounds of the Office's role was reflected in the radio program–making process we describe in this book. If arguments about ongoing federal funding for education went nowhere in this period, the ones about federal policy leadership in education fared only a little better. What began to shift, however, was the valence of pro-democracy education, as the world plunged into war against fascism. By 1940 the Office of Education was able to position some of its democratic education programs as part of the national defense effort, and hence as a necessary part of federal government activity. Even then, however, the climate of suspicion of government activism in education continued to shape the content of the Project's programs and the mode and extent of their funding.

Approach to Research and Analysis

Due in part to the Radio Project's efforts to make transcription recordings of its programs for distribution to radio stations, schools, and universities, audio recordings of a number of Project programs are available for listening and research. At least some recordings are available for all later series, and we made use of these audio records to evaluate the style, format, and sound of the programs, paying particular attention to the role of music. But because recordings are incomplete and difficult to access for some series, we also rely on printed scripts and production materials, interoffice memos discussing program production, listener letters where available, and news coverage of the Radio Project.

Using both program recordings and scripts, we examine the dialogue, characterization, and narration of the shows. In the case of dramatized documentaries, we pay attention to the substantive claims and arguments made through dialogue and narration, as well as the emotional context established by music and drama. In the case of fictional shows, where characters were more fully developed, we consider how identities were constructed in relation to the drama and the larger cultural context. We view Project programs as rich cultural texts that must be interpreted in relation to broader historical understandings of 1930s media and culture. Close readings of these texts offer insight into how Office of Education leaders approached mass education via the new medium of radio and how they translated New Deal policy goals into broadcast content.

The Radio Project's government-network partnership demonstrates the inextricable entangling of commercial and public goals in American broadcasting.

In the U.S. context, government intervention in the economy and culture prompted by the Great Depression was typically mediated by commercial interests such as trade groups, industrial organizations, and large corporations—including broadcasting networks. The Office of Education's Radio Project was *both* an archetypal New Deal project displaying and promoting the enhanced role of government *and* an excellent example of Hooverian associationalism—voluntary partnership between government and private enterprise—in action. The Project reflected the growing authority of state agencies, but this was government radio in a very collaborative and associational sense. It had government employees working through commercial radio networks and yet operating with temporary "relief workers" as staff, adding, as we have noted, several extra degrees of difficulty to the ambitious aim of forging creative new paths in educational broadcasting.

As the Radio Project and other government agencies took to the airwaves in the 1930s, they framed their projects of civic engagement in ways that would conform—for the most part—to commercial conceptions of radio programming and audience tastes. A provocative version of this idea was voiced by Evan Roberts, director of the Federal Theatre Radio Division, when he stated: "I believe you can sell government the way you sell soap."[67] At the same time, commercial broadcasters and sponsors embraced the ideals of education and the language of citizenship to gain audiences, build positive public relations, and hence gain some sort of political cover for what they did.[68] By investigating the specific case of the Radio Project and its interactions with commercial networks, we shed new light on the broader process by which commercial and public visions of broadcasting influenced and supported each other—despite the real tensions and conflicts also in play.

We draw extensively on archival materials produced by the Office of Education and housed at National Archives in College Park, Maryland. Educational Radio Project memos, production materials, and correspondence with network executives and others form the backbone of our documentary research. Although these materials offer detailed information on institutional practices, they do not illuminate all Radio Project activities evenly. For example, we know quite a bit about the writers on *Americans All, Immigrants All* and *Democracy in Action*, but almost nothing about the writers on *Pleasantdale Folks*. While the files for most of the programs we study include only a small amount of listener mail, the *Brave New World* file includes a large cache of listener letters. Our studies of the programs, then, necessarily follow the contours of the available documents and in different cases emphasize the writing process, production process, or listener responses to the programs. Unfortunately, there is a notable absence of information about the Project's WPA relief workers in the materials we have consulted. Despite these limitations, however, Educational Radio Project documents do often contain frank and unfiltered insights

FIGURE 3 Educational Radio Project staff in Washington, D.C., sort and respond to listener letters. Most letters requested educational pamphlets offered during broadcasts. (National Archives photo no. 12-E-32-534. "Radio-Mailing Section," Radio Project-WPA Photographs, 12-E-32, Box 39, RG 12 Office of Education, Still Picture Branch, National Archives, College Park, Maryland.)

into how Project staff members negotiated with educators, other government agencies, and commercial broadcasters in pursuit of their goal of interjecting educational programs into the commercial network schedule.

The Project worked hard to cultivate listener engagement and learning by offering information pamphlets to those who wrote in to the programs, and these offers generated large amounts of listener mail (figure 3). In the case of a sample of over 1,100 letters sent to *Brave New World*, we look systematically at how these listeners responded to the program, analyzing the language used by letter writers and comparing it to the language used in the broadcasts. These letters offer insights into the ways that members of the American public interpreted government-sponsored educational programs in relation to the more ubiquitous commercial network offerings.

Chapter Overviews

Chapter 1 explores how the Educational Radio Project combined commercial entertainment methods with educational ends and fused documentary and dramatic styles into a dramatized documentary format. We investigate the educational and entertainment origins of this format and examine debates over the relationship between dramatization and documentary. We discuss in turn three concepts that help us think about these hybrid programs: *dramatization, documentary,* and *governmental.* Finally, we situate this tradition of dramatized governmental documentary in an international context. We argue that, rather than being viewed as latecomers to transatlantic actuality-based documentary, U.S. broadcasters should be understood as pioneers of dramatized documentary and innovators in its use for both corporate and governmental communication.

Chapter 2 investigates both the production and reception of *Brave New World*'s dramatized documentary format.[69] Boutwell observed that the series, which promoted the Good Neighbor Policy, was an example of "education contributing toward declared national goals."[70] We situate the series within the broader history of U.S.–Latin American relations and focus on its use of emotive music, engaging historical narratives, and distinctive "Good Neighbor" language to promote cooperation and mutual respect between the "Americas." Analyzing letters sent in response to the program, we find that some listeners expressed a level of dissatisfaction with commercial radio and a deep interest in what educational radio had to offer, and they voiced support for a government-sponsored alternative to commercial radio. We argue that these listeners constituted an emergent audience for public broadcasting.

Chapter 3 examines *Americans All, Immigrants All* (AAIA) with a focus on the tensions between education and propaganda that inevitably surrounded a radio series about cultural tolerance. We examine AAIA as a product of the Project's cooperation with the intercultural education movement led by Rachel Davis DuBois and explore the internal debates that shaped the production process—the arguments about how best to use radio's adult education potential to combat racism and intolerance. We find that the educators and broadcasters associated with the Project believed that democratic values and democratic behavior were cultural traits that had to be taught and learned anew each generation. Debates over *Americans All, Immigrants All* reveal how Project participants thought about the possibilities and limits of radio as a means of addressing contentious issues and about where to draw the line between education and propaganda.

Chapter 4 examines *Wings for the Martins*, which departed from the dramatized documentary format and embraced the emerging situation comedy genre. With this program the Radio Project aimed to combine network radio's growing interest in family-oriented shows with the parent education movement's focus on "modernizing" parenting (and the family home) as a necessary support for modern approaches to education and child development. We show how the program negotiated the tensions between the movement's educational ideal of participatory fatherhood and the comic trope of the bumbling father. Although Arnold Martin's domestic incompetence was similar to that of other 1930s radio comedy patriarchs, his nuclear family looked and sounded like a postwar television sitcom family. We argue that *Wings* contributed to the development of the sitcom as a space for citizenship education, which would become a central characteristic of postwar television.

Chapter 5 examines *Democracy in Action*, a series about "how Americans have used representative government to solve problems which they could not meet individually or in private groups—problems arising out of a swiftly expanding, changing civilization—problems which have grown more complex with each succeeding decade."[71] In the light of the post–Cold War drift of American society toward attitudes of hostility to government, these public education campaigns stand out as of particular significance—a small part perhaps of the explanation for the higher faith in government of these generations of Americans.

Chapter 6 explores *Pleasantdale Folks*, an electrical transcription series developed by the Social Security Board to explain the new family-oriented Social Security provisions being rolled out in 1939–1940. We take a closer look at the soap opera genre as it was developing in network radio at this time and investigate how the message of *Pleasantdale Folks* fit within the generic expectations and practices of the soap opera. Specifically, we investigate how the program framed New Deal social policies as continuations of community traditions within the generally socially conservative context of the soap opera. We conclude that *Pleasantdale Folks* and *Wings for the Martins* operated like entertainment-education productions—exploiting broadcasting formats that created emotionally engaging, didactically structured and nationally relevant stories for purposes of propaganda and education.[72]

The conclusion tells the story of the end of the Radio Project—including the loss of congressional funding that had a great deal to do with the concerns about where to draw the line between education and propaganda that had run through the Project's life. It assesses the Office of Education experiment in its historical context and considers how the Project addressed larger questions of documentary authority and dramatization.

In the next chapter we turn to the program format that dominated Project production: dramatized documentary. We explore the complex history of this hybrid format in both national and international contexts, and we highlight the significant role it played in U.S. network broadcasting in the 1930s. By looking closely at the historical, political, and ideological development of this broadcasting format, chapter 1 grounds our investigation of Project productions in the context of the 1930s and helps us understand their implications for broadcasting history more broadly.

1

An American
Documentary Tradition

The Educational Radio Project's mission was to bring the entertainment skills of the broadcasters and the instructional expertise of the educators together in a best-of-both-worlds hybrid that was also governmental—helping citizens understand both what government did and what active citizenship was. William Boutwell and other Project leaders believed that the marriage of educational content and dramatic form would help realize the potential of radio for adult education in a democracy. The philosophy was that unless people were interested and engaged emotionally, they would not listen; if they did not listen, they would not learn. Those beliefs, and the deeply collaborative production arrangements, shaped the sound as well as the form of Project series. For example, the series *Brave New World* opened with a network announcer—the kind whose exuberant and precise tones had likely been used to sell Chevrolet cars or Maxwell House coffee in other programs—gushing about "the democratic ideals we share" with Latin America. The opening of *Gallant American Women* had lush music behind a narrator extolling women "whose deeds are rooted deep in our past and whose influence will reach far into the future." Over its five-year history, Project series adapted in this way a broad repertoire of commercial radio techniques to the goals of civic education.

These hybrid programs were part of a long American tradition of merging entertainment and education. The nineteenth-century Lyceum movement, for example, combined lectures, dramatic performances, music, and other modes of entertainment and drew increasingly large audiences.[1] More sensationally, from 1841 to 1865, Barnum's American Museum in New York offered access to edifying "wonders" of the natural world in a dramatic format that titillated and thrilled audiences.[2] By the late nineteenth century, the Chautauqua movement was bringing a combination of secular and religious lectures, speeches, and music to rural America. At the same time, "respectable" vaudeville circuits emerged, mixing instructional lectures with drama, comedy, and musical performances, reaching urban and rural communities alike.[3] From 1883 to 1916, Buffalo Bill's Wild West show re-created and documented the western frontier, traveling the United States and the world replaying historical battles and recasting them as lessons about good versus evil; as Joy S. Kasson notes, the show "blurred the line between fiction and fact, entertainment and education."[4] The popular press was another important medium that blended entertainment and education—by the late nineteenth century, mass-circulation newspapers and serials offered highly dramatic "true" stories. In the twentieth century, new technologies of communication further expanded the reach of these hybrid forms, including into cinema and radio.[5]

Many Project series not only combined commercial entertainment methods with educational ends but also fused documentary and dramatic styles into a dramatized documentary format. Derek Paget defines this "docudrama" format as a fact-based portrayal of real events that makes use of dramatization, invented dialogue, and music to excite and engage audiences.[6] In addition to this hybrid documentary format, the Project produced a small number of fiction-based series (we focus on two of these—*Wings for the Martins* and *Pleasantdale Folks*—in chapters 4 and 6).[7] In this chapter, we investigate the dramatized documentary format that emerged in radio in the 1930s and played a prominent role in both commercial and public service broadcasting systems through the 1940s. The original radio version of *March of Time* (CBS, 1931–1937; NBC, 1937–1944)—with its emotive "Voice of Time" narration and re-created world news events—is perhaps the best-known example of this genre. But thematic dramatized documentaries dealing with crime, history, and other subjects were also frequent features of network radio. As documentaries based on recorded actuality became more common and recognized by the mid-to-late 1940s, the dramatized documentary lost favor with practitioners and critics and became increasingly characterized as a flawed and crude approximation of actuality documentary.

Despite its fall from critical grace, the dramatized documentary (known as "docudrama" from the 1960s on)[8] reemerged in the United States toward the end of television's classic network era. In this period, programs such as *Brian's Song* (American Broadcasting Company [ABC], 1971), *Roots* (ABC, 1977), *The Holocaust* (NBC, 1978), and *The Burning Bed* (NBC, 1984) engaged TV audiences in the United States and internationally.[9] The format proved resilient in the cable and streaming eras with productions such as *The People v. O.J.*

Simpson (FX, 2016) and *Chernobyl* (HBO, 2019) drawing large global audiences. While our study focuses on governmental dramatized documentary, it also contributes to an understanding of the historical origins and development of this popular broadcasting, cable, and streaming genre.

In the rest of the chapter, we take apart the concepts that shape our understanding of this radio format—namely, *dramatization, documentary*, and *governmental*—in a way that helps us understand the civic and cultural mission of the Educational Radio Project. We discuss each of these elements in turn to explain its meaning at the time and its significance for the Project and its work. To begin, however, we briefly lay out debates about documentary as a mode of communication whose claims to authority were grounded in access to factual reality. We address the relationship between government-sponsored and corporate-sponsored documentaries and identify the key roles played by American advertising-supported media and public relations practices in the rise of radio and film documentary.

Documentary Debates

Much of the history of radio and film documentary has been written from the perspective of an ascendant actuality-based documentary format that proports to capture a slice of lived reality. While audio and visual recording technologies such as photography, phonography, and film had longer-standing claims to representing "the real," broadcasting presented both new problems and new possibilities for documentary expression. Although the transmission of actuality sound had always been part of live-event radio broadcasting, the controlled environment of studio production was *preferred* for most regular radio features, yet histories of radio documentary have tended to explain the prevalence of studio-based dramatized documentaries as the result of technological and institutional constraints. Focusing on the U.S. context, Matthew C. Ehrlich argues: "Technological limitations and a network recording ban compelled many radio programs of the period to employ dramatizations, and hence they were akin to what today would be labeled 'docudrama.' But they were called 'documentaries' in their time, and their claims to truth are no different from those of the documentaries rooted in recorded actuality that had become the norm by 1951."[10] Ehrlich thus attributes the ubiquity of dramatized documentaries to the absence of portable recording technologies and the presence of network limits on recorded programming. He then identifies the public service requirements of the 1947 Blue Book as inspiring a wave of actuality documentary production in broadcasting in the late 1940s and early 1950s. We argue, however, that the prevalence of dramatization in interwar documentaries was a creative choice: radio writers and producers viewed dramatization not as a make-do but as the *best* strategy to bring real-world events to life and draw in mass audiences.

At about the same time that CBS first aired *March of Time*, the BBC established a department to conduct documentary radio research and production called BBC Features, after the feature film. This unit began by producing dramatized documentaries in studio with the goal of promoting "original forms of expression, peculiar to radio."[11] These productions employed "montages of narrative, dramatic dialogue, music, verse, sound-effects and, later, sound actuality."[12] Due to its public service ethos, "auteur" approach to production, and the absence of commercial competition, BBC features were often more experimental, modernist, and aesthetically ambitious than Project productions. Paddy Scannell argues that radio features represented a new method of social documentation that "oscillated between the two poles of drama and journalism"—and it is possible to see the influence of John Grierson's administrative documentary tradition and of a more critical documentary impulse in BBC feature productions.[13] Both Scannell and Paget identify the central role played by leftists such as A. E. Harding in creating these features. Paget characterizes this "very vigorous tradition of radio montage documentary" as an example of a radical documentary tradition, in contrast to the liberal Griersonian one.[14]

From the first BBC feature based on real events—*Crisis in Spain* (1931) produced in London by Harding—these programs show the dynamic interplay of real events and dramatization.[15] *Crisis in Spain* narrated the events leading up to the abdication of the king and establishment of a republic in Spain. Produced by Lance Sieveking, the story unfolded through dramatic reenactments of the way the event was reported and relayed by international press agencies and reporters using radio and telephone "ambiences." *Crisis in Spain* combined dramatic montage with stirring music to generate what Scannell describes as the sense of an "irresistible march of events towards the proclamation of a republic."[16] In Manchester, Harding also worked with D. G. Bridson to produce a series about the region's major industries. The first program, *Steel* (1937), augmented dramatization with recorded actuality—sounds gathered on site at steel mills by a mobile recording unit.[17] Scannell observes that music and verse choruses intermingled with recorded sound in the program, creating "a heroic vision of the abstract power and energy of modern industry."[18] Features came into their own during the war, Kate Whitehead explains: "Because it was . . . something of a hybrid between documentary and drama, it was a very useful tool for putting across the facts in an entertaining, even emotive way."[19] A similar logic was at work in New Deal radio productions.

The shared mass medium of radio broadcasting, the larger context of economic depression, and the spirit of social reform inspired governmental dramatized documentary in both the United States and the United Kingdom. Grierson's influential theory and practice of documentary is another important connector—although not just in the direction of the United Kingdom influencing the United States, as is often assumed. Grierson viewed dramatization as fundamental to documentary in all media, explaining in 1942 that "the documentary idea was not basically a film idea at all": the "underlying concept" was that "the world was in a phase of drastic change affecting every manner of thought and practice, and the public comprehension of the nature of that change vital."[20] In pursuit of the goal of public comprehension, Grierson claimed to have learned a great deal from the American popular press. This interest dated back to his first visit to the United States in 1924, when he was studying in Chicago. He became, he recalled, "highly admiring of the dramatic approach implicit in the journalism of William Randolph Hearst. Beyond the sensationalizing of news we thought we recognized a deeper principle, and I think Henry Luce at very much the same time was recognizing it too . . . that even so complex a world as ours could be patterned for all to appreciate if only we got away from the servile accumulation of fact and struck for the story."[21] Grierson thus saw, in a way that many American intellectuals of the time did not, how the fundamental need of commercial mass communication to engage and hold reader interest had encouraged something new and effective—the dramatization of news.[22] Grierson was an insider/outsider, influential but also controversial on both sides of the Atlantic—on the one hand, championing American advertising, dramatization of the news, and yellow journalism; on the other, advocating progressive, socially concerned, actuality-based documentary.

Charles Siepmann, who worked for the BBC for twelve years before coming to the United States in 1937 on a Rockefeller fellowship to study educational broadcasting, similarly recognized commercial innovations like dramatization as key to the effective presentation of documentary and educational content.[23] In 1941 he asked, "Can Radio Educate?": "Success depends on our power to elicit interest and hold attention. Radio in fact has means of doing so. Techniques have been devised and have brought money to advertisers and pleasure to vast audiences."[24] Siepmann thought that educators had to study, rather than scornfully turn away from, the attention-holding techniques of entertainment radio. In fact, these kinds of hybrid entertainment and educational forms flourished in American broadcasting in the 1930s, on both the local and national levels. They provided, as we will see, precedent and example for the Educational Radio Project.

Dramatized Radio

As one of the main entertainment techniques of commercial broadcasting, dramatization was everywhere on 1930s American radio. According to the *Oxford English Dictionary*, the word means "conversion into drama," implying something preexisting that gets converted. Most radio dramatizations were adaptations of fictional works (novels, plays, films), which do not concern us here. But there were also many dramatizations of actual events, both current and historical, on local, regional, and national radio and it is on this *dramatization of the real* that we focus here. The phrase conveys some of the paradox of what was being attempted—the deployment of scriptwriters, actors, composers, and musicians to turn real events, sometimes very recent real events, into something with the form and sound of radio drama.

American radio dramatizations of the 1930s had a particular focus on crime, accident, and disaster. In Sacramento, a local station carried a dramatization of "a recent auto accident tragedy" as part of a safe-driving campaign.[25] In Miami, station WIOD donated three five-minute periods a week, plus "talent and sound effects," to dramatizing the worst car accidents of the week.[26] Georgia stations carried a dramatization of the 1936 Gainesville tornado disaster.[27] The *Philadelphia Inquirer* offered a monthly Hero Award for the city's police and firefighters, and WCAU made radio dramatizations of the heroic acts "a regular feature of the monthly awards."[28] Such programs were designed to be experienced both realistically and emotionally by the listening audience.

Dramatizations of real crimes sometimes had real-life consequences. Several Pittsburgh residents called the police after hearing a holdup that was actually a dramatization coming from a neighbor's radio.[29] In a Tampa case, lawyers argued that a radio dramatization of a crime had influenced jurors and thus skewed the trial's verdict.[30] The warden of a prison in Salem, Oregon, turned off a 1936 network dramatization of a 1923 train robbery and murder case because he believed it would not have been "good policy" to allow convicted criminals to hear the broadcast.[31] Professional car thief and murderer Martin Durkin lost a court bid to stop CBS in Chicago broadcasting a radio dramatization of his career, on the grounds that it would "injure the feelings of his aged parents, relatives and friends residing in this vicinity."[32]

As the number of radio dramatizations of true stories increased, so did production values. A 1939 article based on an interview with a regional NBC music director explained that at first music in dramatizations was "usually restricted to snatches from popular compositions" but "it is becoming the rule now to write tunes especially for the broadcast."[33] Radio series produced by the Project featured original music, much of it composed by musical director Rudolph Schramm (figure 4). Along with music, radio dramatizations made ample and innovative use of sound effects—especially those about policing and criminal activities. The popular crime series *Gang Busters* (NBC, CBS, ABC, 1935–1957) was known for its striking sound effects and dramatic introduction—inspiring the expression, "coming on like gangbusters."

Although they have not been studied systematically, many dramatized documentary radio series aired on national and regional networks in the United States in the 1930s and 1940s, under a range of descriptors including

FIGURE 4 Educational Radio Project music director Rudolf Schramm (left) conducts a small orchestra. (National Archives photo no. 12-E-32-538. "Radio Schramm and Orchestra," Radio Project-WPA Photographs, 12-E-32, Box 39, RG 12 Office of Education, Still Picture Branch, National Archives, College Park, Maryland.)

"documentary drama," "dramatized human interest," "police drama," "crime drama," and "true crime drama."[34] For each of these programs, the claim of documenting real events was foundational, although the real events were represented with varying degrees of dramatization, embellishment, and invention. Stories based on criminal and legal cases informed the earliest and most common programs, beginning with *True Detective Mysteries* (CBS, 1929–1930; Mutual, 1936–1939; 1944–1958) based on *True Detective* magazine. Crime programs included well-known shows such as *Gang Busters*, along with many lesser-known programs, such as *Police Headquarters* (NBC, 1932), *The Court of Human Relations* (NBC, CBS, Mutual, 1934–1939), and *Twenty Thousand Years in Sing Sing* (NBC, 1933–1939). Other dramatized documentaries included the American Medical Association's *Doctors at Work* and *Doctors at War* (NBC, 1938–1945) and NBC's *The Colgate Sports Newsreel* (NBC, ABC, 1937–1956).[35] The University of Chicago's *The Human Adventure* (CBS, 1939–1940; Mutual, 1943–1946) was a slickly produced dramatized documentary series with episodes featuring both University of Chicago professors speaking as experts and dramatized scenes from history, sociology, science, and medicine.

Scholarship on radio crime shows explores how they promoted practices of scientific documentation in the course of celebrating police professionalism.

Kathleen Battles argues that crime dramas shifted over the course of the 1930s from the *True Detective* model of sentimental confessions to a focus on police procedure. In shows like *Gang Busters* and *Calling All Cars* (Don Lee/CBS West Coast, 1933–1939), police achieved access to facts due to professional training and scientific methods of investigation. Detectives' access to facts, in turn, "validated the authority of the version of the story being told," and of the police themselves.[36] The modern technology of radio was one of the tools that allowed police to collect facts, coordinate policing, and inform the public. Radio reinforced the authority of police, just as dramatized documentaries reinforced the authority of radio to represent the real.

These police series were in some ways similar in form to dramatized documentaries developed by corporations and governments that aimed to guide and manage public perceptions. Following the propaganda produced during World War I—particularly the informational campaigns of George Creel and the Committee on Public Information—advertising and public relations entered a new era of organizational and procedural development. Dramatized documentaries emerged as communicative and cultural strategies for securing positive public images for large corporations and other institutions.[37] Although many such programs aired on commercial networks, *The March of Time* and *Cavalcade of America* (CBS, 1935–1939; NBC, 1940–1953) were two of the most successful examples. In both cases, dramatized vignettes positioned listeners in immediate proximity to real events.

With its weekly mission of dramatizing current events, *The March of Time* was one of the most influential dramatized documentary series of the period and one of the most relevant for understanding the Project's ethos. It deployed stirring drama and music, while validating the accuracy and authority of *Time* and *Life* as news sources.[38] The program was the brain child of WLW Cincinnati director, Fred Smith, who had pioneered radio dramas in the 1920s when radio was still dominated by music and information programming. In 1926 he came up with the idea of putting news to music, and in 1928 he made an agreement with *Time* magazine to dramatize a ten-minute summary of news, which was syndicated widely. In 1930 Smith wrote a long memo to Roy Larsen, *Time* vice president and general manager, suggesting that "dramatized news be done as a network show."[39] The resulting show, *The March of Time*, impressed both audiences and critics, and inspired a monthly film series of the same name from 1935.[40] The program was organized as if the listener were flipping through a radio "magazine" from one leading news story to another, except that each news story was dramatized rather than narrated—including dramatic dialogue that could be based on what was actually said or imagined and fictional—and the newsmakers were impersonated by actors. Listeners encountered each dramatic vignette as if finding themselves on the scene of an ongoing national event or eavesdropping on a conversation between world leaders. Along with using radio actors to bring the news to life, Smith's dramatic sensibilities were also evident in the central role of music in conveying the show's sense of progress and uplift. In 1936 John Grierson told John Marshall of the Rockefeller Foundation that he hoped to return to the United States and wanted to work with the *March of Time* unit, "which he regarded as the most promising of American producers."[41]

Cavalcade of America featured dramatic reenactments from American history based on current scholarship, written by top radio writers and performed by film and radio stars.[42] The DuPont chemical company engaged the advertising agency Batton, Barton, Durstine & Osborn (BBDO) to develop a radio program that would improve the public image of the company. DuPont had been investigated in 1934 as part of the Nye Committee's "merchants of death" public hearings in which companies like DuPont were accused of encouraging U.S. entry into World War I and reaping enormous profits by selling munitions. As Cynthia Meyers argues, *Cavalcade* was meant to be a radio extravaganza that promoted "positive Americanism" in an innovative format: "It was to be a cultural event and an effective educational vehicle reflecting actual scholarship. *Cavalcade* would simultaneously prove radio's capacity for uplifting the public through engaging educational entertainment while reshaping public perceptions of a misunderstood corporate patron."[43] As the benevolent sponsor, DuPont was situated within a national tradition of industry that promised to improve the lives of all Americans. The slogan created by BBDO claimed that DuPont brought the public "Better Things for Better Living—Through Chemistry."[44] As with *The March of Time*, BBDO also invested heavily in music—including hiring the New York Philharmonic Symphony Orchestra—to deliver the uplifting message of American progress and ingenuity.[45] American feats of industrial, scientific, and engineering success signaled the inevitability of human progress under the American system of free enterprise and thus provided moral and political justification for the current economic system in which large corporations accrued enormous wealth and influence. It was, as Ian Tyrrell summarizes, not just an "ideologically conservative program that aligned well with commercial interests," but also one that "sought to use the past to legitimate the present."[46]

In programs such as *Cavalcade* and *March of Time*, radio sound positioned listeners within a forward-moving flow of real events in a way that was impossible with visual media. While visual media (before virtual reality and other three-dimensional visual forms) required a distance between the viewer and the thing being viewed, listening made no such demands. Sound had the ability to surround and envelop listeners, which gave them a unique position of intimacy and access to events being represented.[47] In the case of radio crime dramas, Battles describes this characteristic as the "dragnet effect," in which criminals and listeners alike were ensnarled in a net of police presence through radio sound. Neil Verma uses the term *kaleidosonic* to capture the sense in which listeners were positioned at the center of dramatic action as events swirled around them like colorful shapes in a kaleidoscope.[48] In many of these commercial dramatized documentaries, as well as in series produced by the Radio Project, listeners were located within the acoustical space of the massive historical tableaux—or the small, private meetings—that shaped world events. The positioning of listeners within unfolding soundscapes was critical to both the dramatic and documentary functions of dramatized documentary.

Educational Dramatizations

In the area of educational radio, practitioners and researchers became increasingly interested in dramatization as a means of activating the emotional and intellectual interest of audiences. In 1939 the National Association of Broadcasters published a short guide, *How to Use Radio in the Classroom* (based on an FREC research project at Ohio State University), that emphasized the way that radio could give "remote" and unengaging instructional material "new and vital significance by the technique of spoken drama."[49] A University of Wisconsin study of high school and college students published by Edgar Willis in 1940 found that dramatizations were most effective in changing attitudes among high school students, likely due to the variations in presentation style and emotional appeal.[50] An Iowa study, also published in 1940, contrasted the use of radio talks, discussions, and dramatizations in classrooms, concluding that talks and dramatizations were both more effective than discussions and that drama was regarded as more interesting than talks.[51] Educational radio dramas prioritized the importance of engaging students, which was a central value of progressive education.[52] For educators, then, there were multiple pedagogical reasons to favor dramatization as a technique for educational radio.

Project educators favored dramatization in general and *historical* dramatization in particular. Talia Brenner observes that history dramatizations were "the most frequent form of radio drama, so ubiquitous that many broadcasters and education experts describing the different forms of radio in education would refer to 'history dramatization' as itself a genre."[53] Historical dramatizations on radio were so common in the late 1930s that novelist Arnold Mulder worried that while "history books are becoming more accurate and scientific" the "knowledge of history on the part of the great masses of the people" was becoming "more and more romantically inaccurate" because of movie and radio dramatizations.[54] There was, as we will see, debate at times inside the Project about whether writers on particular series leaned too historical in their development of themes and investigation of issues.

The term *dramatized documentary* then captures three key features of reality-based dramatizations that are important for interpreting the Radio

Project's most popular productions. First, music played a critical role in weaving the facts of the event into a larger emotional story designed to persuade, inspire, and "move" listeners. Second, dramatizations put listeners at the center of the events being documented. Through radio sound, listeners had direct access to all the action presented, and they ear-witnessed the events as part of an anonymous community of radio listeners. Third, dramatized documentary series importantly drew on both the factuality of the events being represented and the emotional architecture of music, language, and drama.

Documentary Radio

The word *documentary* was in fact little used in relation to radio during the interwar period.[55] The Manchester *Guardian* in 1939 referred to the BBC's Olive Shapley as "author of many radio 'documentaries'"—the quotation marks emphasizing the relative unfamiliarity of the term.[56] Searches of digitized newspapers, radio magazines, and industry publications confirm that the term *radio documentary* was barely used in the United States before 1940—in contrast, a search for *radio dramatizations* gets thousands of hits in the publications of the time. It was during World War II that the term *documentary* became used regularly in relation to American radio, but Robert Landry in 1943 still felt the need to explain what he meant: "radio documentary programs, those lectures in dramatic form."[57] William Stott, however, pointed in retrospect to a broader worldview of "documentary expression" that infused cultural production in the Depression era. He argued that radio's documentary mode aimed "to make the listener believe he was there."[58] Those who practiced documentary believed that "a fact to be true and important must be felt," that documentary was "the presentation or representation of actual fact in a way that makes it credible and vivid to people at the time."[59] Accepting Stott's point means that even if producers did not always use the *word* documentary, we can identify and name a documentary aesthetic and intention in 1930s radio.

Significantly, Project staff members *did* sometimes refer to their work as making documentaries; they clearly shared the view of the time that documentary could and should be a dramatized rendering of actual events. We can see them attempting to find the right label for what they were doing, using various combinations of the words *documentary* and *drama* or *dramatization*. *Let Freedom Ring!* was described as "a series of documentary radio dramas."[60] Chester Williams wrote to Studebaker that Project scripts should "avoid as much as possible the presentation of purely imaginative episodes and present that which is 'documentary.'"[61] An early draft script for the show that came to be called *Democracy in Action* described its mode as "documentary dramatizations utilizing full studio production, i.e. actors, chorus, and orchestra."[62] Laura Vitray wrote to Merrill Denison as they were working on writing *Democracy in Action*: "This is 'documentary radio': that should hold the listeners . . . and the dramatizations have more character than those used in *Americans All*, although the overall treatment is similar."[63] Distinguished historian Mary Beard, adviser on *Gallant American Women*, criticized an episode of the series as "not documentary according to the pretensions of the whole program."[64] Project staff members, it seems, did think of what they were producing as documentary *and* as dramatization.

Within that broad agreement, there were plenty of internal disagreements about the relationship between documentation and drama and the relative importance of each. Boutwell believed that educational radio could not provide all the facts and hence needed to provide the stimulation to learn more; for this reason he advocated engaging emotions in Project programs. He told the writer Gilbert Seldes, for example, that *Americans All, Immigrants All* was weak in dramatic structure and that this was a problem because "drama provides the emotional voltage which is required to transfer ideas to the minds of the mass audience."[65] A handwritten document headed "Chester's Position on Am All," probably written by one of Chester S. Williams's colleagues (most likely Boutwell), exasperatedly summarizes Williams's position in a debate during the making of *Americans All, Immigrants All*:

> That education and dramatic programs are two different worlds. That educational radio lies between them in an area defined as "like 'Third of a Nation' without propaganda" or "like a textbook."[66] That to organize a script in order to create an attitude such as "tolerance of all races" or "faith in civil rights" is an error for three reasons: If the attitudes are open to question, then for Government to promote them is to indulge in farcical tactics. If the attitudes are broadly accepted there is no use promoting them because every one agrees with them anyway. That it is futile for us to use drama anyway because we can never be as good as Orson Welles.[67]

Boutwell wrote to Cohen in February 1939 about the "very important argument" he and Williams were having: "Chester argues that the rules and opportunities of the dramatist should not be extended to educational drama. He wants something between education and drama."[68] That space could be very difficult to define, yet a great deal was at stake in it for the Project. It could not simply be argued that educational radio was legitimately only about teaching facts; all agreed that educational radio was more usefully and importantly about stimulating a desire to learn. Should it, however, aim to encourage being an alert citizen who understood the need for and the workings of government, who was tolerant in social relations and understood that democracy demanded of citizens more than just voting? That raised a question—in a pluralist democracy, could a value such as tolerance legitimately be presented as an educational goal of the state? What if the democratic majority was proudly and self-consciously intolerant? That was the troubling question that Chester S. Williams was apparently posing to his colleagues in 1939. These internal discussions plunge us into the heart of Project staff members' sense of what they were doing, the possibilities and the constraints of their situation.

Actuality Documentary

While the Educational Radio Project remained focused on dramatized documentary, some broadcasters at the BBC and the Canadian Broadcasting Corporation (CBC) began experimenting with deploying actuality sound in documentary. In Britain, where the radio feature developed under an auteur model of experimentation and in proximity to Grierson's General Post Office Film Unit, the incorporation of recorded sound was an early innovation. Along with Harding and Bridson, Shapley also began using recorded actuality in the later 1930s in her programs about working-class lives.[69] CBC broadcasters incorporated actuality recordings of everyday voices and local and regional activities in the 1930s. Some examples of series produced in the 1930s were *Les Actualiés Canadiennes*; *Street Scenes*, an interview program focusing on ordinary people from across the Dominion; and *Forgotten Footsteps*, produced by Toronto station CFRB, which used interviews, re-creations, and music to document exhibits at the Royal Ontario Museum. This program resembled the Project's highly popular *The World Is Yours* series, which documented and dramatized stories based on items from the Smithsonian Museum. David Hogarth notes that in Canada, actuality documentary was less a product of an auteur system than of a "factory" approach to broadcasting, involving a fixed division of labor and standardized content and style regulations and practices, all designed to encourage audiences to return to documentary content on a weekly basis.[70] By the late 1930s, the CBC had acquired mobile equipment for recording "events where they happened and when they happened," particularly in preparation for the 1939 Royal Tour.[71] Although the use of actuality sound in Canada remained limited until the postwar period, it was highly valued by Canadian radio producers, even when it had to be staged, re-created, or enhanced by sound effects in the studio.[72]

Project staff members were familiar with the actuality mode of radio documentary because of their connections with the BBC. In 1938 Philip Cohen held a Rockefeller Foundation fellowship at the BBC, where he worked with Alistair Cooke on a documentary about a drought: "This is real documentary stuff," he wrote back to Boutwell.[73] Boutwell recommended the twenty-seven-year-old Cohen to Sterling Fisher at CBS as director of the *Americans All, Immigrants All* series: "he is doing increasingly fine work and has had the benefit of excellent experience in England. His work over there was so highly esteemed that BBC tried to keep him in England."[74] Cohen recalled what he had learned at the BBC: "Documentary radio is analytical; it is graphic; it is developed in a real setting. Its actors are the people actually found in that setting." He noted that "the United States has made little progress with this kind of program" and that "England has moved forward rapidly"—although most of the acclaimed documentary programs had been on regional stations rather than the national one.[75]

The Educational Radio Project came at a moment of transition then, on the cusp of actuality documentary but not a part of it. In May 1941 Philip Cohen, speaking to the Institute for Education by Radio, defined *documentary broadcasting* as "the presentation of the people themselves at work or at play; it does not mean the presentation of skilled, dramatic actors surrounded by elaborate sound-effects and orchestra." He did not intend, he hastily added, "to condemn the dramatic technique in the presentation of cultural materials"—they were, after all, the techniques with which he had worked so effectively at the Project.[76] When Cohen lauded the "presentation of the people themselves" over the use of actors, sound effects, and music in making dramatized documentary, he was in part situating himself generationally but also identifying himself with the then-prestigious British actuality model rather than the dramatization techniques pioneered in U.S. commercial popular media. As an ambitious young man, and perhaps with an eye on his Rockefeller sponsors, Cohen sided with the British over the Americans.

Cohen finally had an opportunity to produce actuality documentary in the United States when, in 1940, Librarian of Congress Archibald Macleish appointed him to direct the Experimental Radio Project at the Library of Congress. Charles Harrell, the program editor, had also recently been on a Rockefeller fellowship to the BBC. The Library's Experimental Radio Project itself received funds from the Rockefeller Foundation—further evidencing the foundation's interest in importing British documentary techniques into the United States and, Michele Hilmes argues, nudging U.S. radio in "a more explicitly national and public service direction."[77] The key element of the Experimental Radio Project's work was on-site recording, allowing the subjects of the documentaries to speak (or sing) for themselves. Cohen directed a series on American regions and communities; several programs were researched and scripted but only one gained network broadcast—*Rebirth in Barrow's Inlet*. Although the story of this coastal South Carolina town was based on recordings of local citizens, the October 1942 broadcast was written by Joseph Liss and dramatized and spoken by actors.[78] The Library of Congress Project series appears to be a repurposing of an idea developed at the Educational Radio Project—a proposal for a follow-up to *Americans All, Immigrants All* drafted in 1939. Writing at the time, Cohen described a proposal for a series about American regions treated "in much the same way that the BBC has treated various parts of England in its documentary programs," emphasizing "the growth of democracy through cooperative effort," and featuring the voices of actual people, "leaders of groups or communities."[79]

Other Library of Congress productions, including John A. Lomax's *Ballad Hunter* programs and the *America in the Summer of 1941* series of oral history interviews (six fifteen-minute documentaries over the summer and early fall of 1941, recorded on transcription disks) experimented with first-person interviews and recorded actuality.[80] A sample of the kind of work in which Cohen was most interested at this time includes the "Man on the Street" interviews he and Alan Lomax conducted on the day of the Pearl Harbor attacks.[81]

Governmental Radio

A final distinguishing characteristic of Project radio productions is that they were *governmental*—produced with the specific aim of informing citizens and exhorting them to more active citizenship and explicating the role of government in civic life. This is where the aims and ambitions of the international documentary film movement guided by John Grierson entered the orbit of the Educational Radio Project. As noted above, Grierson's documentary movement became a source of inspiration for public broadcasters in Canada and the United Kingdom, and thus indirectly influenced Cohen and others at the project who looked to the BBC as a model for educational broadcasting. In addition, the Rockefeller Foundation became an intermediary between the civic goals and techniques of the documentary film movement and U.S. educational initiatives such as the Project.

The most recent characterizations of Grierson's documentary movement depict it as fundamentally about governmentality. Writing of the Grierson-era National Film Board in Canada, Zoë Druick argues that documentary production was a "means of governance" that identified and "nurture[d] a sense of belonging"—she labels this "government realism."[82] Lars Weckbecker makes a similar case about New Zealand, explaining that the aim of the documentary movement was "providing citizens with an appropriate vision by which they would govern their selves and others into the future"—"documentary film's function was to realise a docile, homogeneous and self-disciplining population through a corporatist vision." Rob Aitken also wrote of the way in which Grierson's "broad commitment to progressive forms of social and cultural change" lent documentary film "a kind of *governmentality*." This governmental understanding of documentary was promoted in the United States at the time by the Rockefeller Foundation, which "integrated Grierson's conception of documentary as a technology of social citizenship into the core of its motion picture programs."[83] The foundation was Grierson's most important institutional ally in the United States, and his vision was clearly evident in the film program of the Museum of Modern Art in New York. Writing in 1940, the museum's film library curator, Richard Griffith, observed: "By dramatizing public issues in terms of human need, the documentary film endeavors to show each individual how the great impersonal forces of the modern world affect his life, and thereby persuade him to accept the responsibilities of citizenship."[84] Those were also the goals of the Educational Radio Project: the creative work of its dramatized documentaries was in awakening citizens to the various contexts (local, national, international) of their citizenship responsibilities.

Grierson's strong views on creative governmental communications can be glimpsed in a long memorandum he wrote in February 1944 for the Henry Luce–funded Commission on the Freedom of the Press. Grierson complained that the U.S. members of the Commission tended to think of government involvement in communications only in the negative terms of "regulation" and "control." He pleaded instead for "a larger statement of the necessity of communications to modern government, articulated in respect of growing responsibilities of government," criticizing too sharp distinctions between factual and dramatic communications. While the American intellectuals on the commission worried about government control, Grierson exhorted government to learn from *Time*, *Life*, and *Look* in "dramatizing the new world of the air" and from the American sensational press in "reporting event in story patterns." If government also used a "dramatic form of presentation," breaking down "the unreal distinction between the 'intellectual' and the 'emotional,'" it would become possible to "present or interpret the most difficult matters to a wide non-specialized audience."[85] Grierson thought the United States was exceptionally slow to institute a governmental information service. In "every country except the United States," government had "the power and the means to inform the people what it is doing and what it intends," but in the United States "the fear of partisan political use of information services looms very large in the public argument."[86] These were precisely the kinds of attacks that would be launched against the Project by conservatives in Congress.

Grierson is important to our story because he consistently argued in this way that there were American commercial traditions of dramatizing news and information that government could and should harness. Placing him in the history counters a tendency in the historiography on documentary to depict the United States as a laggard in the international documentary stakes, slow to embrace the socially progressive forms of actuality-based documentary. Grierson suggests a way of telling the other side of that story—of viewing the United States as *leading* development in dramatized documentary rather than as coming late to actuality documentary.

Whichever way we tell it, these transatlantic comparisons have had far more attention than any other transnational influences. What if we looked south rather than east for comparisons? Documentary dramas played a key part in one of the most prominent national programs in Mexico, *La Hora Nacional* (*National Hour*), first aired in 1937. The Mexican government produced *La Hora Nacional* through its newly created Autonomous Department of Press and Publicity (DAPP), and required all radio stations to rebroadcast the program every Sunday evening. Although originally broadcast by DAPP station XEDP, the program was relayed to commercial station XEW and from there broadcast nationally over its powerful long-wave and short-wave transmitters. The program included cultural and educational features, such as Mexican popular and classical music, poetry readings, and dramatized documentaries treating aspects of Mexican history, interspersed with government announcements and progress reports.[87] Renfro Cole Norris found that more than half of broadcast time of *La Hora Nacional* was devoted to music, drama, and history, with the goal of strengthening "the sense of civic responsibility in all Mexicans."[88] In 1939 the DAPP offices closed and the program was transferred to the Ministry of Interior. However, instead of enlisting a government station to produce and distribute the program, President Manuel Ávila Camacho asked media mogul Emilio Azcárraga to produce the program at the XEW studios. Paralleling the Radio Project structure, *La Hora Nacional* became a coproduction of the government and commercial networks until the late 1950s.[89]

A similar partnership between the state and commercial radio broadcasters emerged in Argentina—particularly after the military coup of 1943. Christine Ehrick shows that actress Eva "Evita" Duarte began cultivating an association with the military junta even before she began a relationship with Colonel Juan Perón. After the coup, she "successfully pitched an idea to the military official in charge of radio for a series of documentaries focused on famous women in history." The series, *La Mujer en Historia* (*Women in History*), promised "high morals and historical themes" but in a dramatic style that incorporated elements of popular theater and radio soap opera.[90] The series of historical dramas was sponsored by the state but broadcast in prime time over popular commercial station Radio Belgrano. The series positioned Duarte as an "everywoman" who could inhabit the personas of famous women from Elizabeth I of England to Empress Carlota of Mexico to Madame Chiang Kai-Shek of China. The role made Duarte famous and foreshadowed the political role she would play as a powerful political wife, radio star, and populist representative of the women of Argentina.[91]

Conclusions

Citing as examples *Cavalcade of America* and *March of Time*, Hilmes identifies a mode of U.S. radio production she calls "public service documentary drama": "original works written especially for radio, mixing drama and documentary in creative ways, with a frequent emphasis on the idea of nation and national identity—history, issues and problems, concepts such as democracy and freedom—and an underlying aesthetic of factuality, even when scripted and performed by actors."[92] This describes the style of dramatized documentary that emerged in network radio—and much of the output of the Educational Radio Project—very well. We have argued that Project programs were influenced by both commercial and non-commercial documentary traditions. Along with commercial practices, Project creators drew on educational progressivism and New Deal liberalism to shape a distinctly educational and governmental approach to democracy and citizenship. Additionally, key staff had been exposed to international models of public service media production in radio and film and brought those sensibilities to bear on Project series.

Having surveyed the broader context of radio documentary, we conclude that the major outputs of the Project can best be characterized as *dramatized governmental documentary radio*. Identifying it in that way helps us understand its civic and cultural mission. In the following chapters we draw attention to the ways in which Project series worked creatively to illuminate the role of government and of citizens. We also examine the ways in which the intrinsic tensions in the model—between documentary and dramatization and governmentality—were debated and resolved in the production process of each series.

2

Brave New World

Reframing and Reclaiming
the Americas

In the five-year history of the Educational Radio Project, *Brave New World* was one of the earliest dramatized documentary series to explore a unified theme over an extended period of time—twenty-six episodes over about six months. The series consisted of historically situated dramatic plays combined with fictional sketches and brief interpretive narration. It was created in cooperation with CBS and the Pan American Union with the goal of promoting awareness and understanding of Latin America and Latin Americans, and building support for the Good Neighbor Policy. *Brave New World*, like other Project series, distributed free educational material to listeners to encourage reading and study by individuals and organized groups (and as a tool for audience measurement). It focused on Latin American history and the historical development of U.S.–Latin American relations for two key reasons. First, writers and producers used an historical approach to situate the Good Neighbor Policy as a culmination of historical efforts to improve inter-American relations. This allowed them to position New Deal policy as an evolution of historical practices rather than a radical break from American traditions—a strategy we find in many Project radio series. Second, this approach gave historical legitimacy to claims that the United States and Latin American countries were "sister republics" sharing experiences of European colonialism, independence, and republican government. Specifically, *Brave New World* used Latin American history as a source of allegorical examples that reinforced the need for hemispheric cooperation in the present.

Although dramatizations of Latin American history were the centerpiece of the series, some episodes used fictional sketches and other theatrical techniques to underscore the message of that history for the present. A notable example was the December 20, 1937, broadcast of "Christ of the Andes," which documented the peaceful resolution of a boundary dispute between Chile and Argentina in 1902. We have a firsthand account of the making of this episode in director Earle McGill's 1940 book, *Radio Directing*.[1] Following the heroic choral theme and brief introduction, the episode opened with a dialogue between First Voice and Second Voice that guided the listener through the interweaving of a fictional sketch of a young wife and husband discussing their fear of war in the present, with a depiction of the conflict and resolution of the boundary dispute in the past. McGill noted that he directed the Voices to use a separate microphone and to perform their lines close to and across the mic "to give them a quality of intimacy, to project them so that they would seem to be with the listener rather than a part of the broadcast."[2] The Voices guided the listeners through the events of the dispute and its peaceful conclusion and commemoration with an enormous statue of Christ the Redeemer. Historical events were re-created using the voices of military commanders urging war as the only solution, women organizing in both countries for arbitration of the conflict, and mothers protesting emotionally against war. While listeners were meant to relate to the Voices—who could traverse time and space and make sense of the past for the present—they were also encouraged to hear themselves in the fearful and isolated couple listening to the radio with their young child. In the final scene, the Voices spoke to the listening audience:

SECOND VOICE: Each of you . . . listening . . . do you know this young wife singing to her child? Do you know this young husband, bright with his pride of fatherhood?
[FIRST] VOICE: Tell them of the Christ of the Andes![3]

By positioning the listeners between the Voices who had learned the lessons of history and the couple who had not, the play encouraged the listeners to help promote education for peace and democratic action. In the end, McGill described the broadcast as "spectacularly successful." Producer Philip Cohen criticized it as "peace propaganda." Some listeners expressed appreciation for both the historical drama and the message of peace offered by this episode, as we explore further below.[4]

After a brief overview of the approach and objectives of *Brave New World*, this chapter situates the series in the larger context of U.S.–Latin American relations and the Good Neighbor Policy. We look closely at program scripts,

memoranda, and recordings to investigate how writers and producers incorporated New Deal policy goals into the series through specific narrative and aesthetic strategies. We also examine what these choices tell us about the evolving
form of the dramatized documentary. Finally, we analyze listener letters sent
to the show—most requesting free educational pamphlets offered during the
broadcast. Some listeners asked for more programs that would grapple with
important social and cultural ideas related to Latin America and would connect them to other national and international listeners. Some expressed a level
of dissatisfaction with commercial radio and a deep interest in what educational
radio had to offer and voiced support for a government-sponsored alternative
to commercial broadcasting.[5]

Reframing the Americas

The weekly lead-in to *Brave New World* promised listeners an innovative educational experience by opening a "living book" of Latin American history and
culture: "Open the book of Latin America! Let the pages come alive with saints
and sinners, beggars and kings, tyrants and rebels, scholars and adventurers,
blood and tears, laughter and comedy! The chronicle of countries from the Rio
Grande to the Straits of Magellan—twenty nations with a history and culture
to be admired, and a democratic ideal we share! We, the people of the United
States have common hopes and common dreams with our southern neighbors!"[6] *Brave New World* presented the region as colorful and exotic, while it
emphasized how similar the region was to the United States in terms of history, political values, and economic interests. This paradoxical framework
mimicked the contradictions at the heart of the Good Neighbor Policy. Along
with deploying a language of hemispheric independence from Europe to
encourage Latin American dependence on the United States, the Good
Neighbor Policy also, Amy Spellacy argues, used the rhetoric of friendship
and neighborliness "to both promote a sense of inter-American community
and facilitate continued U.S. economic and political domination in the
hemisphere."[7] Although the contradictions of both the policy and the radio
series were many, *Brave New World*'s strongly positive view of Latin America is
striking in contrast to today's prevalent populist discourse disparaging Latin
America and Latin Americans.[8]

CBS aired *Brave New World* from November 1937 to April 1938 on Mon-
days at 10:30 P.M. EST on a national network of over 80 stations.[9] The Office
of Education employed its administrative network to encourage teachers, students, and local communities to listen to the series and use it as a tool for learning. We know from listener letters that teachers and students of Spanish,
history, geography, and other subjects incorporated the show into classroom
teaching. In addition, members of social clubs and other groups requested

educational pamphlets for use in group activities and events. After the initial network broadcast, the series was circulated to radio stations and schools via transcription disks and scripts.[10] Overall, *Brave New World* brought acclaim to the Office of Education's Radio Project and raised expectations for future network series, such as *Americans All, Immigrants All*, which aired the following year on CBS.[11]

The foremost goal of *Brave New World* was to foster a positive view of Latin America on the part of the American public. As John Studebaker put it, this was the first time the U.S. government had spent time and money on a sustained effort to "help its own citizens appreciate the ideals of people across the border."[12] One reason for this effort was the belief that, without a positive view of the countries of Latin America, Americans would not support the cooperative relations that were critical to the success of the Good Neighbor Policy.[13] As historian and program adviser Mary Wilhelmine Williams argued, one of the main goals of teaching Americans about Latin American history and culture was to combat "prejudiced and patronizing attitude[s]" about the region.[14] At the same time, government officials hoped that by improving U.S. attitudes about Latin America they would also improve America's image in the region and counteract German and Italian propaganda designed to fan the flames of anti-U.S. sentiment. By the late 1930s, some Washington policy makers were seriously concerned about the influence of fascist propaganda and the possibility of anti-American "fifth column" movements in the region. *Brave New World* and other media projects helped address this concern.[15]

A promotional poster distributed to public libraries and schools provides a bird's-eye view of the series. It describes *Brave New World* as a "dramatic RADIO program" that aimed "To Further the Friendship Between the United States and Latin America."[16] The poster features a detailed map of Mexico, the Caribbean, Central America, and South America (figure 5). It lists all twenty-six proposed episodes organized in historical and topical clusters, ranging from "The Conquistadores" to "Leaders in Nation Building" to "Modern Interests of [the] United States in Latin America." The programs are presented in ten boxes that are connected by an electric charge representing the electronic medium of broadcasting.[17] The ten boxes are linked together in a horseshoe shape that surrounds the map of Latin America. Visually, the *Brave New World* series was portrayed as an electronic lasso encircling the countries of Latin America and tying them to the United States.

The poster also captures the energetic, processional style of dramatized documentary that had proven commercially successful for CBS with shows like *The March of Time* and *Cavalcade of America*. It is perhaps not surprising, then, that Edward R. Murrow, CBS's director of Talks and Education at the time, originally chose *Brave New World* from several program series proposed by the Office of Education.[18] The series was overseen by Radio Project director

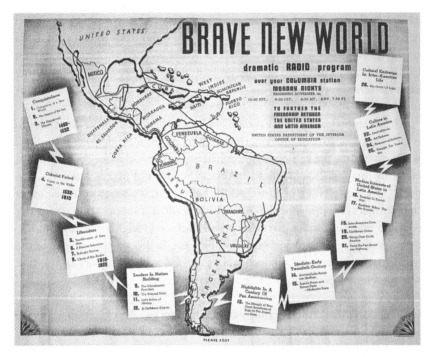

FIGURE 5 *Brave New World* promotional poster. (National Archives (U.S. GPO). Poster, File 19-85 Closed, January 1929–December 1937, Box 125, RG 173 Federal Communication Commission, National Archives, College Park, Maryland.)

William Boutwell and was produced by Shannon Allen, Philip H. Cohen, and music director Rudolf Schramm. Philip Leonard Green provided research, Bernard C. Schoenfeld wrote the scripts, and an Office of Education Committee of five and an advisory committee of ten specialists in Latin American affairs edited and approved the scripts. CBS provided studios and network distribution, along with production support from director Earle McGill and orchestra leader Bernard Herrmann. WPA funds were used to employ actors, singers, musicians, clerical workers, and others.[19] Radio Project staff were relatively young in 1937—Cohen was twenty-five, Schoenfeld thirty, Schramm thirty-four, and Boutwell only thirty-seven—contributing to the atmosphere of energy and excitement that surrounded the production.

The Policy and Ideology of the Good Neighbor

One of the main architects of Roosevelt's Good Neighbor Policy, Samuel Guy Inman, also played a role in developing *Brave New World*. Inman was a missionary, scholar, and social reformer from Texas who, by the 1920s, was a well-known speaker and writer on pan-Americanism. He strongly opposed U.S.

military intervention in Latin America and directly advised Roosevelt on the formulation of the Good Neighbor Policy in 1933 and 1936.[20] Inman began consulting on *Brave New World* in the spring of 1937 and brought not only expertise on the Good Neighbor Policy but also a broader framework of pan-Americanism as embodied in the Pan American Union (forerunner of the Organization of American States).[21] Founded in 1890, the Pan American Union was one of the first international organizations created to promote regional commerce, cooperation, and security in the Americas. Headquartered in Washington, D.C., and supported by the U.S. government, however, it was largely captured by U.S. interests.[22] Richard Cándida Smith argues that the union became a model for the exercise of U.S. power abroad in the form of state-supported private commercial initiatives.[23] In the case of *Brave New World*, the union contributed information on U.S. companies doing business in Latin America, particularly travel and tourism businesses, including the U.S.-government-subsidized Pan American Airways. The radio series promoted U.S. companies as essential bridges between the United States and Latin America—both ambassadors and beneficiaries of good relations in the region.

U.S. ties to the region were historically based on the export and import of raw materials and agricultural goods, and U.S. corporations came to dominate export industries in Cuba, Honduras, Guatemala, Mexico, Chile, and Peru in the early twentieth century.[24] In this environment, the United States frequently deployed military force and economic coercion to safeguard North American investments. The use of force was rationalized, in part, by the Roosevelt Corollary (1904) of the Monroe Doctrine (1823), which asserted the U.S. right to intervene in Latin American political and economic affairs. During World War I—as George Creel's Committee on Public Information promoted U.S. mass culture throughout region—U.S. policy began to depart from the Roosevelt Corollary. As war-torn European nations withdrew economically from the Latin American arena, U.S. financial and commercial interests exploited new possibilities for trade and investment. American business took new interest in the region as a market for industrial and consumer goods and services, and as a fertile environment for financial investment. From this perspective, policies promoting market stability—along with a positive image of U.S. economic life and culture—were better for U.S. business in Latin America than a destabilizing, interventionist foreign policy.

During the 1920s, unsuccessful military interventions, along with changing economic relations, pushed U.S. policy toward a more conciliatory approach.[25] Herbert Hoover, as commerce secretary and then as president, espoused a noninterventionist approach to Latin America.[26] He embraced an associative state model of state-building in which a small central government coordinated, guided, and protected the activities of a "private government" of trade associations, financial interests, and corporations that would act as instruments of

U.S. policy.[27] Infrastructural industries, transportation, and communication, including All American Cables, the Radio Corporation of America, Pan American Airways, and the United Fruit Company, played a key role in associative state expansion in Latin America.[28] The expansion of transportation and travel in the 1920s became a notable feature of *Brave New World*. Three episodes focused on travel and tourism in the region: "A Caribbean Cruise," "A Trip through South America," and "Down the Pan American Highway." The Pan American Union provided information on U.S.-backed projects such as the Pan American Highway and U.S.-owned cruise lines and airlines. These episodes of *Brave New World* affirmed Roosevelt's continuation of the associative state strategy of leaving inter-American cooperation largely in the hands of private U.S. corporations.

The Good Neighbor Policy was also shaped by two interconnected ideological forces: the anti-imperialism of the 1920s and the nationalism of the 1930s. U.S. military interventions in the region—particularly in Nicaragua (1926–1933) and Haiti (1915–1934)—provoked dogged armed resistance, catalyzed anti-U.S. sentiment in the region, and reenergized the anti-imperialist movement in the United States itself.[29] Among the critics of U.S. imperialism were two advisers to the *Brave New World* series: Inman and Ernest H. Gruening, a muckraking journalist from New York, who was well known for his passionate opposition to U.S. intervention in Haiti. Roosevelt appointed him to direct the Division of Territories and Island Possessions, which administratively controlled Puerto Rico, from 1934 to 1939.[30] Along with anti-imperialism, Latin American responses to the economic upheaval of the 1930s had an immediate impact on U.S.–Latin American relations. Latin American states and social groups responded to the contraction of U.S. financial investment and commerce in the region with broad movements of economic and political nationalism. David Green argues that this tide of economic nationalism—and the threat it posed to vast U.S. agricultural, mining, and other holdings—prompted a transformation of U.S. imperialism in the region.[31]

Historians identify three main planks of the Good Neighbor Policy during the New Deal period that incorporated Latin American demands and created a hegemonic pan-Americanism. The first was nonintervention in the internal and external affairs of Latin American nations. Secretary of State Cordell Hull agreed to nonintervention in 1933 when pressed by Latin American delegates to the International Conference of American States in Montevideo.[32] This agreement led to the withdrawal of U.S. forces from Nicaragua and Haiti, repeal of the Platt Amendment, and renegotiation of the U.S. treaty with Cuba. In 1936 the State Department publicly repudiated past acts of violent intervention.[33] With direct military intervention off the table, the United States relied on domestic dictators to enforce an atmosphere of "law and order" in which they believed U.S. investments would thrive. During the early years of the Good

Neighbor Policy, dictators came to power or consolidated power in Nicaragua, Guatemala, El Salvador, Haiti, Cuba, and the Dominican Republic.[34] The second and third components of the Good Neighbor Policy were reciprocal trade and anti-imperialism. The 1934 Reciprocal Trade Agreements Act, also negotiated by Secretary Hull, gave the U.S. president the ability to negotiate bilateral trade agreements with Latin American countries, reducing tariff barriers and encouraging increased communication and interchange between the United States and Latin America.[35] The anti-imperialism plank was more than the repudiation of military intervention: it was a strategy of economic aid and social reform designed to counteract the long-term effects of imperialism. Robert David Johnson chronicles Gruening's attempts to implement such reforms in Puerto Rico, and his ultimate failure. This was, perhaps, the most important but also the weakest component of the policy.[36]

While *Brave New World* presented these three aspects of the Good Neighbor Policy, it focused primarily on what could be characterized as a fourth plank: the ideological transformation in American perceptions of Latin America. This took the form of an effort to eliminate or counteract negative stereotypes found in U.S. media, particularly film, including representations of Latin American nations as "helpless women in distress, unruly children, or savages."[37] Latin American countries began formally protesting negative film stereotypes in the 1920s and 1930s, eventually turning to boycotting and blocking U.S. film imports. Not only did these demeaning portrayals offend Latin Americans, they undermined American support for more reciprocal and cooperative relations with Latin American countries.[38] Negative stereotypes of Latin America in U.S. media also provided fodder for anti-U.S. propaganda beamed at the region by Germany and Italy. In response, *Brave New World* aimed to disseminate positive images of Latin America to the U.S. public.

Because *Brave New World* was engaged in this ideological project of reframing Latin America for a U.S. audience, it is helpful to look at the rhetorical work that the metaphor of the "good neighbor" accomplished in the process. As Spellacy argues, the metaphor of the neighborhood not only carried ideals of community, harmony, and equality but also presented Latin America as a place that was limited, contained, and knowable. Despite its immense geographical space, the metaphor of the neighborhood made the Western Hemisphere ideologically manageable. This was essential for a project like *Brave New World*, which worked to make a region that was little known to people in the United States seem relatable and easily understood. Furthermore, the neighborhood rhetoric was "particularly useful in promoting a sense of community and homogeneity in the Americas."[39] While several episodes of *Brave New World* emphasized the cultural differences within the hemisphere, particularly for purposes of tourism, the program maintained a strong emphasis on the homogeneity of the region in terms of political history and values. In addition, while the metaphor of the neighborhood had the potential to break down barriers of distance and ignorance, it also provided a justification for U.S. control and containment of Latin America.

In sum, *Brave New World* reflected the interwar transformation of U.S.–Latin American relations and gave ideological expression to the Good Neighbor Policy. The policy made some real concessions to Latin American nations (for example, on military intervention and reciprocal trade), but it was more focused on representations and perceptions than on structural inequalities. This same orientation shaped the *Brave New World* series. It offered a positive representation of Latin American countries by emphasizing the fundamental sameness of the "American" historical experience. Members of the advisory board, including Inman, Gruening, and Williams, brought their progressive and anti-imperialist concerns to the series. However, the pan-Americanism advocated by *Brave New World* focused primarily on edifying examples of mutual respect and cooperation from the past, rather than on contemporary efforts to reform U.S.–Latin American relations.[40]

Music, History, and Language in *Brave New World*

In a progress report sent to NBC in 1937, Radio Project officials described the "thrilling adventure" of building a dramatic educational series like *Brave New World*: "It is a terrific undertaking to write a one-act play per week, make it truly dramatic, incorporate into it essential content material, and write a musical mounting for a chorus of 16 and an orchestra of 22 pieces."[41] Along with the scripts, music, and vocal performances, even the narrator was embedded in the action and became a vehicle for dramatization. The report concluded that producing a complex drama like *Brave New World* was a "hard assignment"; however, it was worth the effort to advance the cause of educational radio.[42] Internally, however, Project officials and producers were sometimes less upbeat. Cohen observed that while some episodes were clear and well performed, others were "cluttered" with extraneous material. "We seem to be developing an amazing capacity for telling everything but the actual story," he lamented. Simple and eloquent stories were, he felt, being overwhelmed by complex and distracting material that was only meaningful to the "Latin-American expert."[43] Striking the right balance between educational content and engaging drama was an ongoing struggle for *Brave New World* and other Project programs.

What did *Brave New World* sound like and how did that sound express the show's ideological objectives? Rudolph Schramm composed the music for the series and directed an orchestra and mixed choir made up of WPA musicians and vocalists.[44] Each episode opened with a rousing orchestral prelude, underpinned by a rolling timpani drum, which evoked the forward momentum of a moving train. This was followed by soaring vocals and the announcer's exclamation: "Brave New World!" After this, the choir resumed in a slightly lower key with a processional that suggested a group of people marching purposefully onward. This led directly to the introduction: "Open the book of Latin-America! Let the pages come alive with saints and sinners, beggars and kings . . ." Both the choral theme and bridging music conveyed a forward march of hemispheric progress and expressed emotional attachment to an ideal of pan-American unity.

Documentary makers and scholars have long recognized the important role of music in engaging audiences and dramatizing the real.[45] As Holly Rogers observes, music positions listeners emotionally in relation to the narrative or event being documented.[46] The theme composed by Schramm was a moving choral anthem in the vein of the "Triumphal March" from Verdi's Aida or the French national anthem, "La Marseillaise." The necessarily small size of the orchestra and choir (reflecting the budget of the series) created a more intimate sound similar to a Protestant processional hymn like "Onward Christian Soldiers." Schramm could not compete with the orchestra assembled by Du Pont's *Cavalcade of America*, for example, which included "master musicians" from the New York Philharmonic Orchestra.[47] However, Schramm had a similar purpose of sweeping listeners into the emotional energy and forward momentum of the music to build a sense of unity and shared purpose.

But what kind of unity and purpose did Schramm's theme—and *Brave New World* more broadly—evoke? Because the United States was expanding its political and economic connections with Latin America in the interwar period, it seems likely that Schramm's anthem was heard as an expression of U.S. national unity and purpose. The opening lines of *Brave New World* addressed the audience as "We the people of the United States" and references throughout the program—and in all Radio Project programs—identified both the subjects of the dramas and their listeners as being first and foremost "Americans." These repeated references to national identity constitute what Michael Billig describes as "banal nationalism," that is, everyday representations of the nation that create a shared sense of national belonging and identity.[48] Within this context, Schramm's purposeful theme may have signaled the extension of the values and interests of the United States throughout the hemisphere. On the other hand, in light of the progressive and anti-imperialist thrust of the Office of Education's Latin American project, the music may have suggested a kind of "Internationale" or regional anthem for a newly united and interconnected hemisphere. Perhaps the most likely possibility is that both creators and listeners blurred the themes of U.S. national expansion and interhemispheric solidarity. In this way, the music and drama of *Brave New World* promoted a spirit of "American" unity that was fundamentally tied to the dominant position of the United States in the region, much like the Good Neighbor Policy itself.

In addition to music, *Brave New World* used historical examples to illustrate the core Good Neighbor values of cooperation, anti-imperialism, and mutual respect. History served policy objectives by illustrating the similarity of the historical experiences of Latin American nations and the United States. In particular, the series worked to equate the colonial experiences of people living in the hemisphere by connecting them as neighbors, friends, and family. The first episode, "Conquerors of a New World," used a fictional sketch of two American travelers—one older and one younger—to introduce listeners to the history of Europe's conquest of Latin America. The fictional travelers' conversations were interspersed with historical vignettes of European adventurers, conquistadores, and priests in the New World. The older American traveler encouraged his younger companion to recognize the sense of brotherhood that connected the countries of the Americas. Specifically, he praised the lighthouse being planned to honor Christopher Columbus in the city of Santo Domingo, Dominican Republic: "This lighthouse will symbolize the friendship of the Americas—will be a beacon of democracy and more and we shall be neighbors, friends, comrades. And there will be no more conquistadores! There will be no need for them."[49] A shared geography and historical destiny tied all "Americans" together as neighbors, friends, and comrades. The idea of the Americas as a "beacon of democracy" foreshadowed World War II propaganda that pitted freedom-loving "Americans" against the Axis powers.[50]

Schoenfeld, the series scriptwriter, worked for various government agencies between 1936 and 1943. A liberal, he was briefly a communist between 1945 and 1947.[51] In *Brave New World*, he made a concerted effort to connect each historical episode to the goals of the Good Neighbor Policy. Although "Conquerors of a New World" began with European adventurers and used Christopher Columbus as an icon of hemispheric unity, it was critical of the killing and plundering of the conquest. The fictional American traveler in the story observed that "those conquistadores . . . men who cared for only selfish ends were made immortal by their bloody deeds."[52] In condemning their actions, the episode placed the conquistadores in the same category as the aggressive, militaristic powers of the 1930s, particularly Germany, Italy, and Japan. While the episode praised the cathedrals, universities, and new culture created under European influence, it explicitly compared conquistadores to modern warmongers. This was part of the program's larger strategy—and that of the Good Neighbor Policy—to condemn European influences as dangerous to the hemisphere. The next two episodes, in fact, focused on Latin America's non-European roots and highlighted the efforts of present-day Latin American nations to recognize and valorize those roots. "Empire of the Sun" and "The Magnificent Mayans" explored the achievements of the Incan and Mayan civilizations, highlighting recent findings of archaeologists from Latin America and the United States.

These episodes were followed by one episode on the colonial period (covering indigenous rights) and eight episodes addressing independence and nation-building in the nineteenth century. The first episode documenting the Latin American Liberators, "The Damon and Pythias of the Revolution," opened by celebrating independence leader Simón Bolívar and the founding of the Latin American republics of Venezuela, Peru, Colombia, and Ecuador in 1825. In the spirit of the "beacon of democracy" mentioned in the first broadcast, this script declared that, since the founding of these republics, "democracy has soared above the clouds of tyranny like an eagle high above the Andes."[53] Another episode, "The Schoolmaster President," focused on the life of Domingo Faustino Sarmiento, educator and president of Argentina. The broadcast told how Sarmiento matured as an author and activist in neighboring Chile, and how he was forced to struggle against a series of "dictators" who ruled Argentina against the will of the people.[54] When a woman asked young Sarmiento whether he had a score to settle with Argentine strongman Juan Facundo Quiroga, he replied, "I have a score to settle with all of the tyrants of the world!" Although he was occupied with homegrown dictators, Sarmiento's fight for democracy was projected through late 1930s geopolitical priorities to encompass "world" tyrants.

Other episodes developed a clearer contrast between American democrats and the foreign dictators who threatened the republican values and institutions of the New World. For example, episode 11, "Little Indian of Mexico," focused on President Benito Juarez's efforts to defend the hemisphere against foreign intervention in the form of the French Invasion of 1862–1867 and the proclamation of Maximilian I as emperor of Mexico.[55] In reviewing the scripts, Boutwell emphasized the need to highlight the "danger of non-American forms of government gaining a foothold in the New World" and to demonstrate the "need for the nations of the New World to stand united against the possibility of a threat of non-American intervention."[56] While he found the script successful in showing that "Mexican democracy wins against forms of imperialism," he suggested that the scriptwriter do more to emphasize the contemporary significance of foreign intervention. In particular, he encouraged the writer to develop more of a "feeling of resistance to foreign intervention" on the part of the people of Mexico.[57] This would allow the episode to address "present problems of resisting European or Asiatic intervention."[58]

The episodes that followed the era of independence and nation-building focused on the history and institutions of pan-Americanism, education and the arts, and commerce and tourism. The pan-American episodes documented the activities of four U.S. secretaries of state in relation to Latin America and the institutions of government and learning that served as "Temples to Friendship," such as the new Pan American Union building in Washington, D.C. Two episodes covered trade and three dealt with travel and tourism. Much of the research for the travel scripts came from the Pan American Union, and Boutwell's remarks on the script for "A Caribbean Cruise" suggest that he found the episode to be more promotional than educational. While he allowed that "it probably succeeds in making people want to go to the Caribbean," he complained that the script did not provide a broader orientation to the geography and culture of the region.[59] The remaining episodes addressed educational and cultural topics ranging from poetry, art, and music to philosophy and science.

In *Brave New World*, Latin American history and political traditions were depicted as following the same path as the United States from European colonization to independence to republican democracy. South American liberators Simón Bolívar and José de San Martín were compared to George Washington. Similarities between the United States and Latin America were celebrated even in the unlikely case of Brazil, in which a Brazilian monarchy (not a revolutionary republican movement) declared its independence from the Kingdom of Portugal in 1822. Episode 10, "The Beloved Ruler of Brazil," examined the enlightened and benevolent rule of Emperor Dom Pedro II. The narrator described Dom Pedro, because of his intellectual curiosity, abolitionist views, and focus on the common people of Brazil, as "a man who should have been a Lincoln, but was born a king."[60] Despite ruling the Empire of Brazil for over fifty years, Dom Pedro was nevertheless portrayed as the humble, beloved "Lincoln" of his native country.

Finally, the language used in the series and in pamphlets and other program materials relentlessly characterized the nations of the Americas as similar and familiar. Specifically, the idea of the region as a harmonious neighborhood was conveyed in descriptive terms—such as "Americas," "republics," and "neighbors"—that blurred national boundaries. Indeed, the series title, *Brave New World*, taken from Shakespeare's *The Tempest*, also expressed the idea of a wondrous world that included North, Central, and South America. An undated pamphlet that was sent to interested listeners opened as follows: "Dear Listener: Thank you for your interest in our endeavor to further better understanding among the Americas."[61] *America*, listeners were informed, was an expansive term that enveloped all the countries of the Western Hemisphere. The pamphlet went on to explain that, "Latin America is a convenient term to describe all the countries of America colonized by Latin European nations: Haiti (by France), Brazil (by Portugal) and the eighteen Spanish American Republics (by Spain)."[62] In the United States, however, the primary use of *America* was as a shorthand for the United States of America, rather than as a shorthand for North, Central, and South America. Like the significance of "Americanism" in "pan-Americanism," the meaning of *America* in both "the Americas" and "Latin America" was ambiguous. This language might invoke a new hemispheric multilateralism, or it might signal a process of regional consolidation under U.S. hegemony.

Production Challenges and the Contradictions of the Good Neighbor Policy

Records indicate that at least three scripts dealing with relatively recent events in U.S.–Latin American relations posed challenges for the series.[63] The original "Inter-American Commerce" script was rejected by the committee and had to be revised before it could be broadcast. The source of concern is not clear from the available documents, but Boutwell's comments on the revised script suggest that the episode offered a contentious interpretation of the 1934 Reciprocal Trade Agreement. Boutwell advised less editorializing and more reporting: "Our committees, the State Department, and listeners will not quarrel with honest reporting, but they can take exception to dramatizations and dialog which argue a case which is still controversial."[64] Boutwell frequently expressed skepticism about objections to "controversial" material raised about this and other Radio Project broadcasts by program advisers or network administrators. However, he took a cautious approach of emphasizing facts and minimized arguments that could be interpreted as propaganda.

"*Ariel* and Latin America Idealists" was another episode that had to be postponed for weeks while the script was revised. Although we have not found a final script or recording to evaluate the outcome, it is helpful to look at this case in some detail because it illustrates the contradictory goals of the *Brave New World* series. The *Ariel* script told the story of Latin American youth finding "inspiration in their struggle for social progress and international understanding."[65] The story opened in Montevideo, Uruguay, with José Enrique Rodó discussing his essay, *Ariel*, with a young student activist. The essay encouraged Latin American youth to reject materialism and utilitarianism, and to devote themselves to the pursuit of spiritual fulfillment through the exploration and celebration of Latin American culture. Rodó's strong critique of U.S. materialism was only slightly diluted in the *Brave New World* script: "In the North, young friend, people keep their eyes on the glitter of gold . . . their blood pounds out the rhythm of machinery . . . of industry . . . beauty is thought less of than success . . . but Latin America need not imitate our northern neighbor."[66] Idealism, combined with the effort to end human suffering, was recommended as the best path for Latin American youth to follow. In the depths of the Depression crisis, this message may have had relevance for American listeners as well. The script then went on to provide dramatic vignettes from Argentina, Mexico, and Cuba of students demanding educational and social reforms and taking their protests to the streets. "Today in every country in Latin-America and now in the United States the student movement grows!"[67] The story culminated in the organization of the Ibero-American Student Federation, which included U.S. student participation.

This script provoked a negative response from Boutwell and most of the advisory committee. With typical understatement, Boutwell observed, "If the Latin American student movement stands for terrorist activities as the script indicates and condones (and I'm afraid that's exactly what happened in Cuba), I question whether we should point to it with praise."[68] William Montavon, director of the National Catholic Welfare Conference, objected more strongly in a letter sent to Commissioner Studebaker. He argued that the script should not be broadcast because the only impact it might have would be "the effect of fomenting the revolutionary youth movement."[69] Along the same lines, C. F. Klinefelter, Chair of the Office of Education Committee for *Brave New World*, conveyed the opinions of several committee members that the *Ariel* script was not ready for broadcast. In particular, he quoted Dr. F. J. Kelly's objection: "The script still glorifies rebellion as a means of gaining one's ends and will be interpreted as an endorsement of practices where students take the law into their own hands."[70] Such a broadcast would imply that the U.S. government was taking the side of the students against Latin American governments.

Mary Wilhelmine Williams, an internationally known historian of Latin America and professor at Goucher College, offered a different critique of the *Ariel* script. She observed that the episode seemed to celebrate student rebellion for its own sake without addressing "the really worthy political and economic reforms for which the students stood in various places—as in Cuba, Peru, etc."[71] She also suggested that the program include dramatization of "the great demonstrations made by university students in many parts of South America against the United States intervention in Nicaragua in 1926–1927. That was a fine thing." Williams had toured universities in fifteen Latin American countries in 1926, and may have witnessed some of these protests firsthand. She argued that the student movement should be examined in relation to concrete political impacts, rather than being used as a prop for celebrating a vague idea of inter-American cooperation.[72]

The controversy surrounding the *Ariel* script highlights some of the central contradictions of *Brave New World* and the Good Neighbor Policy more generally. Importantly, the treatment of the student movement elided the very real role of U.S. imperialism as a focus of student—and, more broadly, political—opposition. The series avoided contemporary questions of power and politics in the region and instead focused on the policy goals of "building good feelings," celebrating Pan American cooperation, and telling historical allegories about the need to resist European intervention and dictatorship.[73] Overall, though, *Brave New World* offered a positive image of Latin American history, politics, and culture that was unprecedented in North American media.[74] However, the larger aim of this revisionist history was arguably to convince the American public to embrace an inclusive, "neighborly" strategy of inter-American relations that was viewed by New Deal policy makers as the best way to preserve and strengthen U.S. hegemony in the region.

Listener Responses to *Brave New World*

Along with its ambitious radio productions, the Radio Project devoted considerable energy to cultivating audience feedback. As many as 20,000 listener letters arrived at the Office of Education each week to request pamphlets and comment on shows.[75] Although these letters were not saved for most Project series, fortunately a group of *Brave New World* letters were preserved. At the time, Boutwell made the case that fan letters were a useful measure of audience interest. As he stated in a 1937 presentation: "I would agree that mail is not an *accurate* measure, but I still believe it to be a measure. More than that, a person who has taken the time and trouble to write a letter to a radio program has, to that degree, participated in the program and, chances are, will become a regular listener."[76] Boutwell interpreted listener mail as evidence of audience engagement in educational programs and a step toward "self-education," which he viewed as the ultimate goal of educational broadcasts. While listener letters cannot be taken as representative of the audience as a whole, and there is no explanation of why these particular letters were preserved, the surviving letters do provide valuable first-person reactions to program content that are valuable and cannot be found anywhere else.

Because all the letters saved included pamphlet requests, it is not surprising that they offer no negative appraisals of the program. Radio researcher Jeanette Sayre observed that "almost no program draws very much derogatory mail."[77] Letters were not limited geographically, which is one indicator of a diversity of perspectives among the letter writers (figure 6).[78] The relatively large percentage of letters from the Plains and West Coast is likely a result of the 10:30 P.M. East Coast broadcast time, which was heard in western states during prime time when audiences were larger. It is also possible that those regions had historically closer ties to Latin America and therefore greater interest in a program about that part of the world.

The letters can be divided into four broad groups: 1) simple requests for pamphlets; 2) pamphlet requests that mentioned an educational interest in the show; 3) pamphlet requests that mentioned an interest in travel to Latin America; and 4) pamphlet requests that expressed an interest in economic opportunities in Latin America (figure 7). Nearly all the letters took the general format of a thank-you note, with writers expressing their appreciation for the series and offering compliments to the actors, writers, and producers. Half of the letters simply asked for the pamphlet and mentioned that the writers enjoyed the

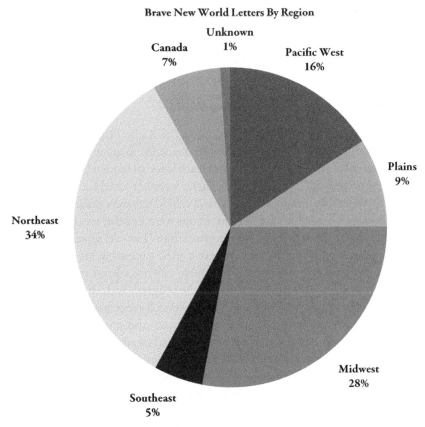

Brave New World Letters By Region

Unknown
1%

Canada
7%

Pacific West
16%

Plains
9%

Northeast
34%

Midwest
28%

Southeast
5%

FIGURE 6 Regional breakdown for a sample of over 1,100 letters sent in response to the *Brave New World* radio series. (*Brave New World* listener letters, Boxes 2–3, Entry 187, RG 12 Office of Education, National Archives, College Park, Maryland.)

program. The second group of letters (42 percent) commented on the educational impact of the program on the listener, and most of our analysis focuses on this group. These letters came from a broad range of people, including students studying Spanish or working on school projects related to Latin America, teachers, and others involved in educational activities with social clubs and groups. The last two groups of letters were much smaller and focused on travel (5 percent) and employment opportunities in Latin America (3 percent).

Although letters from people looking for economic opportunities in Latin America were the smallest group in the sample, the Radio Project staff found these letters troubling. Boutwell created a form letter to dissuade listeners in no uncertain terms from seeking employment in Latin America.[79] Letters in this category were written by people from a range of backgrounds, including laborers, teachers, ranchers, and business people. One listener from Brooklyn wrote, "We are a group of fellows that would like to know if their [*sic*] is any

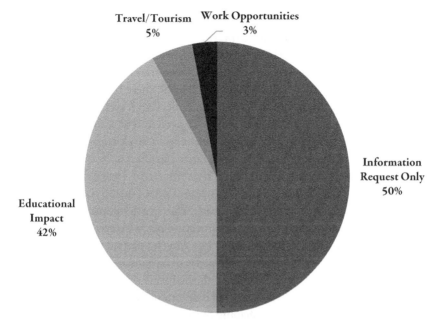

Brave New World Letter Themes

FIGURE 7 Thematic breakdown for a sample of over 1,100 letters sent in response to the *Brave New World* radio series. (*Brave New World* listener letters, Boxes 2–3, Entry 187, RG 12 Office of Education, National Archives, College Park, Maryland.)

possibilities for us securing work in South America, we are skilled laborers."[80] Another listener wrote on behalf of a group of ranchers in Washington state, asking: "Could you send me literature concerning wheat raising and cattle grazing in frontiers of Brazil, Argentina, and Bolivia?"[81] *Brave New World*, it seemed, had been somewhat *too* successful in selling Latin America to a U.S. public suffering through nearly a decade of economic depression. In particular, episodes promoting travel to fertile, temperate, and bountiful countries during the depths of the winter of 1938 may have inspired hopes of finding economic opportunity in Latin America.

The second smallest group of letters came from listeners responding directly to episodes about Caribbean cruises, air travel, and the Pan American Highway. Some writers expressed romantic aspirations to see the "glorious sites" and visit the "fine old cities" mentioned in the broadcasts. Listeners enjoyed the way that travel to distant locales was brought to life in their living rooms. A listener from Sheboygan, Wisconsin, exclaimed that, since hearing the inspiring program, "I'll never rest until I get to Rio!"[82] Another letter praised the Pan American Highway broadcast for "describing actual scenes and events as would be the case of a tourist over the new Pan American Highway to Mexico City."[83]

Although several letters came from people who were no longer in a financial position to travel, most were from listeners with international travel experience writing on elegant stationery or business letterhead. For example, several letter writers mentioned that they had just returned from a month's travel in Mexico or had plans to visit Latin America in the near future. Perhaps with the shadow of war hanging over Europe, wealthier travelers were looking for alternative destinations in the Americas. Overall, these listeners responded enthusiastically to dramatizations of Latin American travel.[84]

The third group of listener letters—the 42 percent that addressed the educational impact of the series—suggests that listeners actively engaged the vocabulary regarding Latin America that was repeated so often in *Brave New World* broadcasts. Listeners experimented with the term *Latin America* and adopted the language of neighborhood, friendship, and even kinship to describe the region.[85] For example, numerous letters made reference to "our neighbors to the south."[86] The importance of the interconnection of the Americas was articulated by several writers. A listener from Los Angeles praised the series' effort to promote positive relations between American nations and opined that "our destiny will be linked more and more with the future of these countries."[87] A listener from Brooklyn similarly predicted that "our neighbors in South America are going to play a great part in shaping our foreign policy."[88] A school superintendent from Nebraska congratulated the program for "doing a great piece of work in welding together the three Americas."[89] In this letter, the metaphor of welding combined the logic of interconnection with the idea of the similarity and familiarity of the Americas that was expressed throughout the *Brave New World* series. Overall, listener letters repeated the idea of "our Western Hemisphere" as a unified and manageable unit.[90]

Letters in the education group also indicated broad approval of the New Deal government's use of radio to promote government policies and cultivate a new perspective on Latin America. Listener letters rarely expressed suspicion of government objectives, and some, in fact, stated support for the government's "propaganda" efforts. In regard to *Brave New World*, a listener from Milwaukee observed, "It is a fine project for the educational department of our government to put forth," and a young listener from Detroit was moved to declare, "The average youth of today respect Our Government and Our Secretary of Interior for sponsoring such programs."[91] Other listeners praised the series as "good propaganda for friendly relations with South America," "peace propaganda," and "intelligent and constructive propaganda."[92] Pacifism was a keen interest of Williams and other program advisers, and it infused several episodes of *Brave New World*, including both "Conquerors of a New World" and "Christ of the Andes," discussed above. After reading the script for "Christ of the Andes," Cohen anticipated listener complaints and protested to Boutwell: "I resent having peace propaganda shoved down my throat especially when I have been told that I am to hear the story of Latin-America." According to Cohen, *Brave New World* scripts were hampered by being "torchbearers" of a political philosophy rather than purveyors of fact.[93] For some listeners, however, this was not a drawback of the series. A vocal portion of the audience identified with internationalism and appreciated the Project's progressive take on Latin American history and culture.

Finally, the educational letter group reflected approvingly on the experiment of education by radio, frequently making comparisons between *Brave New World* and commercial programs. Many listeners commented on the innovative role of dramatization in the series.[94] One identified the main purpose of commercial programs as, "to sell whatever they have to offer." In contrast, "Your program is delightfully different. There are no commercials! This is an unusual thing now-a-days. In fact, some of my friends did not believe me when I told them about this program which is educational but not presented in a formal form, such as a lecture, but is dramatized."[95] The dramatization of historical and contemporary events distinguished *Brave New World* from other educational programs that relied on lectures, interviews, and discussions. Letter writers commented favorably on the performance, music, and overall production of the programs; some described *Brave New World* as their favorite series on the air.

Several listeners commented on the documentary strategy of *Brave New World* and described their appreciation of the ability of drama to bring events to life. "The way the program was dramatized makes me feel as though I was at the scene of happening," wrote one New York City listener.[96] Another listener expressed appreciation for a program in which "true lives were dramatized."[97] A few listeners identified *Brave New World*'s documentary strategy and compared it favorably to CBS's *Cavalcade of America*.[98] In sum, these letters indicate that some listeners expressed interest in the kind of noncommercial, educational, and socially relevant programming that public broadcasting would eventually bring to the air.

Listeners not only interacted with the content of *Brave New World* but also interpreted the meaning of the program within the overall system of commercial broadcasting and the broader social context of radio. For example, numerous letter writers saw the documentary approach of the series as an antidote to commercial airwaves saturated with the "overdone" advertising of products and uninspired adventure, crime, and mystery programs.[99] One writer suggested that *Brave New World*, or a series like it, could be substituted for programs like the *Lone Ranger* to both thrill and educate children. Another writer suggested following *Brave New World* with a bilingual program that could be transmitted to both United States and Latin American listeners simultaneously.[100] Such plans were, however, certainly not on the agenda for CBS and NBC, which saw Office of Education productions as minor, public-minded additions to their sponsor-driven programming.

Conclusions

This chapter uses the case of *Brave New World* to examine the distinctive form and content of the Educational Radio Project's dramatized documentary programs. Within the context of U.S.–Latin American relations, the series informed listeners about the innovations of the Good Neighbor Policy, but more importantly it advanced that policy by promoting a positive view of the region for public consumption. Overall, however, *Brave New World* focused on reframing perceptions of hemispheric relations rather than investigating current structural inequalities. In a couple of instances, attempts to examine current Latin American relations led to scripts that Boutwell and other committee members viewed as too controversial for broadcast.

Analysis of a group of over 1,100 listener letters indicates that some listeners responded favorably to a government radio program that aimed to promote Roosevelt's Latin American policies. Because it was grounded in official U.S. foreign policy and promoted the relatively benign ideas of hemispheric cooperation and friendship, it is possible that *Brave New World* was insulated from anti–New Deal attacks on "propaganda" in ways that Project shows dealing with domestic issues were not. Although some producers and listeners readily understood the series to be "propaganda," those who challenged New Deal policies may have found it less problematic because it dealt with policies directed outside the United States. Unlike later Radio Project programs that attempted to avoid charges of being "government propaganda" by presenting a range of perspectives on policy questions, *Brave New World* directly and unabashedly promoted the major planks of the Good Neighbor Policy. But the program was not just informational—it sought to foster a different kind of American citizenship, alert not just to the national self-interest of the United States but to the neighborly roles and attitudes needed in the hemisphere.

While letter writers echoed the broadcasts' focus on mutual interests and shared values with "our southern neighbors," they offered their own ideas about the meanings and implications of *Brave New World*. In particular, the program inspired some listeners to offer their own visions of radio as a medium of education: from bringing noncommercial programming to the American people to opening U.S. airwaves to Latin American voices. Although legislative recognition and institutional aid for public radio were decades away, listener letters provide additional evidence that the Educational Radio Project helped prepare the ground for public broadcasting. It did so not only by promoting the station set-asides that eventually formed the infrastructure of public radio and TV, but also by revealing a latent audience demand for publicly engaged, noncommercial radio content.[101]

3

Americans All,
Immigrants All

Toward Cultural Democracy

In November 1938 *Americans All, Immigrants All* followed *Brave New World* on CBS; it was the ninth network series produced by the Educational Radio Project. Developed in cooperation with the Service Bureau for Intercultural Education, *Americans All* was designed "to increase tolerance and promote unity among our people by broadening the understanding of the contributions of men and women from many nations to our national life."[1] A popular success, the show generated high listener mail and won prizes.[2] Boutwell told Edward R. Murrow in November 1938 that *Americans All* was "going over swell" and that they had received 2,300 letters and cards in the first four days.[3] He wrote Sterling Fisher at CBS in late December 1938 that the mail for the program was "quite remarkable."[4] The show generated more correspondence than *Brave New World* or *Let Freedom Ring!*, indicating that something about its format and content resonated with the public.[5] The timing was good, as Boutwell acknowledged—"events in Europe have certainly given us a beautiful build-up for Americans All," by showcasing the human costs of ethnic hatred and intolerance.[6] The time of day was also good—CBS had at short notice offered to move AAIA from Monday 10:30 P.M. Eastern to Sunday 2:00 P.M. Eastern, an excellent slot just before the New York Philharmonic broadcast.[7] The Office of Education considered this a flagship series and was proud of its work. Studebaker inquired in November 1938 about the availability of the recordings "since he wants to send a set to Warm Springs"—presumably in the hope that President Roosevelt would listen to them.[8] Producers credited on the series included Earle McGill and William Robson, but Betsy Tuthill is also noted on at least one CBS AAIA script. There were twenty-six episodes in all, the season lasting six months.

Each episode began with a wordless sung fanfare of Rudolph's Schramm's opening chorus, then a narrator through a filter: "Let us raise a standard to which the wise and honest can repair" and the sung chorus beginning "A standard brave and defiant, uniting Americans all." Then the Announcer: "Americans All—Immigrants All. This is the story of how you, the people of the United States, made America—you and your neighbors, your parents and theirs. It is the story of the most spectacular movement of humanity in all recorded time—the movement of millions of men, women and children from other lands to the land they made their own. It is the story of what they endured and accomplished—and it is also the story of what this country did for them. Americans All—Immigrants All!" Then the chorus again, concluding with a rousing sung exhortation: "Remember we're immigrants all!"

Music was very important in *Americans All*. Lead writer Gilbert Seldes said at a planning conference: "Persons listening to the program will think of it as music and drama. If you think of it that way that is the way you will want to listen to it."[9] The Prospectus called for a twenty-piece orchestra, but it is the chorus that makes the more obvious contribution. Sung choruses frequently punctuated, interrupted, or welled up behind the spoken dialogue. The ever-present choir gave a distinctive sound to this series—denaturalizing the stories to some extent. Maybe this is what Boutwell meant when he complained in February 1939 about "a tendency for a slight artificiality to creep into the handling of the music."[10] We might speculate that the series sought not to emulate film, with constant deployment of suggestive background music smoothly augmenting the central action, but rather to use the music more disruptively and intrusively, to remind us that we are listening to a radio dramatization. AAIA often sounded busy. Studebaker complained of episode eight that it had "the most elaborate aggregation of sound effects I have ever heard . . . a background of sound which often became so noisy as to make inaudible the foreground of talk." He was still complaining about "noisiness" at episode ten—there were gunshots, crowd hubbub, shouted dialogue, falling trees, spoken dialogue in many accents, and music.[11] The nature of the series, depicting people from a great range of languages and ethnicities, tested the ability of actors to mimic accents. Ted de Corsia at CBS claimed to have twenty-four dialects "on the tip of his tongue" but also reveled in the ability of New York City to provide dialect lessons—whether in Gullah or Greek—just a subway ride away.[12]

This chapter introduces the team of people who made *Americans All, Immigrants All* and explores the goals and approaches of the series. We draw on the rich archive of their discussions and arguments that reveals the complexity of their task and the extraordinary effort behind making these programs, including the modeling of cooperation between educators and commercial networks. After investigating the tensions between education and propaganda that inevitably surrounded a radio series about diversity and tolerance, we look more closely at AAIA as the product of a collaboration with the intercultural education movement led by Rachel Davis DuBois. In particular, we review conflicts between advocates of a focus on distinct cultural groups and those who thought an orientation to cultural interaction *between* groups was more important. Finally, we take a brief look at audience responses to *Americans All* and assess the significance of the program for CBS and for American listeners. Although individual programs may today sound clumsy, even patronizing, we argue that the series made a significant cultural intervention and represented a remarkable mobilization of the resources of this new model of educational broadcasting based on associative government-commercial cooperation. It was never an easy path to follow. The educators and broadcasters associated with the Project believed that democratic values and democratic behavior were cultural traits that could be learned. The broad goal of AAIA was popular education on how to live in a culturally pluralist democracy—an aim that remains important and relevant more than eighty years later.

Program Personnel and Objectives

CBS assigned its director of television, Gilbert Seldes, as the main writer for the series and lent him to the Project part time. Seldes, born in 1893 in New Jersey to Russian Jewish immigrant parents, had become, by the 1920s, "the most vocal American champion of popular culture."[13] He was on record as opposed to education by radio, labeling it "one of those attractive, utterly wrong notions which come to plague decent citizenry once every five years."[14] He consistently argued against programs designed "in the direction of destroying prejudice" and instead wanted listeners to be able to draw their own conclusions from the material presented about the contributions each group had made to the nation.[15] He believed that commercial broadcasters in the United States had successfully developed a mass listening audience and that educators could learn much about communication from them.

Seldes drew upon research provided by DuBois and the Service Bureau for Intercultural Education. Born in 1892 in New Jersey to Quaker parents, DuBois had been active in pro-tolerance education since the mid-1920s and had collected extensive research materials on American ethnic groups. The American Jewish Committee contributed significantly to *Americans All* by paying her salary. The Office of Education held out to DuBois the idea that if *Americans All* was a success, intercultural work might become a permanent Division of the Office and, hence, that an ongoing job might be found for her.[16]

Additional writing support was provided by lesser-known contributors. In a letter to Boutwell in January 1939, Seldes mentioned that he had engaged "an extremely good script writer to sketch out certain dramatic scenes. . . . The young woman doing the work is exceptionally good at a certain type of brief dramatization and some of the most approved sequences in the scripts have been partly her work."[17] This was Jane Ashman, hired by the Project to work on the series. Born in 1911, Ashman had attended high school in Winnetka, Illinois, graduated from Carleton College in 1932, and a couple of years later took a class in playwriting from Frederick Koch at Northwestern University.[18] She cowrote the final three episodes of *Americans All* and contributed to others. She and Seldes wrote, she recalled, "in the patchwork fashion," she working up details for scenes.[19] The series suffered for that reason, she felt: "The *Immigrants* scripts were never good scripts as such—except in a few cases where either Seldes or I wrote the whole thing."[20] In another letter to Boutwell she mentioned "all the scripts I've written for the Office of Education already (ghostly though they were)," indicating perhaps an even broader and less acknowledged role.[21] In addition, experienced journalist Laura Vitray was brought in midway through the series as editor on the scripts, supplementary publications, and teaching materials.

Production of AAIA was arduous, involving extensive research (Boutwell with all his experience described the research on the series as "tremendous") and consideration of the best means of presenting the material.[22] The dramatized documentary format was labor intensive and project files give a sense of the care and attention to detail, and the time pressures, involved. One publicity letter explained that "on every half hour program we will put 1500 to 2000 [staff] hours of preparation."[23] The networks also, of course, contributed to Radio Project shows in significant ways. Boutwell explained in late 1938 that both CBS and NBC were "contributing very heavily for orchestra, actors, sound effects, studios, and many other factors."[24]

Network broadcast of sustaining programs could mean less than it seemed if numbers of local stations opted to take local commercial programs rather than network sustaining ones. But 102 of the 114 available CBS stations carried AAIA (figure 8).[25] In Kansas City on March 17, 1939, 33 percent of the radios in use were tuned to it.[26] The total radio audience for the series was estimated at 6.5 million. Not just in production but also in distribution, therefore, *Americans All* exemplified the FREC's goal of promoting "actual cooperative arrangements" between educators and broadcasters. Almost inevitably, there were some frustrations and complaints at the Radio Project end—in the case of AAIA about the number of times CBS assigned a new producer to

FIGURE 8 Map showing distribution of *Americans All, Immigrants All* by radio. (National Archives photo no. 12-E-32-2169 dup #. "Radio," Radio Project-WPA Photographs, 12-E-32, Box 39, RG 12 Office of Education, Still Picture Branch, National Archives, College Park, Maryland.)

the series—but, overall, Project relations with CBS seemed to work better than with NBC.

The belief underlying the Project was that the task was not just producing the broadcasts and ensuring stations accepted them but also stimulating audience interest and enabling enduring attitude change. On a commercial show, the networks cooperated with advertisers who undertook that audience-side work. On these Radio Project shows, the cooperating partner was the Office of Education, which undertook publicity and advertising work for its series. "It has been our opinion from the beginning of the Radio Project," Boutwell explained, "that a major task in the use of radio for education is the assemblage of an audience. To wait for an audience to grow through the slow process of chance discovery of programs is a fairly inefficient method."[27] As with *Brave New World*, the Office of Education used its administrative contacts to do that audience building work. Letters about *Americans All* in Studebaker's name were sent to 7,000 school superintendents, 23,000 high school principals, 27,000 PTA presidents, and 9,000 librarians.[28] Publicity was also undertaken by the Service Bureau for Intercultural Education. Investigative journalist (and former student of DuBois) Arthur Derounian was employed to do publicity for

AAIA. Philip Cohen observed that Derounian "almost single-handed . . . has done one of the best jobs in publicity done in relation to any of our programs" and that he was in some measure "responsible for the great increase in our mail."[29]

The subsequent use of the programs in educational and community settings received almost as much attention as the preparation of the broadcasts. The recordings were for sale with a teachers' manual; the scripts were available for local reperformances. Teachers used AAIA in schools; the YMCA was interested in using it in its 1,150 branches. Studebaker wrote: "When I think of the far-reaches not merely of the broadcasts but of the later use of the scripts and the recordings which we expect to make, in combination with manuals and other instructional materials, I feel that we should capitalize every opportunity to do this job better than any series with which we have had experience to date."[30]

Propaganda for Tolerance and Harmony?

Within the Office there was, alongside commitment to the program, constant concern about the potentially blurred line between adult education and propaganda. At the September 1938 planning conference, Studebaker insisted that the Office had "no interest in political propaganda. I have never been asked to spread it. The Office has never been asked to spread it." He understood the purpose of AAIA rather as one of enabling self-expression: "It is to arouse the enthusiasm of people of different races and nationalities living in peace together and working together to strengthen the life of each and make available to all the richness that comes from the freedom to each race to express itself."[31] Nevertheless, a writer in *Radio Guide* in late 1938 described AAIA as "Government propaganda, if you like—propaganda for peace and good-will among men."[32] While propaganda for tolerance and understanding might seem self-evidently a good thing, it was not so to all. A radio series designed to "increase tolerance and promote unity among our people" would have been ambitious at any time, but was especially so in late 1938, in a nation still in deep economic crisis and a world in turmoil.

The association of government broadcasting with propaganda was so strong by the late 1930s that propaganda was discerned even where it was not intended. As AAIA went to air in November 1938, there was national debate about whether more Jewish refugees from Europe should be admitted to the United States. In Congress there was resistance—Senator William Borah predicting "tremendous opposition" to any attempt to increase immigration.[33] Edward Ashley Bayne, director of the Service Bureau for Intercultural Education, wrote to researcher Jeanette Sayre that "some of us have felt that the emphasis on the Jew made by giving him a special program . . . had added fuel to the conception that we are pro-Jew and the whole series is designed as pro-refugee propaganda."[34] Sayre, who was studying the AAIA audience, replied that a couple of respondents had observed that "since the personnel of the Columbia Broadcasting System is largely Jewish, it is likely that they were putting on the program to arouse opinion in this country in favor of letting in the refugees."[35] In this charged and suspicious environment, the Office was understandably anxious that nothing it produced for radio be heard as propaganda.

Project leaders were generally happy to describe their aim as fostering tolerance—that seemed to them a defensible liberal goal in a democracy. Boutwell wrote to Edward R. Murrow in London about plans for AAIA: "it will be devoted . . . to contributions which the various nationalities and races have made to the American culture. Objective: Tolerance."[36] Studebaker described tolerance as a self-evident good in a letter inviting author Louis Adamic to join the AAIA Supervisory Committee: "Thinking people agree that the foundation of our democracy is the spirit of tolerance of the other man's viewpoint, regardless of his race or place of origin."[37] Of course in casting "thinking people" as in favor of tolerance, Studebaker tacitly conceded that not all Americans agreed. The golden door of immigration to the United States had closed only in 1924. Not only did the scars of the nativist campaigns of the 1920s remain, new transnational currents of racial nationalism and anti-Semitism were being welcomed by at least some Americans, and in the Jim Crow South racial inequality and white supremacism had legal and institutional authority.

The idea of promoting tolerance was criticized by both DuBois and Seldes. DuBois described use of the word as "unfortunate": "members of the minority groups and other races feel that by its use there is an assumption of a bit of a superiority attitude."[38] Perhaps we hear her voice toward the end of the episode on the Germans: "Tolerance. What is it? Why is it top column news today? Tolerance is just understanding the other fellow. But in a democracy we need more. We need an appreciation for having in our midst people of many backgrounds who have contributed so much that is essential to our happiness and well being." Seldes was also unhappy with the idea that the mission of AAIA was promoting tolerance. He reminded Boutwell:

> When we first discussed the series together we agreed that we wanted to illuminate the subject, and that we would never make any plea, never expound the underlying attitude. The German script in effect makes a plea for tolerance (which is not the theme of the series) and you note in your letter that Dr. Studebaker favors "something in the nature of a sermonette" at the end of each program. I see the need and value of a summary at the end . . . But to attempt to do more strikes me as extremely dangerous. The underlying purpose of the series is to make people understand that life in the United States is the achievement of many kinds of people, each giving what it had to give, each

taking much from the others. That idea should come out more clearly in the scripts; it should be repeated at the end, and serve as an indicator of future programs. Anything beyond that strikes me as exhortation—not particularly effective on the air, and full of pitfalls.[39]

For Seldes, propaganda—for either tolerance or appreciation—was to be avoided. He thought Americans could be led to embrace appreciation of different cultures largely on self-interest grounds, as they learned more about what immigrants had done for the nation. DuBois, however, wanted exhortation—to push Americans beyond mere tolerance to positive gratitude and affection for each culture's gifts.

Intercultural Education and Activism

Americans All was shaped by DuBois's intercultural education movement, which developed "the most important and widely used antiprejudice curriculum in American schools through World War II." The movement advocated using schools as instruments for fostering harmony and appreciation between Americans of different ethnic and racial heritages.[40] AAIA had a distinguished Supervisory Committee of experts in the field of intercultural and tolerance education.[41] With its key themes of ethnic and class unity—and the celebration of a culturally pluralist version of American nationalism—*Americans All* resonated to some extent with the politics of the Popular Front, but was more directly the product of the liberal progressive educational movement championed by Rachel DuBois and others.

Shaped by her Quaker upbringing, DuBois had a background in movements for international peace. In the early 1920s, however, she had concluded that racial tolerance at home was a precondition for world peace and that better education could foster both. During the 1930s she became increasingly concerned that, while "many teachers are developing activities aimed at increasing international understanding, few were aiming at the development of more harmonious relations among groups within our own country." That work of fostering cultural appreciation, in schools and communities, became her life's work: to "reduce segregation, discrimination, and conflict by breaking down prejudice and developing more appreciative attitudes among the various culture groups which make up America."[42] Her contributions to AAIA were driven by these activist commitments, and hence she understood the goal to be changing attitudes. In her writings through the 1930s she unembarrassedly used the phrase "social control" to describe this process, quite clear that attitudes could and should be changed by expert intervention. In a 1938 memo about AAIA to Seldes, Studebaker, and Boutwell, setting out "Certain Generalizations . . . Which Are to Be Held in Mind During the Preparation of the Programs," the first was as follows: "This is a conscious attempt to use the best means of social control in order to develop more appreciative (not tolerant) attitudes among America's culture groups."[43] While that might sound like a recipe for producing propaganda, DuBois never used the word *propaganda* about her own work, but only about the race-hate inspiring propaganda that she was combating. She wanted AAIA shows—and follow-up educational material—to activate new cultural attitudes and behaviors in listeners. For example, she suggested that the series ask listeners to take part in the sharing of cultural values by "becoming conscious of something in their own background that can be shared with others."[44]

At Woodbury High School in New Jersey in the later 1920s, DuBois had pioneered an assembly program in which students were addressed by people of different ethnicities ("culture bearers") about their group. It all came about after a "boring" speaker on the League of Nations failed to capture students' interest. She thought of a more experiential way to let them learn about diverse cultures *within* the United States—a different route to world mindedness and peace consciousness: "people's interests must be aroused dramatically—that is, their feelings must be reached."[45] The assemblies were to engage students emotionally, intellectually, and socially—so an element of dramaturgy as well as pedagogy was involved.[46] In the assemblies, DuBois favored materials that demonstrated a group's long residence in the United States and its people's participation in the major events of American history—these were to become key ingredients in AAIA as well.[47]

Having made a name for herself with this intercultural work in schools, in 1932 DuBois went back to study. Her mentors at Teachers College in New York included progressive educators Daniel R. Kulp II, William Heard Kilpatrick, and Harold Rugg and anthropologists Franz Boas and Ruth Benedict. She became director of the Service Bureau for Intercultural Education, an organization she had founded in 1933 as a clearinghouse for materials for intercultural education. The Bureau received funding from the WPA and Civil Works Administration, to research American ethnic groups and produce classroom resources on such topics as "The Arts and Crafts of the Pennsylvania Germans," "The Negro in Literature," "Orientals in Science and Invention," and "Jewish Orchestra Conductors in American Life."[48] DuBois was a longtime member of the NAACP and had appreciative and collegial relationships with African American leaders, including William Pickens, W.E.B. Du Bois, and A. Philip Randolph.[49]

Rachel DuBois had the idea for intercultural discussion groups and ultimately a pro-tolerance radio series after listening to Charles Coughlin and wanting to counter his message that the United States was a white Christian nation.[50] John Studebaker was enthusiastic about the idea and about the fact that DuBois had already developed material on sixteen different ethnic groups as part of a WPA-funded project.[51] Network acceptance of the proposal contrasted with a longer history of commercial radio assimilationism, referencing cultural difference to define and sanction the mainstream. Hilmes argues that it was "precisely the task of radio in the 1920s and 30s . . . to serve as this nation's central institution of cultural unification and definition. Radio told a nation of immigrants what it meant to be an American, and how an American should think and behave."[52] *Americans All* set about forging national unity at a time of crisis in an ethnically diverse nation in a quite different way, foregrounding earnest appreciation of other cultures and portraying cultural difference as a positive thing. That this was a prestigious series with government backing leant more power and influence to its representations.

In December 1938, in response to *Kristallnacht* in Germany, the superintendent of schools in New York City ordered twice monthly school assembly sessions to teach tolerance.[53] In every public school, assemblies were to be devoted to the "promulgation of American ideals of democracy, tolerance and freedom for all men."[54] The Board of Education added that "the programs for all these assemblies should be based on the social and political history of the United States."[55] Superintendent Harold Campbell advised principals and teachers to find "many opportunities" to inculcate the ideals of democracy and tolerance— not just in history, geography, and literature lessons but also in health, where games and folk dances could help develop a spirit of fair play.[56] DuBois's Service Bureau provided curriculum and in-service materials to support the schools in these programs.[57] Studebaker publicly linked *Americans All, Immigrants All* to this initiative and reinforced the idea that this was a needed response to the international situation, proclaiming it the "historic duty of the schools of our Nation" to "strengthen the defenses of our democratic ideas and practices against the inroads of doctrines . . . so thoroughly lacking in scientific and spiritual justifications."[58]

Conflicting Approaches to Intercultural Education: DuBois versus Seldes

DuBois pioneered the "gifts" approach to intercultural education. Identifying the best each culture had to offer ("the fine courtesy of the Italians," for example), she asked, "Can cultural values be consciously shared?" The attempt to do so was her progressive project. She observed that while modern societies engaged in planning of all kinds, there had been little attempt to plan "for an integration of cultural values."[59] DuBois cast the cultural traditions of minority groups as comparable to natural resources and warned that "America's *cultural* resources are also being wasted because of the tremendous pressure for everyone to act alike, think alike, *be* alike."[60] These two quite practical progressive ideas—that planning could be applied to cultural as well as social and economic matters and that conservation and wise husbandry of the nation's cultural resources could be achieved by valuing and preserving all cultures within the nation—informed her educational practice.[61]

"Intercultural" implied negotiation between existing cultures, understood as distinct and separate. Critics at the time and since have felt that DuBois's approach risked reifying ethnic cultures, thinking of them as static, outside time and change.[62] DuBois was familiar with the anthropological ideas of Franz Boas, Margaret Mead, and Ruth Benedict, citing them in her work and collaborating with Benedict at the Progressive Education Association. She acknowledged the anthropological insight that cultures were always dynamic and in flux, but nonetheless retained her activist sense that changing perceptions of separate single cultures was the most urgent task. She spelled that message out to Seldes, Studebaker, and Boutwell in 1938: "There are no appreciative or world brotherhood attitudes in general; therefore if specific misconceptions exist toward certain groups and are to be changed . . . it is necessary that such groups be dramatized separately."[63] This separate cultures approach became the cause of conflict—in the Progressive Education Association's Commission on Intercultural Education, in the Service Bureau, and in the writing of *Americans All*. Benedict put the critique most sharply, accusing DuBois of deploying an unscientific understanding of culture to argue for "immigrant cultural conservation" and calling her "the woman who believed that race problems could be solved by teaching children that Japanese were adept at arranging flowers." Mead was, however, supportive for many years and agreed with the model of seeking cultural change at an interpersonal level.[64] Tensions between pluralist cultural relativism, which saw cultures as open and individuals as able to make and remake themselves, and the attribution of more stable and even determining ethnic characters, ran through American intellectual life at this time.[65] In planning *Americans All*, progressive educational and anthropological ideals of personal growth and openness to experience were thus perhaps not surprisingly always in tension with the recitation of a history about relatively fixed and timeless national/ethnic characters and personalities.

Seldes had a different idea from DuBois about *Americans All*—he wanted it to portray not individual groups but the big picture of how immigrants had contributed to the United States and become Americanized. Studebaker, who was actively involved in early conferences developing the series, worked out a compromise—some episodes on individual groups, some on larger themes.[66] Seldes eventually agreed that treating each group separately would be acceptable *if* they could be associated with one principal gift to the nation:

> I conceived the programs dealing with separate nationalities as units in a complete structure. I should like the listener, at the end of the series, to be able to look back and feel, "Now I know how the essential things came to America."

Frankly I think this of vastly greater importance than the feeling, at the end of any separate program, that "I never knew till now that the Swedes made the first log cabin." In this view, some of the recent programs are concrete building blocks: in the Scandinavian, the idea of cooperation is central; in the German, the idea of fighting for freedom and honest dealing comes out in such varied phases as abolition, civil service, and conservation; the Irish script centered on education through schools and publications—by emphasis if not by amount of time given to the subject; the Jewish deals with several associated efforts to improve the human lot, connected by one central idea—to avoid the need of charity by preventing poverty, and this is worked out through labor relations, settlement work, scientific attack on disease. Various aspects of the establishment of civil rights and political independence were central in the English and Scottish scripts; the use of the land was meant to be the theme of the Hispanic.[67]

This mixing of attention to gifts and groups was the approach taken, as table 3 illustrates.

Americans All then documented the "contributions" of distinguished representatives of each group and attributed each group with one dominant and unchanging personality. For example (from episode one): "Voice: My people brought intelligence . . . My people knew how to cultivate the soil . . . My people brought hatred of the tyrant . . . My people brought strong arms and sturdy back and willing hands." The accompanying brochure explained: "Immigrant Gifts. The brawn, brain, and inventive genius of the immigrants and their descendants have made the United States a world leader in science and industry. In reading about this pageant of achievement, which is unique in human history, you will also learn something about the *diverse racial origins* of those who laid the gifts on the 'altar of America.' Here they are— IMMIGRANTS! SONS OF IMMIGRANTS! AND SONS OF SONS OF IMMIGRANTS!—men and women who have thrilled the worlds of science and industry, the arts and crafts, and social progress and government."[68] Each episode focused on the most distinguished individual representatives of each group and documented their achievements and contributions to the nation, linking them to the attributed group personality.

The focus on immigrant gifts was a means of promoting tolerance, but also raised uncomfortable questions about the criteria upon which the value of those gifts was to be assessed. In the episode on "Orientals in the United States," listeners learned that "the Oriental temperament has elements of nobility all its own" but that "the active rushing method of American industrial and commercial life is not natural to the tradition of the Orient. It is not surprising therefore, that some of the greatest contributions of these immigrants have been in the sciences where long and patient research, rather than quick action, is

Table 3
***Americans All, Immigrants All* Episode List**

Number	Theme	Date of broadcast
1	Opening Frontiers	Nov. 13, 1938
2	Our English Heritage	Nov. 20, 1938
3	Our Hispanic Heritage	Nov. 27, 1938
4	Scotch, Scotch-Irish and Welsh	Dec. 4, 1938
5	The Winning of Freedom (Colonial and Federal Periods)	Dec. 11, 1938
6	The Negro in the United States	Dec. 18, 1938
7	French Speaking Peoples	Dec. 25, 1938
8	The Upsurge of Democracy (Jacksonian Period)	Jan. 1, 1939
9	The Irish in the United States	Jan. 8, 1939
10	Germans in the United States	Jan. 15, 1939
11	Scandinavians in the United States	Jan. 22, 1939
12	Closing of the Frontiers	Jan. 29, 1939
13	Jews in the United States	Feb. 5, 1939
14	Slavs in the United States Part 1 (Russian and Polish)	Feb. 12, 1939
15	Slavs in the United States Part 2 (Poles, Czechs and Slovaks)	Feb. 19, 1939
16	Orientals in the United States	Feb. 26, 1939
17	Italians in the United States	Mar. 5, 1939
18	Near Eastern Peoples	Mar. 12, 1939
19	Immigrants from Small Countries	Mar. 19, 1939
20	Contributions in Industry	Mar. 26, 1939
21	Contributions in Science	Apr. 2, 1939
22	Contributions in Arts and Crafts	Apr. 9, 1939
23	Contributions in Social Science	Apr. 16, 1939
24	A New England Town	Apr. 23, 1939
25	An Industrial City	Apr. 30, 1939
26	Grand Finale	May 7, 1939

needed."[69] Episode two aimed to show that, although the English were not the first to arrive in North America, they "mostly with their numbers, and also with their spirit, impress upon our country, and establish firmly here, their culture; language, laws, their burning desire for personal and political freedom, etc." For the episode on Near Eastern peoples, the prospectus said the aim was to "stress the law-abiding qualities of these peoples (Greeks, Turks, Armenians, Syrians, Arabians, etc.), respect for learning, manual skill and fine artistic sense. Near Easterns bring excellent food habits—well balanced meals."[70] The aim of tolerance was thus, in line with Seldes's views, not made obvious, but one can discern some shaping of the evidence in counter-prejudice directions—the Germans are introduced as a "frugal and hence prosperous people," while the

Jews are innately philanthropical and concerned for the common good. DuBois's propensity to connect the case for respect and appreciation to a group's longevity in America, and on the basis of distinctive contributions made and characteristics demonstrated, had some obvious problems—one conceivable extrapolation of the argument was that equality was something earned by groups through achievements and contributions and embraced by the host culture out of self-interest.

The gifts approach not only, as Diana Selig argues, "erased differences within groups and froze each culture in time," it also seemed to ignore the reality that many or most Americans were descended from more than one group.[71] In contrast, Teachers College progressive educator Harold Rugg's 1938 school text *Our Country and Our People*, a comparable and contemporaneous piece of progressive intercultural education, acknowledged that "most Americans have ancestors of several nationalities."[72] *Americans All* portrayed the *cultural* mixing of ethnic groups within the United States as a source of strength; its persistent didacticism about this was in context brave and timely. A companion pamphlet suggested activities and questions for classroom discussion relating to the first program: "Have you observed that every great culture in history is the result of the mingling of many cultures?" The series prospectus explained why Americans could hope for immunity from the race politics of Europe: "Europe's desperate plight with neighbor set against neighbor cannot be suffered in the United States because the men and women who have come here from the four corners of the earth have accepted the idea that there is both strength and beauty in the new alloy which comes from the melting pot."[73] In the actual United States, of course—most obviously in the South—"mingling" was often controversial, which is perhaps why the culture mixing theme only rarely led to discussions of mixed ancestry like this one: "How many different 'racial' strains, as described in the broadcast, can you trace in your own family history?"[74] Cultural mixing was safer terrain than intermarriage. Philip Leonard Green, research supervisor at the Office of Education, referred in correspondence to the "racial groups" whose stories were to be treated in the radio series but the intercultural education people were in contrast always clear that the focus was on "culture groups."[75]

Seldes thought that the point of the series was neither stimulating ethnic pride nor mainstream appreciation of particular ethnic achievements or characteristics, but rather disseminating the understanding that American society was the product of many contributions. He made this case at the September 1938 planning conference: "If the purpose of the entire thing is that America was created by the immigrant and the immigrants were created by America then I think you will have to have these general subjects. . . . If we cut out these general things we will get back to glorifying and fragmentizing the entire thing."[76] Barbara Savage astutely summarizes the internal debate: DuBois was about reducing prejudice and fostering intergroup appreciation, while Seldes empha-sized the unifying rather than differentiating aspects of the national history; he had a "more nuanced yet more conservative" approach.[77] Seldes recalled years later that his favorite episode was the first one that dealt with "America as a whole, not with any one group."[78] He was interested in *connections*: "If we want to illuminate the inter-relationships of various groups, and to bring emphasis on the mutual dependence of America on them and them on America, we use material quite differently. The ... negro spiritual, it happens, has musical con-nections with Scotland; connections through the hymns with England; and the music was developed into American idioms by a third group of immigrants, the Russian Jews."[79] This was the ground of compromise—both DuBois and Seldes wanted to celebrate connections between groups, what DuBois called "creative use of differences."[80] Episode one stressed that "nothing in America is ever done by any one group alone" and invoked a kind of invisible hand of immigration: "the thrifty immigrant cannot enrich himself without contrib-uting to the greatness of the United States."

This win-win version of U.S. history left exploitation and hierarchy largely out of the story—its benign inclusiveness came at the price of removing things such as conflict over scarce resources, and structural advantage or disadvantage, from the story. *Americans All* was so busy documenting "gifts" and "contribu-tions" that it had little to say about prejudice and intolerance. There was plenty about hardships and struggles, but in most episodes hard work met its just reward. The "Negro" episode obviously posed challenges in this regard. W.E.B. DuBois read a draft script (Rachel DuBois sent it to him, warning it was "pretty bad") and he had some strong advice—noting, for example, that it discussed the effect of slavery on the plantation mistress yet "the effect on the slaves them-selves is not mentioned."[81] In the final version however, slavery was bluntly described as "theft" and "the most appalling trade in history," the spread of slave cotton plantations west was described as "dispossessing the Indians and the small farmers" and African American achievements were celebrated. In con-trast there was a general absence of Native American perspectives on contact history—for example, episode one reports early colonial conflict with the com-ment that "the French incited the Indians to raid the English settlements" then cuts to Cotton Mather's advice to recruit hardy Scots to settle the most danger-ous frontiers and narration that the Scots and Scotch Irish did just that with their "spirit of independence"—in other words, the fortitude of the settlers, not the Indigenous peoples whose land was being taken, claims our attention.

One of the most vexed questions confronting *Americans All* was whether the Jews should be treated separately as an ethnic group or as members of a reli-gion. Rachel DuBois, in line with her general position, argued that "as long as the Jew is separated negatively then the only way to separate the Jew is to separate him positively in the minds of the people." Studebaker agreed: "My leanings personally are somewhat in the direction of frank recognition of the fact that there is a Jewish problem."[82] The representative of the American Jewish Committee, Frank Trager, was, DuBois recalled, opposed to a separate episode. DuBois was influenced by the Reconstructionist school of thought that saw Judaism historically, as the folk culture of the Jewish people rather than eternal religious truth, while the American Jewish Committee leadership, including socialist Trager, believed that Judaism should be understood as a religion.[83] DuBois recalled that she had been adamant about having a separate episode: "'But,' I responded, 'we have found that fascinating story of Haym Solomon who gave his whole fortune to George Washington during the bitter winter at Valley Forge.'"[84] This was, of course, quite literally a gift story. After a vote, it was decided to produce a Jewish episode, and it garnered the highest mail response of the series.

Iphigene Ochs Sulzberger, wife of *New York Times* publisher Arthur Hays Sulzberger, wrote to say it was a "great mistake" to treat Jews as a race rather than a religious group: "I do not think it is to the interests of the United States or of its Jewish citizens to take Hitler's propaganda along these lines seriously."[85] Chester S. Williams in the Office had a similar criticism. He argued internally that *Americans All* episodes "over-emphasize racialism and under-emphasize humanism." The series, he wrote, "asks for tolerance of Germans as Germans, for Jews as Jews, when we are after a spirit of genuine cooperation—man with man—in the spirit of the Constitution which uses the words 'irrespective of race.'" He worried about the separate cultures approach in a world threatened by virulent racial nationalism: "The international threat to civilization comes from the philosophy which emphasizes race and blood. By these programs we do not seek to promote a feeling of tolerance among second or third generation immigrants for the racial or national characteristics of later immigrants. Rather, do we want to stress the fact that we have no minority problem and will have none so long as we repudiate the race and blood theory by a practice based on the collaboration of peoples, irrespective of racial or national origins, in the achievement of social welfare."[86] Boutwell defended the series to Studebaker against this charge: "Strenuous efforts have been made to report incidents revealing immigrants from specific groups working with Americans of other origins. The closing paragraphs of every script have emphasized the fact that we are indeed Americans All."[87]

But, as war loomed and race hatred grew in Europe, key supporters and funders of anti-prejudice work, as Selig observes, looked "with suspicion on a philosophy that emphasized difference among groups" because "Americans had only to look to the totalitarian regimes of Europe to see what might result from excessive cultural pride."[88] The New York Public Schools' tolerance education program did not develop along the cultural gifts line and Selig reports that "teachers frequently emphasized democratic ideals and individual rights rather than intercultural understanding."[89] Many liberals had also concluded that this was a time to assert universal principles and rights, not just intercultural dialogue. DuBois was thus losing support, even within her Bureau.[90] Bruno Lasker, brought in to review the Bureau's publications in 1940, concluded bluntly that "the effort to credit ethnic groups as such with the individual achievements of persons of renown is fictitious, fails in its purpose of raising respect or liking for the particular group, and should be abandoned."[91] New Bureau chair William Heard Kilpatrick was also not in favor of increasing ethnic consciousness. The board sought DuBois's resignation, which it received in 1941.[92] DuBois described it as a "forced resignation." She then founded a new organization, the Workshop for Cultural Democracy.[93] "Cultural democracy" had become her mission through the later 1930s. She wrote to Louis Adamic in 1938 that the concept, which she described as being "about sharing cultural values," had been "growing in my mind."[94] In her 1940 doctoral thesis she further explained that cultural democracy at home could help build "a world which would have learned to recognize the oneness of humanity in its diversity of expression."[95]

Given all this sharp debate at the time, it is not surprising that historians' discussion of *Americans All* has dwelled upon the now-obvious limitations, awkwardnesses, and condescensions of its "gift-bearing," pro-tolerance account of immigrants.[96] But it is surely more remarkable that a governmental program of tolerance education happened at all and on this scale, than it is that it did not measure up to twenty-first-century expectations. We can, in retrospect, see 1938 as a pivotal moment, at which DuBois' gift paradigm came under intense pressure—it might have been an adequate answer to anti-immigrant prejudices, but it seemed completely inadequate against the racial hatreds and mass killings being reported from Europe and Asia.

Dramatic Form

The arguments about focus on one ethnic group or many, about actively promoting tolerance in the abstract or less polemically demonstrating the positive results of cultural mingling and contributions in specific cases, had implications for the *form* of these radio programs. The issue, as always, was balancing the competing demands of dramatized documentary—keeping the documentary true and the drama compelling. Commenting on a draft of the first episode, Boutwell made clear that he wanted the "authentic realism of the documentary approach," "emotional drive and force," and "the mounting thrill of the successive waves of immigration" (figure 9).[97]

The characters in the story of *Americans All* were national types endowed with distinctive (and always positively valued) personality traits but the listing of gifts and successes created dramatic and narrative problems for radio.

FIGURE 9 Educational Radio Project director William D. Boutwell (seated wearing glasses) takes notes while listening to a transcription recording of a program rehearsal. (National Archives photo no. 12-E-32-535. "Radio Division," 1940, Radio Project-WPA Photographs, 12-E-32, Box 39, RG 12 Office of Education, Still Picture Branch, National Archives.)

Seldes thought rapid movement over scenes more effective for a historical presentation than longer dramatic passages—he wanted "an epic quality, a sense of constant movement . . . music and symbolic voices, with a counterpoint of fact."[98] Episode one, Seldes's favorite, moved rapidly in this way: "We invite you to the greatest spectacle in history—the making of America by your forebears and yourselves—by dozens of racial strains—combining—interacting—cooperating." The episode featured live-sounding radio: "We take you now to the Tower of London." Boutwell thought the technique "very good": "it gave a quality of bringing history up to date."[99]

Perhaps as a consequence, however, lack of dramatic coherence was a regular self-criticism within the project. Laura Vitray wrote in November 1938 that one draft AAIA script had "the same general defect which characterizes all Seldes scripts. There is no real dramatization, but rather it is history in dialogue. The rapid succession of brief scenes presents an even flow without emotional climaxes."[100] Jane Ashman complained to Margaret Cuthbert at NBC that the series "was completely lacking in dramatic construction—and therefore lost most of its potential force."[101] Boutwell was also critical of Seldes's writing—he constantly advocated narrative and emotion in Project series and he felt that

Seldes's scripts sometimes lacked those elements. He observed in November 1938 of the second episode: "One of the questions which it seems to me we may always ask of a program is this: Does it pull the heartstrings, put a lump in your throat, etc.? This program was not over-strong in this respect."[102] He wrote similarly in January 1939 that Seldes's scripts lacked drama and that this was a serious matter because drama provides the "emotional voltage" required to transfer ideas to the minds of the mass audience. He complained to Seldes directly: "The very nature of your kaleidoscopic approach to script writing and the broad canvass of these programs lay serious pitfalls. There has been considerable criticism that the succession of voices without identification led to confusion on the part of listeners." Boutwell reported that Studebaker was very concerned about these issues—so much so that he wanted Seldes to submit with each script "an outline which will show the central purpose of the script and a-b-c the subsidiary themes bearing on the central purpose."[103]

We can see the tensions clearly—DuBois wanting celebration of each group and its gifts, Seldes a kaleidosonic presentation about diverse contributions on a theme, Boutwell emotional impact and narrative drive, Williams clearer distancing of ethnic pride from blood and soil nationalism, and Studebaker something recognizably pedagogical and pro-tolerance. Inevitably, *Americans All* in the end was all these things in part but none of them perfectly realized.

Responses to *Americans All*

Much of the mail to *Americans All* came from people interested in the episode about their ethnic group. Decades later Seldes attached a memo to his copy of the series manual to say that the makers of the series had been especially gratified that "20% of the letters came from other groups than the one we treated that week."[104] That was putting the best face on the situation—80 percent came conversely from the group featured. The suspicion that the popularity of the show derived from already-existing ethnic pride rather than newly created tolerance was articulated by radio researcher Paul Lazarsfeld in his *Radio and the Printed Page*: "There are reasons to suppose that the bulk of the listeners are the immigrants themselves, who receive comfort from being told how valuable they are to this country. Then an analysis of the structure and the motivation of the audience reveals that the effect of the program cannot possibly be the one intended originally: to promote tolerance in the native-born."[105] Nicholas Montalto goes so far as to call *Americans All* a "fiasco" because of this finding that the show was mainly reaching the ethnic groups themselves, not the mainstream whose tolerance needed boosting.[106] That goes too far and wrongly assumes that the target was only the nonimmigrant population. And, of course, part of the point of the show, expressed in its title, was that there were relatively few "nonimmigrants" and many whose family connection to immigration was recent. The 1930 U.S. Census reported that 11.6 percent of the population was foreign born and about another 21 percent had at least one foreign-born parent—so a third of the population was immigrant or second generation. DuBois was, like Adamic, very concerned about the second generation—that they should feel pride, not embarrassment, about their origins—and that led her to reject the "melting pot" metaphor in favor of "cultural pluralism" or "cultural democracy."[107]

A Sequel?

There was much discussion about a possible second series. In late 1939 Boutwell wrote to CBS's Sterling Fisher:

> Last spring when it was evident that AMERICANS ALL, IMMIGRANTS ALL had enjoyed very warm reception, Mr. Seldes and Mrs. DuBois put their heads together and outlined a plan for a sequel series. This plan was forwarded to me and I am reasonably sure that Seldes has a copy. They reasoned that, having shown the contributions which various nations and races have made to the growth of American civilization, the next logical step was to show what different regions in the United States had contributed to our civilization. They have in mind that in so doing we would again bring out the special contributions of national and racial groups arriving in respective regions. The program would not be limited to the story of immigrant groups, but would tell what the 3rd, 4th, 5th, and 6th generations of immigrants in New England contributed to the development of New England, and also what New England contributed to the United States.[108]

The aims became more therapeutic over time: when DuBois, Ruth E. Davis, and Seldes were pitching for a second series, they talked about promoting "social and psychological health" and producing "more of a *community of feeling* on the part of all Americans." The second series was envisioned as moving beyond dramatized documentary to including the voices of real people in the broadcast. Philip Cohen championed this aspect of the planning. It was to have been, as we saw in chapter 1, a series about American regions treated, Cohen wrote, "in much the same way that the BBC has treated various parts of England in its documentary programs."[109] By July Cohen was pushing alternative ideas: "Arousing interest by having the listeners develop a feeling of identity with a particular fictitious family could be used. This could be a colonial family starting in the East, with their descendants scattering to different parts of the country, meeting new immigrant families—and by cooperating with them and struggling and overcoming all obstacles new states are carved out."[110]

CBS cited the looming war situation as a reason to reject a second series. Sterling Fisher wrote back to Boutwell: "I have discussed in the Program Department the question of a new series of "Americans All" to begin next Autumn. The consensus is that it would be not only unwise, but impossible, for us to attempt to make a commitment of time so far in advance. As you know, too many uncertain factors are involved to enable us to have any fair idea of programming possibilities until Autumn 1940 is much nearer."[111] The networks were doing other pro-tolerance programming at this time, but it may be that the political controversies beginning to surround the Project had as much to do with the CBS decision as the content of the proposed series. As noted in chapter 1, Cohen returned to this program idea in his work at the Library of Congress in the 1940s. Stewart Cole of the Service Bureau for Intercultural Education was also discussing a possible series titled "United We Stand" with CBS and the Office of Education in the fall of 1940—he told Boutwell his organization was keen because the new series would "continue the 'Americans All—Immigrants All' idea in the minds of the people."[112] Studebaker sought defense funds for the series.[113] But this planned series also fell through due to lack of budget to produce it.

Conclusions

Americans All, Immigrants All was a critical and popular success that put on display some of the ambitions and tensions in the cooperative production model. It more or less successfully negotiated the perils of government involvement in making educational material, even propaganda, in the public interest at a highly volatile and politicized moment. Its subject matter—tolerance and understanding—might appear at first to be beyond controversy, but actually that was not the case. Plenty of Americans would have disagreed with the gifts model and with the placing of all the gifts alongside one another as equally valuable and important in shaping the nation. Those Americans who clung to the idea that theirs was a white Christian nation, those many Americans who thought that race purity was better than race and ethnic mingling, would also have objected to the program and its message—although most likely they did not tune in at all. The Americans most sympathetic to the message were themselves immigrants, descendants of immigrants, or those who identified with the heritage of one ethnic group or another. The effects of government intervention in the communicative economy as advocate for pluralism and tolerance are, of course, difficult to assess. Individual programs may sound clumsy, even patronizing, today, but this was a significant cultural intervention and a remarkable mobilization of the resources of this new model of associative government-commercial cooperation in educational broadcasting.

Jill Lepore wrote recently: "There is no twenty-first-century equivalent of Seldes's 'Americans All, Immigrants All,' because it is no longer acceptable for a serious artist to write in this vein, and for this audience, and for this purpose."[114] Seldes's willingness to write in this way was one necessary ingredient, but so was the existence of a government-sponsored program willing to run the risk of accusations of state propaganda in producing governmental dramatized documentaries that encouraged values such as tolerance, equality, and diversity. *Americans All* was made possible by the belief that democratic values and democratic behavior were not innate nor a racial trait but cultural—and hence had to be taught and learned anew by and for each generation. The goal of *Americans All* was to teach Americans how to live in a culturally pluralist democracy. It was a particularly successful example of the Educational Radio Project's broader governmental mission to develop radio for democratic education.

4

Wings for the Martins

Cit-com

Wings for the Martins was a domestic situation comedy that aired over the NBC Blue network on Wednesday at 9:30–10:00 P.M. EST from November 1938 to May 1939. This twenty-six-episode series, which focused on the fictional Martin family as it encountered the everyday problems of raising and educating children, was produced by the Educational Radio Project in cooperation with the National Congress of Parents and Teachers (PTA), NBC, and the WPA. The Martin family included father Arnold, who owned and operated a hardware store; homemaker, Myra; and their children, Patty (seventeen), Jimmy (twelve), Barbara (nine), and Dicky (five). These characters represented idealized white, middle-class Americans, and the objective of *Wings* was to explore how the "typical American family"—with a little help from educators and community organizations—could build a nurturing environment for future citizens (figure 10). Every week the series was introduced as "Wings for the Martins! A program for all of us who stand by while the younger generation tries its wings!"

As a comedy based on a fictional family, *Wings* was a major departure from earlier Project productions such as *Brave New World* and *Americans All, Immigrants All*, which dramatized real historical events and promoted values of democracy, unity, and tolerance. This chapter interprets this departure from the dramatized documentary format as a product of twin pressures from the parent education movement (PEM) and commercial broadcasting. The PEM was a well-financed, middle-class movement that included the PTA and other

FIGURE 10 *Wings for the Martins* family portrait. (National Archives (U.S. Office of Education). "Wings for the Martins"—Publicity Material, Box 6, Entry 182, RG 12 Office of Education, National Archives, College Park, Maryland.)

organizations; it aimed to modernize parenting (and the family itself) as a necessary step toward implementing progressive education in the schools. In order to meet these goals, PTA and Radio Project educators created a fictional nuclear family—with children at several different stages of development and schooling—that could be used to explain and popularize the many educational, psychological, and social objectives of the PEM. At the same time, the desire of Radio Project producers to create a successful and popular broadcast led them to emulate the sitcoms and family-oriented programs that advertising agencies were developing in the late 1930s. *Wings* borrowed some elements from the top-rated primetime serial, *One Man's Family* (NBC, 1932–1959), and harnessed the emerging sitcom format to present parenting advice in an inoffensive and engaging way. Through light comedy and humorous situations, *Wings for the Martins* dramatized new approaches to parenting—carefully modeling how families could benefit from the lessons learned by the Martin family.

The use of a fictional family in *Wings for the Martins* and *Pleasantdale Folks* (discussed in chapter 6) also represented a shift from dramatized documentary as a mode of informing and persuading to modeling as a means of influencing audiences. The dramatized documentaries included short fictional vignettes; as we will see in the next chapter, *Democracy in Action* included longer fictional stories to illustrate the working of government in the present. *Wings* was different, however, in that it was all fiction. At its best, dramatized documentary could bring cultural values "to life" for listeners and inspire feelings of purpose and solidarity. In contrast, a fictional family could demonstrate ideal responses to New Deal initiatives in vital areas such as education, housing, and social security—providing both a guide to action and a framework for interpretation. Radio researcher Herta Herzog, who began studying radio serial audiences around this time, found that listeners learned specific life strategies from fictional serial programs and that daytime serials provided listeners with a number of "gratifications," including emotional release and escape from the drudgery of everyday life. She concluded that, to many listeners, the serials "seem to have become a model of reality by which one is to be taught how to think and how to act. As such they must be written not only with an eye to their entertainment value, but also in the awareness of a great social responsibility."[1] *Wings for the Martins* was designed to be just such a model of reality for listeners, providing cues on how to integrate scientific educational practices into their daily lives. Although the Radio Project continued to work to extend learning beyond radio listening by offering pamphlets and encouraging listeners to join local PTA groups, the shift to fictional programming signaled a new awareness of, or willingness to use, radio as a medium for governmental and civic modeling of how to live.

Marrying Education and Entertainment: The Ideal

In late 1938, expectations for *Wings for the Martins* were running high in Washington, D.C., and New York City. Commissioner of Education John Studebaker wrote to NBC president Lenox Lohr: "This series has every promise of being the most successful approach to the difficult problem of applying radio to education itself that has yet been attempted."[2] He bolstered his claim with a letter from the chair of the FCC, Frank R. McNinch, who praised the Office of Education for developing program techniques "by which increasingly large numbers of listeners are attracted to programs of real educational value."[3] An NBC press release described *Wings* as focusing on "an average American home" in which "every familiar situation on which parents of children have to make decisions" was explored, including questions about exposure to movies and radio, planning for college, homework, clothes, report cards, health, and children's clubs.[4] NBC's James Rowland Angell, retired president of Yale University hired to be the network's "educational counselor," sent letters touting *Wings for the Martins* to national opinion leaders, including Eleanor Roosevelt. He characterized the program as addressing "one of modern education's most pressing problems . . . securing the cooperation of parents in the schooling of today's children." Angell's letters included a smart-looking "illustrated NBC broadside promoting the whole series" and he assured his correspondents that *Wings* "is a human story, told without moralizing."[5]

The confident publicity masked some doubts within NBC where, while executives supported the program, they had also decided that it should only air after the 1938 midterm elections: Angell observed in a memo that "it could scarcely fail to be taken as New Deal propaganda" if aired immediately before or during election week.[6] By late 1938 NBC was sensitive to any suggestion that its collaborations with the federal government were producing New Deal propaganda. Angell himself was, in the words of historian John Boyer, "a staunch Republican" with a "profound dislike of the New Deal."[7] It is important to situate NBC's response to *Wings* in the context of the network's larger reaction to the FREC and the government's activist approach to public service broadcasting. While NBC complied with the cooperative production arrangements required by the FREC, it was less interested in any particular educational content than in cultivating an image of highbrow public service. To this end, it competed with CBS to promote highly visible "prestige" programs and to present itself as a medium of cultural uplift and adherence to what Goodman has described as broadcasting's "civic paradigm"—in 1937, for example, NBC hired both Angell and world-renowned conductor Arturo Toscanini as evidence of its commitment to public-interest broadcasting.[8] Internally, however, educational programming staff members felt they needed more resources and support. Back in 1936 NBC educational director Franklin Dunham had complained of a loss of Education Department personnel despite the fact that the average proportion of educational programs had increased from 18 percent to 26 percent between 1935 and 1936. He recommended to Vice President John Royal a number of strategies for improving educational programs, including the suggestion that "any continuity presenting the common daily happenings of a family has first chance of success" in educational broadcasting.[9] *Wings* answered Dunham's call for family-oriented educational programming and Angell's subsequent public endorsement lent it further cultural prestige.

Wings for the Martins was an ambitious effort to popularize the latest educational and psychological insights into child rearing by presenting a story of family life that also met network standards of entertainment. Radio Project director Bill Boutwell's decision to hire two scriptwriters with network experience to work with a supervisory committee of educators held the promise of threading the needle of commercial radio with educational content. It also had the potential for conflict, as the educators' values clashed at times with the conventions of commercial radio. Nonetheless, Boutwell's aim was to present parent education in a way that was nationally relevant and realistic. Publicity focused on the show's relevance for American families: "'Wings for the Martins' answers through the marvel of radio the oft-repeated wish of so many American families 'to see ourselves as others see us.' Here is the family that lives next door—or the brood that lives down at the corner of Vine and Maple,—or even our very own!"[10] Listeners were encouraged to see themselves in the Martin family and to learn from the everyday challenges that the family members faced. Producers hoped that most parents could relate to topics ranging from Jimmy not making the baseball team to parents' struggles with budgeting to Patty's decision to "go steady" with a boy.

The realism of *Wings* was attested to in listener letters. Although the Radio Project papers do not hold a significant collection of listener letters sent to *Wings*, they include a few letters along with selected quotes culled from thousands of letters received. Listeners from New York, New Jersey, and Wisconsin described the Martins as "a very real and interesting family," "so realistic and very unusual," and "true to life." "These true to life family skits are doing more actual parent education than a ton of textbooks or hundreds of lectures!"[11] One letter writer from Pennsylvania complimented the program for presenting "many problems which beset my own family and possible solutions." The listener continued by suggesting several possible problems that *Wings* might address, such as "a more profound understanding and friendship between a teen age boy and his father?"[12] This listener's request for an episode dealing with father-son relations aligned closely with the program's focus on the father's parenting role.

Wings opened each week with a simple, light musical theme that evoked a familiar—even old-fashioned—middle-class domestic scene. Composed by Rudolf Schramm and performed with violins and piano playing in harmony at a slow tempo, the *Wings* theme was upbeat yet genteel. It created a musical setting that precisely anticipated Arnold Martin's hope for an evening of "comfortable dawdling in his own home," only to be interrupted by humorous domestic complications that would inevitably end in a lighthearted yet informative resolution.[13] Most episodes were concerned with educating Myra and Arnold about problems faced by one or more of their children. Although the younger children had relatively simple reactions to learning (typically delight or trepidation), Jimmy and Patty were old enough to deploy creativity and initiative in their efforts to solve everyday problems. While Myra was normally patient and resourceful, Arnold was often befuddled and frustrated when it came to dealing with his children's problems. Much of the comedy came from his confusion, although in the end Arnold grew closer to his family and expressed pride in his children. At the conclusion of each episode, listeners were encouraged to write to "Wings for the Martins, Washington, D.C." for a free pamphlet with information and further reading to help them apply the lessons learned by the Martins in their own lives.

Taken as a whole, *Wings* promoted three broad educational goals and provided resources for answering specific questions about educational practices. First—reflecting the PTA's primary goal—it aimed to strengthen communication and cooperation between families, communities, and schools. The Martins modeled the roles of parents and students in this triangle of learning; they represented the family not as a self-enclosed unit but "as a web of relationships with ties to the larger community."[14] For example, *Wings* encouraged parents to seek information about recent changes in schooling across the country, including new kinds of report cards, new strategies for learning to read, and a new focus on physical education. It also promoted educational resources available in the community and discussed how to make the most of the public library, how to join local groups and clubs, and how to find wholesome (and free) entertainment in local parks and historic sites. The series also included programs on how to integrate movies and radio into family life (in the case of movies, this included a discussion of how to select and advocate for family-appropriate films). By emphasizing the connection between families, communities, and schools, *Wings* exemplified the citizenship function of American public education. Second, *Wings* emphasized the need for parents to treat children as distinct individuals with distinct needs at different stages of development. This perspective reflected advances in the psychological and educational study of child development from the 1920s.[15] Every episode in the series expressed this underlying value, but it was stated particularly clearly in the synopsis of the first episode, "Jimmy Runs Away: 'None of you ever ran away before!' moans Mrs. Martin. 'Why is Jimmy so different from Patricia, Barbara, and Dicky?' Through Jimmy's trials, the Martins learn that children need help to solve their individual problems."[16] *Wings* was organized so that each Martin child represented a different stage of development and education. The youngest child, Dicky, was used to promote early childhood education and kindergarten and address ways of making the home more accessible for a small child. For nine-year-old Barbara, the show discussed ways to encourage reading and suggested that even small children would benefit from social activities outside the home. For seventeen-year-old Patty, the show focused on planning for college and applying new knowledge about adolescent psychology and socialization to everyday problems faced by teens and their parents.

Jimmy, age twelve, was the child who received the most attention in *Wings*. Several episodes focused on the role that parents should play in encouraging a male child's independence and individual initiative.[17] For example, in "He Didn't Make the Team" (April 12, 1939), Jimmy decided to organize his own baseball league with all the boys in town who did not make the Junior High team. After two weeks of playing for his own Maple Street Orioles, Mrs. Martin observed the benefits of so much exercise for Jimmy: "I haven't seen him eat so well nor look so well nor be so awfully sweet tempered in I don't know how long."[18] The episode also includes criticisms of school athletic departments that focus on winning teams rather than encouraging physical activity and sports for all children. When the star pitcher of the Junior High team is unable to play in the championship game due to poor grades, the coach looks to recruit Jimmy to pitch based on the skills he has developed over months of play. Jimmy is initially excited by the offer and is about to accept it when he realizes that he is supposed to play for the Orioles in their own championship game at the same time. The coach tries to convince Jimmy to play by telling him that the honor of the school and the town is on the line. Although Jimmy is tempted, his final response is, "Sorry mister—I'm playing for the Orioles." Throughout the episode, Mr. and Mrs. Martin expressed vocal support and enthusiasm for Jimmy's independent baseball league. When it came time for Jimmy to choose between the Junior High team and his own, they remained largely silent. While the parents were present for support, they gave Jimmy room to come to his own decisions about right and wrong, responsibility and commitment.

Finally, *Wings for the Martins* focused not just on individual children but on the family as a whole, with a particular emphasis on Arnold Martin's relationships with his children. By the 1930s, educational and psychological experts were emphasizing the essential role of the father as a companion to his children and as a model of masculinity and successful citizenship. The father's enhanced parenting role was designed to strengthen and safeguard the heteronormative ideals of gender identity for both parents and children during a time of social upheaval.[19] As will be examined below, *Wings* focused particularly on the relationship between Arnold Martin and his son Jimmy as a means of modeling idealized New Deal citizenship.

Wings differed somewhat from previous Project programs in that women played a larger role in developing and supervising the program. Director Bill Boutwell still oversaw the series and appointed Phil Cohen to direct production. He also hired the script-writing team of Pauline Gibson (later Pauline Gilsdorf) and Frederick Gilsdorf, who had achieved recent success with a play,

"The Ghost of Benjamin Sweet," broadcast by the CBS Columbia Workshop.[20] However, much of the planning and supervision of the scripts was done by women. Assistant Commissioner of Education, Bess Goodykoontz, directed research and chaired the Planning Committee and the Script Review Committee, while Effie Bathurst supervised the program. Both women worked with an Office of Education committee of twelve (seven of whom were women) and a PTA committee of seven (five of whom were women). To understand their roles in producing *Wings*, it is necessary to take a closer look at the PEM that shaped their development as education professionals and the progressive education environment in which *Wings* was conceptualized.

The Parent Education Movement

The PEM has aptly been described as a form of "scientific utopianism"—including progressive educational values along with elements of nativism and eugenics—that coalesced as a response to a deep sense of social dislocation in the early twentieth century. Julia Grant defines it as "a movement to reform families, and ultimately American society, through the popularization of information on child development to parents nationwide."[21] This middle-class movement emerged in the 1920s in response to fears about a looming generation gap between parents born and raised at the turn of the century and children raised in a modern era shaped by World War I, the consequences of mass immigration, urbanization, new forms of mass media and mass culture, and the struggle for women's rights.[22] Revelations about the purportedly low cognitive and emotional aptitude of most Americans, gleaned from intelligence tests administered to World War I recruits, provided a sense of urgency for citizenship training in the 1920s. Overall, the PEM mobilized educators and parents (primarily mothers) who organized at a grassroots level to apply scientific principles of learning to the home and school. It also trained a generation of professionals in child development, psychology, and education.[23]

Historians emphasize the extent to which the PEM was influenced by first-wave feminism and the growing access of women to higher learning. Given cultural fears about the declining fertility of educated middle-class women, the PEM was an effort to transform motherhood into something more appealing to those women—something scientific, respected, and more like a profession. By the 1930s, the movement came to focus on the importance of adapting male behavior to the new expectations of women. Specifically, this took the form of transforming the role of the father in the home to increase paternal participation in child-rearing and education.[24] The project of "domesticating" Arnold Martin was a central focus of *Wings*, as will be examined below.

The PEM had a significant impact on both scientific and popular views of the family, largely due to the support it received from the Laura Spelman

Rockefeller Memorial Foundation (LSRM) beginning in the 1920s. The foundation provided funding for professional organizations including the PTA, Child Study Association of America, and the National Council on Parent Education. Between 1923 and 1930, LSRM initiated or financed child-welfare research institutes at six universities: Iowa, Columbia, Yale, Minnesota, Toronto, and Berkeley. The LSRM made five-year grants to these universities that were later renewed and increased; the University of Iowa (then the State University of Iowa) received almost $1 million.[25] These institutes trained large numbers of women in child-related fields.[26] The goal of these research institutes was not only to promote scientific study of the problems of child care and development but also to train personnel to apply scientific knowledge to parent education.[27] LSRM was directed by Beardsley Ruml with the aid of the energetic and persuasive Lawrence K. Frank, who "incubated, launched, and nurtured most of the child-research programs" with the aim of advancing the PEM.[28]

Many of the women who gained leadership in the PEM were trained in these institutes, including those who worked on the PTA-Radio Project collaboration for *Wings*. Many started out in elementary education, trained at Iowa or Columbia, and gained faculty positions in universities. They published regularly, founded national organizations, and participated in national and international conferences. They were independent women, most of whom did not marry or start families. Goodykoontz was unusual in that at the age of fifty she started a family by adopting and raising two girls.[29] Without knowing precisely why these women migrated from school administration and higher education into government service, we might conjecture that it had to do with access to resources and the potential to effect educational change on a national level. In some cases it may have been a hopeful response to the expanded role of women in public life promoted by the Roosevelt administration and made visible in the strong leadership roles of Eleanor Roosevelt, Frances Perkins, and Ellen Woodward, among others.[30] Although no woman was appointed to the top leadership in the Office of Education until the creation of the Department of Education in 1979, the agency did offer some women opportunities for lateral movement, as well as national and international travel, research, and intellectual exchange.

The two women who played the biggest role in developing *Wings for the Martins* were Bess Goodykoontz and Effie Bathurst. Born in Iowa, Bess Goodykoontz (1894–1990) was an elementary school teacher and administrator who received her bachelor of arts (BA) and master of arts (MA) in education from the University of Iowa, where she taught in the Elementary Experimental School and served as its principal in 1921–1922. She served on the education faculty at the University of Pittsburgh for five years before joining the Office of Education, where she served as assistant commissioner of education from

1929 to 1946.[31] At the time she supervised *Wings* in 1938, she had almost two decades of experience in progressive education and administration under her belt.

Effie Geneva Bathurst (1886–1970) was a specialist in rural education and curriculum and was also from Iowa. After serving as a teacher and administrator for rural schools for fifteen years, she earned her BA in education from the University of Northern Iowa (then Iowa State Teachers College) and became a research specialist at Teachers College, Columbia University in New York before becoming a senior specialist at the Office of Education. Eight years older than Goodykoontz, she also brought decades of educational experience to the PTA collaboration. Over her career, she published hundreds of articles and books on a broad range of curricular topics including conservation and inter-American education.[32]

Other women on the general planning and script review committees for *Wings* shared similar professional trajectories. Another Iowan, Helen K. Mackintosh (1887–1980), was a specialist in language arts and general education at the Office of Education from 1938 until her retirement in 1963. She received her BA, MA, and PhD in education from Iowa and served as a faculty member at both Miami University in Ohio and the University of Pittsburgh before taking a position in the Office of Education.[33] Mary Dabney Davis worked as assistant superintendent of schools in Duluth, Minnesota; graduated from Columbia; and directed the Department of Elementary Teacher Training at Geneseo Normal and Training School in New York, before joining the Office of Education, where she was a specialist in kindergarten and primary education.[34] Finally, California native Elise H. Martens (1889–1961) was a specialist in exceptional children and special education who worked at the Office of Education for thirty-five years.[35] During Goodykoontz's tenure as assistant commissioner in the 1930s and 1940s, the Office of Education attracted a large number of educational specialists who were women.[36]

While the LSRM invested in educational professionals such as Goodykoontz, Bathurst and Mackintosh to bring the PEM message to the people, it also funded mass media initiatives for more direct popular messaging. Most notable was *Parents' Magazine*, which was oriented to middle-class families and exists in much the same format today.[37] Although LSRM's Frank expressed some doubts about successfully disseminating scientific child development information in a popular format, the foundation supported the media enterprise from its beginning in 1926 and it turned out to be a singular success. As historian Steven Schlossman observes, *Parents' Magazine* "was the only commercial periodical whose circulation and advertising revenues climbed steadily upward during the course of the Great Depression."[38] The commitment of advertisers and readers to the magazine, even during a decade-long economic crisis, indicates the deep cultural significance the magazine held for its middle-class audience. A study of representations of fatherhood in *Parents' Magazine* indicates that it was an important medium for promoting the concept of participatory fatherhood. A content analysis of the magazine reveals that the percentage of articles mentioning the benefits of active parenting for fathers rose from about 42 percent in 1930 to over 60 percent in 1945.[39]

Other institutes and groups funded by the LSRM also explored radio as a tool for parent education. The Child Study Association of America began to create radio talks in 1925.[40] Two years later the staff at the Minnesota Institute of Child Welfare began airing radio talks about parenting and initiated a narrated series, *Up the Years with the Bettersons*, that ran until 1942. That series was designed and delivered by three institute faculty members: Pearl Cummings, Esther McGinnis, and Marion Faegre. *The Bettersons* was a fifteen-minute daytime series that targeted an audience of women who worked in the home. At the center of the program was Mrs. Betterson, an idealized mother who "keeps abreast of the latest psychological theories and expert child rearing advice" and applies them successfully to her four children who ranged from kindergarten to high school age.[41]

The family portrayed in *The Bettersons* is almost identical to the family in *Wings for the Martins*. We have not found any evidence to suggest that the creators of *Wings* were influenced by the *The Bettersons*; however, it seems likely that ideas of this kind were shared at educational conferences and meetings, and the idea of creating a "model family" with children at four different levels of development and schooling was possibly a common strategy used by parent educators for teaching purposes. According to Ann Johnson and Elizabeth Johnston, *The Bettersons* also addressed two of the three themes highlighted by *Wings for the Martins*: the need to treat children as unique individuals with distinct needs, and the ideal of companionate marriage in which men participate in the educational and emotional upbringing of the children. Mr. Betterson was often referred to informally as "Dad" rather than "Father," and in one episode he explicitly stated that he wanted to be liked more than respected by his children.[42] Along with training researchers and educators and supporting educational organizations then, LSRM funding promoted the mass dissemination of parent education through radio broadcasting projects and the highly successful *Parents' Magazine*.

Marrying Education and Entertainment: The Reality

In the case of *Wings for the Martins*, we have a window onto what happened when the values of the PEM as expressed by government educators met the practices of commercial broadcasting. This section examines the conflict that arose at the Radio Project between the scriptwriters and their educational supervisors. First, there was general tension between the cultural expectations of the educators and the norms of commercial radio production. Second, there were specific conflicts over the representation of Arnold Martin and his relationship with his children. While educators wanted to portray a serious father engaged with and guiding his children's lives, writers drew on the well-worn figure—then widespread in U.S. popular media and gaining a foothold in domestic radio comedies—of the bumbling father and husband. The next section takes a closer look at the origins and meanings of the incompetent father stereotype in popular media generally and radio in particular. In this section, however, we focus on how *Wings* negotiated the tensions between the PEM ideal of participatory fatherhood and the comic trope of the bumbling father.

Almost as soon as *Wings* went on the air, disagreement emerged between the educators in Washington and the producers in New York. Effie Bathurst sent a memo to producer Phil Cohen in early December 1938 summarizing the script committee's criticisms of the series. While she acknowledged that the acting was spirited and the music engaging, she conveyed the committee's view that the drama was too dependent on "an accumulation of turmoil and hair-raising incidents." These situations represented Mr. Martin, in particular, in what they viewed as an unflattering light. For example, she complained that in one episode "Mr. Martin was childish and too blustery" and in another he was "bombastic" rather than humorous and needed a "more wholesome spirit."[43] Cohen shared Bathurst's memo with Boutwell with a sense of disbelief: "Bill, it would be the easiest thing in the world to make this family into a bunch of milk-sops—humorless, unexcited, unexcitable, and unexciting; but believe me it would be an awful thing to do. Here for the first time we have the perfect combination of education and entertainment and the girls seem just unable to face the prospect of success."[44] Cohen expressed his solidarity with the writers and offered to visit Washington to explain things to the educational specialists supervising the series. Boutwell and Studebaker attempted to make peace between the parties and suggested bringing the committee to New York to observe a broadcast of *Wings*.[45]

By early February 1939, however, months of wrangling between the *Wings* script committee and the writers had come to a head. Pauline Gibson wrote a long memo to Boutwell expressing her frustration at dealing with the committee over script 15, "Places to Learn Outside the School." Gibson and Gilsdorf had written a script in which Jimmy's extracurricular learning activity was to serve as a junior magistrate in traffic court for the day. Through a number of unexpected complications, Arnold Martin found himself in traffic court being judged by his own son. The situation was certainly dramatically compelling, and Gibson noted that it resulted in a "very fine relationship between father and son, in addition to the fact that the boy learned in the process a real respect for the purpose and workings of the law."[46] Goodykoontz and Bathurst objected to this script, and others, on the grounds that children should not be put in distressing, "harrowing," or confusing positions and that family members should not "save the day" in overly dramatic fashion.[47] Like Bathurst's earlier criticism, these suggestions were in direct conflict with the regular use of confusion, distress, and surprise by sitcom writers. Much of Gibson's frustration also came from the fact that the committee's objections were tied to cultural expectations more than educational outcomes. She observed that some of the male members of the committee viewed this as a trying experience for Jimmy but thought that it was ultimately justified because of the positive learning outcomes. Perhaps taking a cue from Cohen and Boutwell, who had referred to the educators as "girls," "crafty cats," and "old maids," Gibson concluded that the real problem was with the female members of the committee.[48]

Gibson's memo indicates that she perceived a cultural divide between her writing team and the Radio Project's women educators. It seems likely that age, regional origin, professional training, and other factors came into play. Gibson chose to use gender as the lens through which to distinguish her "masculine" commercial radio perspective from Goodykoontz's "feminine" educational one. Goodykoontz, Mackintosh, Davis, Martens, and several other women on the committee were often referred to as "Dr." in office memos and in the press because they had postgraduate degrees and had previously held university professorships. Gibson, however, always referred to them as "Miss." She accused the educators of expressing a "predominantly feminine" and "pseudo romantic attitude" about the Martin family. She observed that, unlike the men on the committee, the women were unable to accept "realism" and remarked: "Had they not outnumbered Mr. Frazier and Mr. Jessen at the first committee meeting, I doubt that all this would have come up."[49]

In his efforts to mediate the conflict, Boutwell suggested that Gibson should view the directives of the committee in the same way as she would look at the demands of an advertising agency sponsoring a program. Gibson's response was direct: "In your letter today, you drew an analogy between our relationship to the committee and the relationship of script-writers to an advertising agency. This analogy we do not admit. In dealing with an advertising agency, we should feel that we are dealing with our peers . . . not with amateurs in the field. Outside of yourself, there is no one on that committee who knows radio."[50] *Feminine, romantic,* and *amateur* were the terms Gibson used to describe the female educators. Due to his knowledge of radio (and, no doubt, because he was her boss), Boutwell escaped her scorn. Soon after this, however, Gibson and Gilsdorf left *Wings* and the writing assignment was taken over by Laura Vitray. While Boutwell encouraged the scriptwriters to adhere to the suggestions of the committee, he ultimately seemed to agree with Gibson that the educational ends justified the commercial means. With some moderation, commercial-style characterizations and plot devices remained in *Wings* broadcasts. A closer look at the episodes that focused on the relationship between Arnold and Jimmy helps to clarify how the writers' efforts and the committee's outlook came together.

Several episodes addressed Arnold Martin's role in his son Jimmy's education, including "Places to Learn Outside of School," "He Didn't Make the Team," and "What, No Nightwork?" In both "Places to Learn" and "He Didn't Make the Team," Arnold's role as a father was to be a facilitator for his son's learning—particularly Jimmy's development of his own moral compass and capacity to judge right from wrong.[51] Rather than imposing his own paternal authority on his son, Arnold stood by and supported Jimmy while he made important decisions. This happened in "Places to Learn," when Jimmy was required to enforce the law against his own father, and Arnold accepted the judgment respectfully and gracefully. It also happened in "He Didn't Make the Team," when Arnold withheld his own opinion and allowed Jimmy to decide whether he would pitch for the Junior High baseball team. These episodes demonstrate two key goals of the PEM: promoting participatory fatherhood and making the home into a place of "scientific" learning for individual children rather than a place where parents make all the decisions. In "Places to Learn," however, Arnold's compromised and extremely embarrassing position in traffic court was also a comic strategy that introduced a shocking and humorous plot twist and played on the stereotype of the bumbling father. As Gibson reports in her memo to Boutwell, some of the educators believed that this plot subverted Arnold's authority to such an extent that it would be offensive to listeners.[52] This challenge to patriarchal authority was extreme, but it was also short-lived and limited to a unique circumstance. While comedy had its risks, it offered one means of encouraging new models of parenting without seeming to upend patriarchy as a whole.

In the episode, "What, No Nightwork?" we find another example of Jimmy's learning experience coming as part of a comic challenge to Arnold's authority. The entire episode is premised on Arnold's misunderstanding of the difference between traditional "nightwork" (math or other school lessons done at home) and a new concept of "homework" (practical projects done at home that apply skills and knowledge learned at school) emerging in the 1930s. While he hounds his children about their nightwork, they smoothly avoid his inquiries and trick him into helping them with the various homework projects they are working on (Barbara is churning butter, Jimmy is planning a family trip to Pine Mountain Park, and Patty is trying out a new dress design).

Arnold's interaction with Jimmy is particularly revealing of the father's ineptness and outdated ideas and the son's initiative and ingenuity. Jimmy finds a misplaced map that his father has been looking for and lays it out on the floor with some other maps to plan the trip. Jimmy says, "Get down on your knees, Dad, like this. It makes the maps easier to see." When Arnold makes audible groaning noises, Jimmy asks, "What's the matter, Dad, can't you get down on your knees?" Arnold responds gruffly, as if in pain, "Pfft! What a question. Of course, I can."[53] Jimmy starts talking about which route to take and asks his dad to check his calculations. Jimmy has already collected information about the route and he builds Arnold's interest in the trip by talking about sights they could see, including a new dam on the river and the state capitol. Jimmy encourages his father to believe that the trip to Pine Mountain Park is Arnold's own idea. Eventually Arnold asks Jimmy, indignantly, "How did you know we were going on this trip?" The trickery is ultimately good natured and it becomes a means whereby Myra and the children can reaffirm Arnold's positive and essential role in the home.

Wings in the Commercial Context: Fatherhood, Family, and the Sitcom

Both PEM practitioners and commercial broadcasters desired to bring the family into focus in a new way: for educators, the motivation was a concern with national unity and citizenship training; for broadcasters, it was a need to create programming that would celebrate the family home as a sphere of consumption. While this led to similarities between *Wings* and the emerging family sitcom, there were also significant differences. This section begins by taking a closer look at the bumbling father stereotype to evaluate *Wings* in relation to other domestic sitcoms. It then turns to comparing *Wings* with domestic radio sitcoms and serials of the 1930s and television domestic comedies of the 1950s. This investigation reveals that *Wings*—with its child-centered domestic sphere, engaged father figure, and effort to model normative Americanism—sounded more like a television family sitcom of the 1950s than a domestic radio sitcom of the 1930s.

The representation of fatherhood is a key element of domestic sitcoms, and to understand this feature of the sitcom, it helps to take a closer look at the origins and meanings of the bumbling father stereotype. Sociologists and historians have traced this incompetent father template to the rise of an ideology of separate spheres in the nineteenth century that began both to exile middle-class white women from public and work spaces and to dissociate men from the domestic sphere.[54] The incompetent father emerged in popular media in the late nineteenth and early twentieth centuries as a measure of how distant and unfit he was for parenting given his primary commitment to public life and work.[55] Therefore, although the stereotype seemed in some ways to belittle the father and challenge his patriarchal prerogatives, it was actually a sign of a strongly patriarchal society that could clearly distinguish social standing on the basis of sex. For example, studies of representations of fatherhood in *Saturday Evening Post* cartoons indicate that images of incompetent fathers increased during periods of more secure patriarchal authority and decreased during less patriarchal periods. Less patriarchal periods were defined by rising labor-force participation rates of mothers, declines in birth rates, and increased advocacy for companionate marriages. Ralph LaRossa et al. found that between 1924 and 1944 the portrayal of incompetent fathers dropped from 69 percent to 45 percent in *Post* cartoons. Earlier research by Randal Day and Wade Mackey found that portrayals of incompetent fathers in *Post* cartoons were high in the 1950s and 1960s, and then dropped in the 1970s.[56] It is important to note that although representations of incompetent fathers may have declined during the 1920s and 1930s, they certainly did not disappear from popular media.

In the context of commercial radio, there is a relatively fine distinction to be made between a father who is incompetent in dealing with children and a male authority figure who is generally incompetent in the domestic sphere. The bumbling father as such was not common in 1930s radio comedy because children were largely absent from these programs. Most domestic comedies featured married couples without children (for example, *Burns and Allen, Easy Aces, Fibber McGee and Molly,* and *Blondie*). Only a small number of domestic comedies or domestic serials introduced children in primary roles, and they typically included only one child who was tween or teenaged. For example, Vic and Sade adopted a son, Rush (played by Bill Idelson), in the early 1930s, and Paul Barbour of *One Man's Family* adopted a daughter named Teddy around the same time. These characters became more active as domestic comedies began to focus on teenage characters beginning in 1939 and accelerating in the early 1940s, with shows such as *The Aldrich Family, A Date with Judy, Archie Andrews,* and many others. Nonetheless, the bumbling male authority figure without children became an important tool for constructing comedy in the domestic sphere.

In contrast to the sociological and historical research on incompetent fathers, research on radio comedy has identified an *increase* in the presence of incompetent patriarchs in 1930s radio comedy in general—and the emerging radio sitcom in particular. Male comedians of the 1930s, including Jack Benny, George Burns (*Burns and Allen*), and James Jordan (*Fibber McGee and Molly*), served as humorous, self-deprecating models of failed masculinity. Susan Douglas and others argue that these comedians played an important role in a society in which patriarchal power had been shaken by profound economic crisis. In this situation, actors like Benny—with his traits of stinginess, vanity, and insecurity—provided foils against which listeners could project resilient images of American masculinity.[57] Thus, an increase in the presence of "challenged" patriarchs and a decrease in representations of incompetent fathers with children may have been parallel responses to the increase in working mothers, declines in birth rates, and calls for companionate marriages that accompanied the Great Depression.

At the same time, a certain degree of incompetence on the part of the male breadwinner—which produced confusion, misunderstandings, and topsy-turvy situations—became a frequent and effective generic strategy in the emerging domestic sitcom. As seen in the examples from *Wings*, the sitcom operated by creating situations in which patriarchal authority was inadvertently and temporarily challenged or weakened, such as when the children tricked Arnold into helping them with their homework projects, or when Arnold found himself being judged by his son in traffic court. The patriarch might become disempowered vis-à-vis his wife or children, but his authority was reasserted once the situation was resolved. Indeed, part of the humor came from the fact that paternal authority would inevitably be reinstated. In a more traditional household without a predictably inept father figure, women and children would have little room for comic agency. For a variety of contextual and generic reasons, then, the confused or inept patriarch became a convenient and dependable feature of domestic sitcoms.

If most commercial domestic comedies consisted of childless couples, where did the writers and developers of *Wings* turn for inspiration in network broadcasting? Interestingly, the writers drew on the long-running serial *One Man's Family*. In the late 1930s and early 1940s, *One Man's Family* (*The Family*) was one of the most popular prime-time programs in the country. Written by Carlton E. Morse for nearly twenty-seven years, the program drew on a mix of genres, including serial melodrama, light comedy, and a celebration of the idealized middle-class family. As Hayes explores, evidence suggests that advertisers and networks viewed it as a model for the emerging family sitcom, largely due to its finely crafted family interactions.[58] *Wings* drew on specific aspects of *The Family*—including its representation of the family patriarch, its large, more traditional family, and its orientation to the family as a site of moral education. However, it transformed the traditional family template in significant ways that made it a unique presence on network radio.

The show's catchphrase—"Wings for the Martins! A program for all of us who stand by while the younger generation tries its wings!"—was a clear echo of *One Man's Family*'s tagline: "*One Man's Family*! Dedicated to the mothers and fathers of the younger generation and their bewildering offspring!" In a significant twist on the catchphrase, *Wings* referred to children of the 1930s as the "younger generation," whereas *The Family* referred to young parents of the 1930s as the "younger generation." This reflected the fact that while the Martin family was a nuclear family with four children, *The Family*'s Barbour clan, headed by Henry Barbour and his wife, Fanny, consisted of five adult children; adopted granddaughter, Teddy; and eventually numerous additional grandchildren. Both families included four or more children, but *Wings* scaled the extended Barbour family down to a single nuclear family. As mentioned earlier,

FIGURE 11 The Martin Family "tries its wings." (National Archives (U.S. Office of Education). "Wings for the Martins," Folder Wings for the Martins—Publicity Material, Box 6, Entry 182, RG 12 Office of Education, National Archives, College Park, Maryland.)

Wings's focus on a nuclear family with four children was largely determined by the educational goals of the PEM. However, the shift to a nuclear family may have also been an effort to offer a more modern and progressive take on the radio family (figure 11).

Arnold Martin's ineptitude, gruffness, and tendency to grumble and "humph" at his family (qualities to which the Radio Project educators strongly objected) also appear to be modeled on Father Barbour.[59] John Dunning describes Henry Barbour as a "crusty" and "difficult" character who often expressed frustration and confusion about how to deal with his children's problems.[60] Just as Fanny Barbour was forced diplomatically to triage Henry's various domestic missteps, so Myra Martin stepped in to guide Arnold toward competent responses to his children's problems. While Henry Barbour faced some challenges to his authority on the domestic front from his wife and children, his incompetence in the domestic sphere was generally met with good-natured teasing from the family. As discussed above, Arnold Martin's domestic confusion was likewise treated as a good-humored opportunity for learning. In the case of *Wings for the Martins*, the incompetent father modeled the behaviors that needed to be changed and created space for listeners to learn new educational practices.

Although *Wings* was a short-lived, experimental educational broadcast, it is notable that its image of a middle-class nuclear family looked and sounded almost nothing like contemporary radio sitcoms, but rather prefigured the suburban, postwar television family found in programs like *Father Knows Best* (CBS, 1954–1960), *The Adventures of Ozzie and Harriet* (ABC, 1952–1966), and *Leave It to Beaver* (CBS, 1958–1959; ABC, 1958–1963). Like *Wings*, these shows engaged in "living room lectures" where families faced problems and learned.[61] Studies of postwar domestic comedies have rarely considered the prewar origins of the format, either in terms of the innovations of radio advertisers or in the culturally resonant PEM that took root in the late 1920s and 1930s.[62] *Wings* episodes were didactic, incorporated comedic elements and focused intensively on the family as the site where individual American citizens were nurtured and formed. These are all qualities attributed to 1950s domestic sitcoms. Due to its creative transformation of the developing sitcom genre, *Wings* provides an argument for looking more closely at similarities between family representations in 1930s radio and 1950s television. This is one instance of the genuine cultural innovation that Project shows managed to achieve despite, or perhaps because of, their always troubled and conflicted efforts to bring educational content to commercial radio.

Conclusions

As a comedy based on a fictional family, *Wings for the Martins* was a major departure from earlier Radio Project productions that dramatized real historical events. This shift to fictional programming was shaped by the Radio Project's desire to meet the goals of the PEM and commercial broadcasting. Network programmers and Radio Project administrators touted *Wings* as providing an innovative marriage between radio and education that would demonstrate how American families could contribute to building more creative and competent citizens.

This analysis of *Wings* recordings, scripts, and production documents has shown how the program negotiated the tensions between the PEM ideal of participatory fatherhood and the comic trope of the bumbling father. While

Arnold Martin's domestic incompetence was similar to that of other "challenged" patriarchs in 1930s radio comedy, it was oriented to creating space for learning how to bring scientific principles of child rearing into the American home. It also offered a relatively unthreatening way to introduce significant changes into middle-class families. In addition, it contributed to the development of the sitcom as a space for citizenship education, which would become a central component of Cold War television.

The shift from dramatized documentary to fictional formats in the cases of *Wings for the Martins* and *Pleasantdale Folks* signaled a shift from telling allegorical stories of national unity and purpose to providing specific examples of how Americans should participate in New Deal initiatives on education, housing, social security, and more. While specific actions and behaviors could be modeled step by step in these fictional shows, much of the drama focused on what New Deal innovations would mean for the American middle class and for American workers, and how listeners should interpret these changes. Like dramatized documentary, much of the work of the fictional programs was to create an atmosphere in which large changes in the meaning of citizenship and citizens' relationships to government were normalized and presented as part of long-held American traditions. With respect to *Wings*, the progressive, child-centered nuclear family of the Martins was presented as a "typical American family"—even though it was largely absent from prime-time radio programming and far from a dominant family formation in Depression-era America. In the case of the soap opera *Pleasantdale Folks*, explored in chapter 6, the unprecedented launch of a national system of social security together with enhanced state-level welfare provisions was likewise presented as a logical and nonthreatening extension of practices quite consistent with traditional American values.

5

Democracy in Action

Dramatizing the
Democratic Process

Democracy in Action (DIA) went to air on CBS in May 1939 in the 2:00 P.M. Sunday eastern time slot just vacated by *Americans All, Immigrants All.* The first series of thirteen episodes was written by Merrill Denison; this season was extended to October 1939, with eight more episodes by Allan Wilson. A further thirty-four programs were then broadcast between October 1939 and June 1940, organized in short thematic series on trade, public health, social security, labor, the census, and housing. DIA thus ran for a year, making it the longest-running of the later Project shows. In September 1939, 103 stations were carrying the show—one more than for *Brave New World*, but below the number for AAIA.[1]

DIA was an important series for the Project, an ambitious attempt to make a program that would not only provide information about government but also illuminate democracy as a whole way of life. In a world in crisis, DIA sought to dramatize the case for democracy and spark interest in democratic culture, behavior, and demeanor—the kinds of things that de Tocqueville had written about a century earlier. "How can we make these programs more than descriptive or informational?" asked an early memo. "How can we make them tell a progressive story which emphasizes the functions of government while revealing the mechanism?"[2] More than a civics lesson about how government worked, DIA sought to stimulate in citizens a positive view of government as simply a tool to solve problems, and as something already present in their everyday lives. The series received praise from radio critics. Internally, Cohen enthused of one 1939 episode that it was "one of the finest programs that has ever gone out under our auspices."[3]

But while this was in many ways the most important and timely of all topics for the Project, it was also—in 1939 and 1940—one full of risk. Was it possible to stimulate a positive view of government without being accused of producing propaganda for the New Deal? Radio historian Gerd Horten has described *Democracy in Action* as "clearly partisan," citing its mission of exploring the "contributions of government to solutions of complex problems in American industry, health, social security, foreign trade, labor welfare, etc."[4] That was, unfortunately for the Project, true—in the context of sustained Republican and conservative Democrat attacks on New Deal state expansion, even a bland statement about the "contributions" of government could be heard as partisan propaganda. The New Deal, now on the defensive in the wake of the court-packing controversy and Roosevelt's attempted "purge" of conservative elements in the Democratic Party, was inevitably part of the subject matter of a series about American government. Suspicion of government information and propaganda was rising, both nationally and internationally. Funding for cultural and information programs was under threat in Congress—the Federal Theatre Project, for example, was ended in 1939. Office of Education staff knew that a great deal rested on this series for them. Behind the scenes there was much debate and apprehension. Chester S. Williams warned colleagues: "This is a pivotal program . . . designed to attract the attention of key persons in government," and hence "it must attain a very high standard of perfection, both from the standpoint of presenting meaty material and from the standpoint of dignified and convincing radio production."[5]

Domestic politics was not, however, the only obstacle. Democratic government was also on the defensive internationally, against resurgent fascist and communist alternatives. Williams told a planning meeting in November 1938 that the Office wanted to make a series that would "create the impression and feeling that the system of government which we have now, the way in which Congress functions and the services we perform, is all worth preserving against the major alternative of the efficient dictatorships."[6] Writer Allan Wilson agreed that one of the objectives of the series should be to set up a "contrast of conditions and methods of democracy with those of dictatorship."[7] In order to do that, again much more was needed than explaining the mechanisms of American government. The program should convey, Williams said, that democracy "is not a fixed or finished arrangement" but something that citizens can "amend, change, improve"—they needed an approach that "makes it real and appeals to the feelings as well as informational." Series researcher Selma Goldstone agreed that "democracy is not only a means of government but a means of living."[8]

Like other Project series, DIA utilized historical dramatizations, in this case to explain the growth of government. It also used fictional scenes set in the present to more polemically model exemplary citizenship—the closer the show came to the present, the more it turned to fictional vignettes rather than dramatized documentary. This chapter explores how the climate of debate in which producers, writers, and advisers crafted the scripts for DIA fostered the thematic and aesthetic innovations of the series—the most important of which was the distinctive dissonant spoken chorus that concluded most episodes. We argue that Project producers deployed these discordant choruses to dramatize the complexities of governing in a pluralist democracy and to defuse allegations that the series was New Deal propaganda for expanded government.

Each episode of *Democracy in Action* opened with a choir singing in unison to small string ensemble accompaniment: "United we plan for the needs of our land, democracy in action!" Following this sung chorus came a chorus of individual speaking voices—described in the scripts as a "Choral Montage," and expressed this way in the script for episode one: "Montage of voices across music suggestive of democratic process":

It's a free country isn't it?
There ought to be a law.
Why doesn't someone do something?
Mr. Chairman I move.
Second that motion.
All in favor?
The ayes have it.
Mr. Speaker: the people of this sovereign state.

Then the Announcer: "Out of the needs of men and women have grown all customs, laws, institutions and governments."[9] That apparently simple statement summed up the carefully-crafted argument of the series—that democracy required active government and active citizens; that as society, technology and the economy developed, the American people had wanted and needed an expansion of the responsibilities of government. In later episodes that opening statement was further elaborated: "This is the story of you—a free people deciding what your government should do and should not do. Using your power to determine public policy. Choosing for yourselves the paths you shall follow."[10] This was a polemical opening in the late New Deal context—reasserting popular sovereignty and more specifically the idea that in a democracy the people decided the extent of government.

A Show about Government or a Show about Democracy?

Conveying all that in an entertaining and educational radio series was never going to be easy. The lengthy and somewhat troubled planning phase of the series can be explained by the two goals—to explain American government but also to spark passion about, and explicit commitment to, democracy. National political factors encouraged the narrower functional focus on the workings of government agencies, while international ones suggested the need for a much more ambitious series about why democracy was worth defending. This section shows how DIA moved back and forth between these two goals.

In September 1938, Commissioner John Studebaker appointed Chester S. Williams as supervisor of a series then titled "Government at Work." Irve Tunick, twenty-six years old, had been hired in August as a scriptwriter for the series.[11] He had previously worked at New York station WINS and on the popular children's series *Cowboy Tom's Roundup*.[12] Selma Goldstone, then only twenty-one but with three-years' research experience for the National Committee for Research in Medical Economics and an MA from Columbia University, was assigned to work on the series as a researcher. Boutwell explained in October that the title "Government at Work" was being used for "a number of program ideas having to do with reporting the work of the Federal Government to the people." Included were plans to present "treatment of administrative agencies in various departments one after the other," as well as series on Congress at Work, Social Security, and—note the careful phrasing— "Human Needs, and how the Government is helping our people to meet them." Boutwell enthused that these themes "permit almost unlimited elaboration."[13] Through October and November 1938, Tunick worked on draft episodes about the Bureau of the Budget, the Federal Reserve System, and the Social Security Board. In late October Boutwell reported that Studebaker thought highly of Tunick's approach and that a long series was envisaged: "S is particularly pleased with Tunick's work and he will concentrate on the Gov't series. The first 20 of 150 or more. That's our idea anyway."[14]

As international crises escalated through late 1938 and early 1939, a series reviewing the work of Washington departments and agencies began however to seem less than adequate. Even domestically, defending democracy seemed more urgent than explaining the work of government agencies. Boutwell suggested in October that "Making Democracy Work" would be a better title than "Government at Work": "government," he noted, was "a cold word" that "conveys the notion of control whereas 'democracy' in addition to being a warm word conveys the idea of participation."[15] By February 1939 the show was being called "Of the People," with objectives including "contrast of conditions and methods of democracy with those of dictatorship."[16]

In March, things took a different turn. Boutwell reported that "we have had a definite invitation from the World's Fair Federal exhibit authorities to present a program series in cooperation with them. It is possible that we may adapt OF THE PEOPLE for this series."[17] While the 1939–1940 New York World's Fair is better remembered for its utopian and futuristic corporate exhibits, it also had a strong government presence. President Roosevelt took a particular interest in the federal display, insisting that it be organized thematically rather than just illustrate the work of different departments or agencies. Robert W. Rydell observes that both Franklin and Eleanor Roosevelt saw the world's fairs of the 1930s as "a golden opportunity to restore popular confidence in the government's ability to meet the crisis of the Depression and to show American citizens that the government had their best interests at heart."[18] By April 1939, discussions between the Office of Education and the Federal Fair Commission were underway. The idea was that the twelve thematic exhibits of the federal government's pavilion at the 1939 World's Fair in New York would provide topics for a radio series, focusing on the government's role in areas such as transportation, communications, food, shelter, health, security, and education (figure 12). This helped nudge the proposed radio series away from the bigger issue of democracy and back toward a consideration of government functions over time. Studebaker had decided they would work on the themes of the World's Fair exhibit and "turn to the handling of the democratic process series later."[19] The ambitions of the earlier phase of discussion were still there, but a more practical and immediate set of goals about presenting the work of government gave structure to the show.

Around this time Tunick's contract was not extended and in March 1939, Merrill Denison—an experienced dramatist and radio scriptwriter who had worked both in Canada and with U.S. radio networks—was hired to write the series. Boutwell recalled that "the possibility of cooperating with the World's Fair exhibit" had become "a factor in the situation" of changing writers.[20] Denison visited the fair in early April and quickly concluded, however, that the radio series could not just offer "descriptive accounts" of the federal exhibits: "having prowled around them for three puzzled afternoons I can assure you that such a treatment is out . . . any attempt to describe them would only prove dull and insipid."[21] Instead, he wrote, the new series should "hammer home the fact that every expansion in the functions of administrative government has been the result of definite need imposed by changing conditions—not the result of a desire on the part of a nebulous character known as 'Washington' to extend its powers."[22]

In April CBS rejected the title "Of the People," sparking a new round of name discussion.[23] A document from April listed thirty-six possible names, including "Democracy Must Be Heard," "Let the People Speak," "The

FIGURE 12 Government exhibit on housing at the 1939 New York World's Fair. (New York Public Library photo no. b11686556. "Works Progress Administration—Federal Works Agency—Exhibit on housing," New York Public Library Digital Collections, accessed May 28, 2021, https://digitalcollections.nypl.org/items/5e66b3e9-1995-d471-e040 -e00a180654d7.)

People—Yes!," "Democracy—For Life!," and "Blessings of Liberty."[24] Denison recommended "For the People."[25] Cohen told Boutwell that Denison also favored "United We Stand," but added: "I feel very strongly that "More Perfect Union" is the right title since it expresses the purposes of the program . . . that we are working toward a more perfect union rather than expressing the feeling that it is an accomplished fact."[26] And yet by May, the title was *Democracy in Action*, apparently approved at a very high level—Studebaker reporting he had "checked directly with the President concerning the title and was pleased to learn that he was already familiar with our cooperative plan and in favor of the title 'Democracy in Action.'"[27]

Although Denison was brought in with little time left to pull the series together, his episodes achieved some critical acclaim, to which he proudly pointed in July 1939: "Ben Gross of the *Daily News* (circulation 3,500,000) has spoken in flattering terms about the program four Sundays in succession. This is most unusual. *Variety* (the bible of the entertainment world) gave it the best review it has ever accorded an educational. These reactions seem very important to me, particularly since *Variety*'s praise was won by the 'maturity' of the show. From an audience appeal point of view I regard praise from the hard boiled owls on the New York dailies more indicative than the approval of any self-appointed prize juries."[28] Cohen thought that, after all the indecision, it was Denison who managed to "discover the formula that finally got us on the air."[29] What was that formula? In what follows we describe three key elements: the historicization of active government, the use of dissonant choruses, and the deployment of fictional vignettes within the dramatized documentary format.

Despite Denison's success, he also eventually fell out with the Project leadership, in part over the continuing uncertainty about whether the series was about government more narrowly or democracy more broadly. Boutwell explained to Denison in July that they had "re-analysed previous approaches to the problem of presenting by radio the democratic process" and concluded that it was "an extraordinarily difficult problem to handle effectively and to the satisfaction of all concerned." He defended new plans to extend the series with simpler collaborations with particular government agencies: "It is much easier to present the work of a given group of agencies than it is to present the democratic process and show how it has evolved and changed through the years."[30] Denison wrote back, observing that "from an educational standpoint, *Democracy in Action* is the most important series I have met and from a radio standpoint it is the most mature." He was also highly critical of another plan, from the series consultants, for what he described as a new series "of half hours devoted to the exposition of the philosophic theories of democratic government . . . whether we like it or not radio is no medium for theory or philosophic exposition."[31] The members of the advisory panel for the series—political scientist Catheryn Seckler-Hudson and economist Leon Marshall of American University—were also unhappy. They wrote to Chester S. Williams in July saying that their original plan (for "a constructive and far reaching contribution to the understanding of government on the part of our people") was feasible only if the scriptwriter "will get under the job and spend a lot of time in Washington in detailed conferences with us." They deprecated the revised plan for episodes beyond the first series, of cooperation with government agencies, as "essentially a commonplace one" that also contained perils: "The agencies discussed must surely be conferred with, and this is likely to hold up your progress. Unless the material is kept at a commonplace level there is the possible charge of propaganda. There is at least the possibility of criticism leveled at the Office for expenditures for a venture that is not very constructive."[32]

The biggest practical complaint about Denison was about timeliness. The schedule was so crucial because there were many cooks—Denison as an experienced professional writer thought an insulting number of cooks—in the DIA kitchen. Project staff and writers had to navigate between the strictures of the advisory committee and the constant advice of the broadcasters that drama and engaging the audience were more important than scholarly detail. Established Project procedure called for committee review of draft scripts: "The scripts should be read by the script editor, the director, and the supervisor before a meeting of the review committee is called; the script editor, and supervisor should discuss the criticisms, and suggestions for revision should be transmitted from the program supervisor to the scriptwriter so that the script submitted to the full committee will have been revised in the light of radio division editorial judgement."[33] Denison was not used to his work being scrutinized in this way. He was caught in the middle of the cooperative relationship between broadcasters and educators and the endless debates about balancing drama and documentary, complaining to Williams on one occasion that "Columbia is already objecting to the wordiness and length of the Commentator's speeches and the Committee for its part is objecting to the length of the dramatizations."[34] Boutwell, Williams, and Vitray each marked up Denison's scripts with suggestions. Vitray tested each script on her secretary, Denison on his wife—although even this earned an admonishment from Williams: "I suggest you get illiterate critics and stop reading scripts to your wife."[35] Cohen, however, regularly sided with Denison, praising his scripts as "the most literate writing we have had."[36] One of the functions of the Office—and one of the reasons that deadlines were always sources of tension—was elaborate and careful fact-checking of draft scripts. Denison did not want responsibility for fact-checking, and in June a rearrangement gave Cohen that responsibility and the right to make late changes.

The result of all this input was that Denison found the multiple requests for additions and revisions very difficult to deal with in the time available. He complained to Williams about the academic advisers that, instead of "being a series of straightforward and direct programs dealing with the development of the administrative agencies of the Federal Government . . . I would be asked to discuss abstruse points of democratic government and to attempt to write dramatized lectures on political economy." He had, he wrote, no idea at the start that scripts would go to the advisory committee who were "paid to criticize." Within the Office, he singled out Williams's comments as "either insulting, captious or school-masterish."[37] When Denison objected to the committee looking over his shoulder, Williams attempted to mollify him with the observation that "the fact that the memoranda on the committee meetings contain primarily criticisms and suggestions to consider in making revisions does not alter the appreciation of all of us for your fine draft presentations."[38] Cohen wrote to Williams, rejecting the suggestion that he (Cohen) was responsible for prejudicing Denison against committees: "If Denison has become prejudiced against committees, it is because he has heard the entire history of this series, with the almost endless shifting of plans and policies up to the point where he stepped in and actually began to write the programs." He added that he thought Denison's scripts "far above the standard of our average programs" and reminded Williams of his view that "we wasted an awful lot of time on this series and that it was finally pulled out of the fire by one man's jumping in and working very quickly."[39]

The problem was that the oversight was, from the Office point of view, nonnegotiable because it was the very essence of the cooperative model—a way of maintaining the input of educators, as opposed to just subcontracting writers to deal directly with the commercial broadcasters. Williams told Cohen that the Office had to be a part of the production process, rejecting any suggestion that "we simply for all intents and purposes eliminate the committee. . . . This cannot be done. The Commissioner will not hear of it. If you cut the committee here, you might as well cut out the Office of Education and say that educational broadcasting can be done by competent authors who send their scripts directly to the network production department. There is a principle involved here."[40] The Office also consulted other experts and inevitably they also had ideas about more things that could be covered in the episodes. Belmont Farley of the National Education Association sent three pages of suggestions of other historical topics that might be covered—more attention to canals, carrier pigeons, and Perry's trip to Japan.[41] But the writers faced word and time limits. Denison wrote in May to thank Williams for the many suggestions, "all of which I find most interesting, but most of which, unfortunately, cannot be incorporated in the script because of the limitation of time."[42]

Commissioner Studebaker terminated the DIA series in July 1939, after thirteen episodes had been written (table 4).[43] C. F. Klinefelter, assistant to Studebaker, wrote to Denison on August 16, 1939, that "since apparently you have not been able to follow your schedule . . . providing for delivery of first of four scripts by August 14 . . . your services are terminated August 17."[44] CBS was, however, interested in a further series and the Office was keen to keep its place in the Sunday afternoon schedule.[45] In October, there were discussions about Denison returning to work on a second series, but he found the terms offered insulting: "Even the indentured servant of colonial times got a better break." This he found too much, given it was "proposed to the professional who rescued the Office of Education from a morass of ineffectuality after its long and extravagant waste of public funds had failed to produce a single acceptable script for the series DEMOCRACY IN ACTION."[46]

The DIA episodes that followed were in short series on areas of government responsibility—social security, health, labor, trade, the census, housing (table 5). The writers—Laura Vitray, Allan Wilson, Peter J. Harkins, and Broughton Tall—worked in collaboration with particular government departments. These shows publicized existing government programs and used fictional vignettes

Table 4
***Democracy in Action*, Series 1 Episode List**

Number	Theme	Date of broadcast
	Original Episodes—*written by Merrill Denison*	
1	Transportation	May 14, 1939
2	Communication	May 21, 1939
3	Food	May 28, 1939
4	Shelter	June 4, 1939
5	Conservation	June 11, 1939
6	Trade	June 18, 1939
7	Industry	June 25, 1939
8	Finance and Credit	July 2, 1939
9	Social Welfare	July 9, 1939
10	Education	July 16, 1939
11	Internal Protection	July 23, 1939
12	Foreign Relations	July 30, 1939
13	National Defense	Aug. 6, 1939
	Additional Episodes—*written by Allan Wilson*	
14	Public Health	Aug. 13, 1939
15	Agriculture	Aug. 20, 1939
16	The Arts	Aug. 27, 1939
17	Labor	Sept. 3, 1939
18	Recreation	Sept. 10, 1939
19	The Consumer	Sept. 17, 1939
20	Safety	Sept. 24, 1939
21	Youth	Oct. 1, 1939

to draw attention to, for example, the provisions of the Social Security Act or the workings of health and quarantine regulations. There were strategic incentives for the Office to cooperate with government agencies and departments. Several were keen to utilize the services of the Office of Education for programs about their activities. Boutwell told Cohen in June 1937: "Yesterday I gave Mr. Studebaker three loose-leaf notebooks packed full with requests for service from the Radio Project for next year. This includes requests from . . . the Farm Credit Department, Charles Greeley Abbott of the Smithsonian, and many other high officials."[47] A letter from the same month made the motive explicit: "We are receiving requests from many sources for program series and this all helps to increase the chances that the Project will be continued."[48] Boutwell also told Cohen in September 1937 that the Department of Commerce had requested cooperation on a program.[49]

Table 5
***Democracy in Action*, Additional Series Episode List**

Trade Series: Oct.—Nov. 1939—*written by Laura Vitray*
22. Foreign Trade
23. Farmers Trade Abroad
24. Industries and Foreign Trade
25. Yankee Ships and Yankee Trade
26. U.S. Foreign Trade Comes of Age

Public Health Series: Nov.–Dec. 1939—*written by Peter J. Harkins*
27. Growing Pains
28. Border Stop Signs
29. Case History
30. If the Truth Be Known
31. A New Lease on Life
32. Partners in Prevention

Social Security Series: Dec.–Jan. 1940—*written by Laura Vitray*
33. Security for the Family
34. Job Security
35. Security for Children
36. Caring for the Handicapped
37. Security for the Aged
38. Security—Today and Tomorrow

Labor Series: Feb.–Mar. 1940—*written by Allan Wilson*
39. Life and Limb
40. Immigrants All, Workers All
41. Employment
42. Home and Mill
43. Umpiring Labor and Management

Census Series: Mar. 1940—*written by Allan Wilson*
44. Census #1
45. Census #2

Roof over America Series: Mar.–June 1940—*written by Broughton Tall*
46. What Do You Mean, Home Sweet Home?
47. How We Got That Way
48. What Price Bad Housing?
49. The Villain in the Play
50. Houses That Jerry Built
51. Voices in the Wilderness
52. Streamlining the Home Industry
53. The House Next Door
54. Rooms with a View
55. Uncle Sam and the Housing Frontier

Historicizing Active Government

Returning to Horten's "clearly partisan" description—is it fair to label DIA as pro New Deal? What we can say is that the series consistently portrayed the New Deal as in the mainstream of American political tradition rather than as a radical break from it. That alone might have been enough to alienate those anti–New Deal Americans already convinced that the expansion of government and public employment was alien to American traditions and risked setting the United States on the road to dictatorship by entrenching the president and his party in power forever. But the story DIA told about the expansion of government was carefully shaped to anticipate and counter such anti–New Deal critiques. It offered a strong counternarrative, in which it was the people who wanted and needed government to take on larger roles and responsibilities.

Publicity for the show always emphasized the limited, delegated, and problem-solving nature of American government: "DEMOCRACY IN ACTION—How the Republic has been solving its problems—labor, health, foreign trade, etc.—for more than 150 years."[50] The opening of episode two put it this way: "Democracy in Action . . . will show you how our government functions began—how they have grown—how they exist today for but one purpose—to serve the 132,000,000 people who are America." Government was shown to have taken on roles for common-sense reasons—to enhance safety, protect the vulnerable, defend borders, facilitate trade and communication. In episode three, a doctor explained the need for federal regulation of food: "No state, no city, no matter how large or powerful, can hope to better these conditions by itself. How can they when food may be grown in one state, processed in another, stored in a third and sold for consumption in a fourth? I tell you only the Federal Government can do the job that must be done."[51]

Sensitivities about praising expansion of government as a form of progress were acute. DIA writers were instructed not to make the framing narrative a triumphalist one of the expansion of government activity and responsibility. Williams observed to Boutwell that the more Denison could show "that Government was forced reluctantly into a field," the better: "And that Government ordinarily tried to give aid—land, finances, regulations—almost any expedient rather than undertake the task itself. The crux of the situation, it seems to me, is not that we distrust government but that we trust democracy, which in theory calls for minimum decentralization, maximum individual initiative. Mr. Denison shows the will of the people at work but it is more than that: he should show the people trying to solve their problems according to democratic theories and processes."[52] Williams told Denison that "rather than this emphasis on the government doing the job or playing a role, we would like to see the people getting some of their needs met through democratic government. The chief actors, therefore, are the people and not the bureaucrats."[53] That, however, was too theoretical for Denison. In a long, impassioned letter in June, he complained that he had been told to "refrain altogether from praising the New Deal," but was then criticized for making the programs too historical. In the first-series episode about Shelter, he noted, treating the present work of the federal government had been a problem because

> the mere statement of its agencies is tantamount to the most flagrant praise in view of what has gone before. . . . You complain that again the program is 95% past and 5% present. This is exactly the thing we started out to do. We did not start out to write a series of dramatized lectures about the philosophic principles of political economy or democratic government. We started out to tell the story of the growth of the administrative agencies of the Federal Government of the United States as these agencies were related to the themes of the exhibits in the Federal World's Fair Building.[54]

A strong counternarrative to anti–New Deal depictions of government overreach was evident in the repeated statements that the people *chose* the things they wanted government to do *and* those they did not want it to do. In episode twelve, for example, we are given "the moving story of self government—of a free people deciding what their government should do and should not do." Those moments when government operation or intervention was rejected were emphasized—Abraham Lincoln saying that government should help but not actually build the railroads because "it's the kind of undertaking this country prefers to see left to private enterprise"; the postmaster general telling Samuel Morse that the government was satisfied that the telegraph "may be better entrusted to private enterprise." Episode two had this canny summary of the U.S. government's role in broadcasting: "Technology forced the creation of a Radio Commission. Tradition restricted its regulatory powers to a minimum." The episode concluded: "Whether we like it government must assume new responsibilities as they develop. And why should we resent government? It is ourselves acting through the democratic process." Writer Laura Vitray suggested a more homely and practical metaphor: "a democratic Government letting out its seams to cover the needs of a growing people."[55]

In an overheated political environment, in which conservative critics often accused the New Deal of representing "foreign" ideas, *Democracy in Action* thus worked consistently to domesticate and historicize active government. Tunick had thought the theme of government was best approached historically, a view that aligned with those of many other writers on the Project. As we have seen Denison explain, the historical focus was a practical strategy in the face of the conflicting ideological demands that always worried Project leadership. After his visit to the World's Fair in April 1939, Denison also recommended a historical approach to every topic covered: "the idea of going back in every case to Washington is a good one since the World's Fair is supposed to memorialize the 150th anniversary of his inauguration."[56] Actually, the fair planners had to some extent sidelined the Washington anniversary theme in favor of exhibits depicting the future.[57] But there were as we can see reasons why historical narratives worked well for DIA in particular and the Project shows in general.

DIA episodes in the first series had a common structure—beginning in the colonial or early national past, moving forward in time through a series of dramatized scenes depicting consistency of principles through dramatic change in circumstances. Episode eight about social welfare depicted the continuities of "the people of America in their pursuit of happiness . . . their struggle for security . . . their battle for social welfare." At first abundant land and the family provided security, but then government needed to become active to achieve the same ends—beginning with the Marine Hospital Service in 1798, legislation against child labor, care for Civil War veterans, workman's compensation, old-age pensions, and finally to New Deal agencies such as CCC, FERA, NRA, AAA, and the Social Security Board. Federal support for the arts was shown to be not a new idea in episode sixteen, which traced such efforts back to copyright law in 1790 and the Marine Band in 1798, before eventually reaching the New Deal arts programs. That came from Denison: "I would not deal to any great extent with the Federal Arts Projects except to note them at the end. What I do want to do is point out that the U.S. Government's interest in and assistance to art did not begin with the Roosevelt Administration."[58] Nevertheless, the episode ended with mention of New Deal cultural programs via the introduction of fictional characters—as we will see in the next section.[59] The narrative of historical continuity, then, worked to naturalize and nationalize New Deal government initiatives, placing them in a much longer national history.

The history represented in DIA was full of detail—people, events, ideas from the past—but these were embedded in big narratives about historical change. One such narrative was about a national transition from natural abundance to managed scarcity—of resources such as land, timber—and hence to a necessary role for government. Episode five had Daniel Boone and other frontier settlers enjoying a wealth of natural resources, but then came timber shortages and laws about preserving live oak timber and game animals, so that now "literally hundreds" of federal, state and private agencies, authorities, bureaus, services were operating to conserve America's resources. But still "the old fight goes on—the struggle between those who thoughtlessly indulge in waste—and those who would wisely use."[60] Radio critic Ben Gross heard this as a "stirring history."[61] Episode three on Food moved the other way—beginning with the first Thanksgiving at Plymouth, the larger theme was the move from scarcity to abundance, with government assistance: important steps included the pure milk and food legislation, state cattle inspectors, quarantine and importation laws, land grant colleges, the 1862 creation of the United States Department of Agriculture, knowledge of bacteria and pasteurization. A voice summarizes at the opening: "Where there once was scarcity—there is now abundance— where there were once shortages—there are now surpluses."[62] The episode ended with food stamps in 1939 to show continuity of concern with managing temporary scarcity and surplus. Laura Vitray criticized a draft, saying it sidestepped "the fact that millions of people in America have not enough to eat. I cannot see how a broadcast can purport to deal with the government in relation to food, yet overlook the most vital issue of all." She recalled that Leon Marshall at the advisory committee meeting had said that "the greatest problem ahead for the whole world is one of organization. . . . Isn't this a fair example of that fact? We have the food but we haven't the organization for utilizing it properly?"[63] Perhaps in response, the final script did describe a problem of distribution—the American people "have learned to grow enough food for all of us. Can we learn to distribute it?"

The relentless historicizing in the DIA scripts is the more remarkable because it came under frequent internal criticism from Project leaders. Boutwell commented in November 1938: "Our experience in radio prompts me to be very suspicious of historical leads."[64] "History," he warned in May 1939, "is only useful as a guide to the future."[65] Writing of the script on Conservation he said: "I want to protest again more loudly and strongly against the introduction which takes us immediately back to 1773. Just as sure as the sun rises, the historical lead turns away listeners."[66] The series' advisers wanted the programs to address "the contemporaneous situation as well as the world of tomorrow," believing that would "strengthen the series."[67] Writer Laura Vitray, too, had pragmatic reservations about the historical focus, complaining about the time given in the episode on communication to the travails of delivering mail by horseback, calling for "telescoping of some of the historical matter . . . both in order to leave room for a picture of communications today and because at points the dramatizations lost interest for me."[68] Her own DIA series on Social Security featured more fictional dramatization set in the present and less history.

Clearly, however, there were good reasons why the historical approach stuck and why it became such a key element of Denison's "formula." Amid the controversies swirling around the New Deal, historical narratives provided an ideological buffer for the series: enveloping it in a patriotic mood, providing factual material for the dramatized documentary form, and—perhaps most crucially—allowing for the depiction of New Deal governmental expansion and reform as continuous with the sweep and trajectory of longer national history and tradition.

Dramatized Documentary with Fictional Interludes

DIA also featured many dramatized fictional sections—invented scenes set in the past or the present. The fictional sections created space for more polemical interventions. Fictional characters, for example, expressed opinions that the narrator or commentator could then correct. They could also describe current government programs. The episode on the Arts ended with several fictional characters: a violinist on the Federal Music Project, a former newspaperman working on the Federal Writers Project, a painter at the Federal Art Project, an actor who had been with the Federal Theatre Project. The actor says: "Before it was terminated this year we had about eighty seven hundred actors, designers, technicians, playwrights, theatre musicians, stage hands, ushers and other people working on the project.... Our prices were low or nothing at all—so many times we played to people who had never seen a stage play before. But that's all over now."[69] This episode was broadcast on August 27, 1939, just weeks after the Federal Theatre Project had been axed: "Some Productions Brilliant but Many Piffling Experiments—Taint of Left-Wingers Wrecked Noble Purpose" read the *Spokane Spokesman-Review* front-page story on July 16 about the termination.

Getting the right balance between educational content and dramatic form on DIA was also a topic of constant internal debate. Boutwell reported to Studebaker that there was "a difference in viewpoint with Chester Williams holding one set of beliefs, and myself and the scriptwriters holding an opposite conviction. Chester and I have tried hard to reconcile our difference of opinion, but to no avail."[70] Williams in February 1939 was championing documentary over dramatization: "The objective should be to interest the audience in the subject itself and not primarily in the characters who should always be regarded as convenient vehicles for content. The scripts, therefore, in my judgment should avoid as much as possible the presentation of purely imaginative episodes and present that which is 'documentary.'"[71]

Boutwell, in contrast, placed greater emphasis on the dramatic structure and hence argued that a script needed to treat just one subject at a time: "This principle of unity is as vital for script writing as it is for good speaking or even good teaching."[72] Boutwell favored dramatization in part because he thought the production results were better. He wrote of the October 1939 episode on foreign trade: "I wish more data could be put into dramatization and less into narration and voices since we can't seem to get even moderately respectable production on anything else."[73] But most of all he thought dramatization more efficacious for education by radio. Of a December 1939 episode he observed: "I would call this a grade B program. Adequate but not superior. It did not make any important facts clear nor burn them into my consciousness by the fire of drama."[74]

On the other hand, Boutwell thought the January 1940 episode, "Caring for the Handicapped," was "the best DEMOCRACY IN ACTION program we have ever had . . . a good, clear, stirring script well produced."[75] That episode, written by Laura Vitray, was weighted toward dramatization. It opened with a fictional vignette set in a construction company office. Dixon, the boss, has, at the suggestion of Peterson, a representative of the state rehabilitation service, hired Mabel, a receptionist who is "crippled" and uses crutches. Dixon is very pleased with her work. But now Peterson, arguing that handicapped people bring inspiration to other workers, wants him to hire some men with disabilities: "Dixon, you need a crew of one-armed painters and I can get them for you." Dixon resists, ridiculing the suggestion. They invite Mabel in to get her advice, and she flatters Dixon into agreeing. The episode then turns to dramatized historical documentary mode, canvassing topics such as Thomas Gallaudet's work with the deaf and Samuel Gridley Howe's with the blind and the way both gained government support. In this case the contemporary fictional scene had a clear polemical point, while the historical sections (which also contained some fictional scenes) were more informational—although they also worked, as was common in Project shows, to locate the present in a historical trajectory of slowly awakening conscience and hence increasing government responsibility. The assuredness of the production of this episode, perhaps further evidence of the "maturity" that Denison had detected in DIA, suggested that a working consensus had been found on balancing documentary and fictional dramatization and that there was increasing skill in doing the dramatizations convincingly.

CBS also weighed in on the drama versus documentary debate. CBS executive Max Wylie, Denison reported, wanted "more, bigger and longer dramatizations."[76] In mid-June Wylie was critical of the processes inside the Office, which he said were resulting in "inferior quality" scripts. He implied that Williams's interventions in particular were responsible for producing scripts that, while they were "both accurate and interesting as pieces of prose," had been "almost totally inert dramatically . . . I have a suspicion that whatever Mr. Williams' talents may be they do not lie in the field of dramatics." He added: "It is my feeling that this is bad broadcasting. It is bad broadcasting because it is dull. . . . At the risk of seeming ill-tempered may I say that the privilege to determine the handling of this material is not Washington's but ours, and we shall exercise it. The content is your privilege."[77] Again in September Wylie wrote of Allan Wilson: "Wilson is a high grade writing man. But his shows bumble and stumble all over the place. They are dramatically unattractive; they are great looping documentaries without any buzz in them; chopped up essays, interrupted travel talks, devoid of scenes, devoid of people, devoid of emotion, devoid of dialogue, devoid of characterization. Our feelings are never engaged, never affected. We are mercilessly talked at, monotonously informed, belabored with that Washington genius for being dull. We never meet anybody interesting, never see anything exciting."[78] Project staff continued to resist that kind of simple form/content division of labor, insisting that matters of presentation and style were also the province of the educators. But these heated arguments give us a good sense of how "actual cooperative arrangements" worked in practice and how the tensions between documentary and dramatization were played out during the creative process.

Dissonant Choruses

The political climate pushed the creators of DIA toward new radio production strategies within the dramatized documentary format. Ambient anxiety about the line between propaganda and education constrained the producers, writers and advisers of DIA, but it also encouraged specific thematic and aesthetic innovations. The use of a narrator and a commentator as well as chorus-like assemblages of individual voices decentered these programs on contentious topics—we hear strong opinions about government and democracy, but also strong dissent from them. However, it is worth first distinguishing the use of sung and spoken choruses.

Sung choruses were a common ingredient in the Project shows for a quite practical reason. Williams explained that "the object of having a chorus in the beginning was to provide a means of employing WPA workers in the actual operation of the project." Unfortunately, he added, "the constant criticism of our programs has shown a dislike for the chorus as a means of setting mood and giving musical color to the production. . . . I am convinced that the chorus is a disadvantage to 'Democracy in Action.'"[79] Sung choruses, among other things, aurally foregrounded men's and women's voices in harmony. Boutwell found the prominence this gave to the women's voices unsettling, recommending on one occasion that "maximum use should be made of humming with the male voices dominant."[80] Echoing a long-standing prejudice against soprano voices—and female voices more broadly—in U.S. broadcasting, he thought women's voices too prominent in the opening chorus of DIA: "Couldn't that high soprano note in the theme be re-arranged?" he asked in March 1940.[81]

A few months earlier Boutwell had written to music director Rudolph Schramm: "You know that I have had difficulty in defending in our own office the idea of having a chorus at all. The criticisms have been chiefly (1) the inability to understand the words sung by the chorus, and (2) the chorus singing has interrupted the flow of the scripts rather than provided suitable transitions."[82] The interruption to the flow of the scripts can, on the other hand, be heard as deliberate—a conscious choice of a disruptive musical interlude, as opposed to the smooth transition music then commonly used in narrative film or radio soap opera. Earle McGill, who directed several of the DIA episodes for CBS,

FIGURE 13 Earle McGill directing an Educational Radio Project cast in rehearsal. (New York Public Library photo no. b20726882. "Earle McGill directing cast in rehearsal for the radio program 'Americans All—Immigrants All,'" New York Public Library Digital Collections, accessed May 28, 2021, https://digitalcollections.nypl.org/items/199740c0 -0048-0139-e550-0242ac110003.)

wrote in his 1940 book on *Radio Directing* about his work on the earlier Project show *Brave New World*, arguing that for such "highly stylized" productions, "bald and literal" sound effects were to be avoided because "the use of highly realistic effects" might "take something away from the allegorical quality of the story."[83] Sung choruses sometimes in this way, we argue, deliberately broke up the smooth surface sound of an episode, returning us somewhat jarringly—or as McGill put it, in "highly stylized" fashion—to the context of a radio studio production (figure 13).

Sung choruses in Project shows were almost always in unison, sounding out themes of unity and forward national momentum—that important part of the New Deal aesthetic effectively conveyed the idea of the people united, speaking and singing together. The opening spoken chorus was, in contrast, individualized and multivocal, although relatively consensual in its suggestion of a shared "democratic process." An early draft script (not broadcast) shows Irve Tunick experimenting in this way with a chorus of voices in agreement, representing the people and their affirmation of the necessity of government and law. This sequence builds toward the affirmation of popular sovereignty of the fifth voice:

> NARRATOR: The laws of our land! Why do we have any laws at all? Why not a land without law?
> VOICE 1: The law protects my family and my home.
> VOICE 2: The law guarantees me my personal liberties.
> VOICE 3: The law grants me redress for injury and loss.
> VOICE 4: The law serves me by doing things I cannot do myself. It delivers my mail. It coins my money. It protects my health. It supervises my interests in foreign nations!
> VOICE 5: The law governs me—and I govern the law![84]

Here the chorus depicts the people speaking in multiple voices but with one mind. That more consensual use of a spoken chorus contrasts sharply with the dissonant chorus that became a key part of Denison's formula—used not just through the Denison first series but in later DIA episodes as well.

The dissonant chorus allowed for the presentation of controversial issues while allowing both or several sides to be heard. Most often, the voices disagreed about the size of government. In episode two on communications:

> VOICE 3: Entire industries may be threatened by the rapid advance in communications. . . . Should government do anything about it?
> VOICE 4: No! We say the time has come to restrain government activities.
> VOICE 5: We disagree. Whether we like it government must assume new responsibilities as they develop. Why should we resent government? It is ourselves acting through the democratic process.[85]

In the conclusion to episode three on food:

> VOICE 1: We must reduce production.
> VOICE 2: That's not the answer. We must increase consumption.
> VOICE 3: Agriculture must be made to stand on its feet. Why should it have such enormous subsidies . . .
> VOICE 6: We've got to return to fundamentals—abide by the law of supply and demand.
> VOICE 7: Supply and demand be blowed. We can't let people starve.[86]

In the conclusion to a July 1939 episode on social welfare, the commentator says that economic security "is every man's right—and every citizen's heritage in a Democracy." But then other voices come in. Voice one asks, "Are we attacking the problem right when we place this type of legislation in the hands of the

Federal Government?" Voice two says: "The welfare of the individual is a local matter—a matter for the family, the church or the local community." Voice three disagrees, saying the fight for security "is a national fight." The episode ends with voices four and five asking questions: "Where does government assistance end and paternalism begin? Can we relieve the individual of fear and insecurity—and yet permit him to retain his individual initiative?" Those voices articulated some of the deepest political divisions of the period and provided— or so Project leaders hoped—some inoculation against the charge of pro–New Deal bias.

Here, finally, is another Vitray episode, on "Security—Today and Tomorrow," from January 1940:

(THESE SOUND EFFECTS ARE IMPORTANT AS THEY TELL A STORY)
MONTAGE OF SOUND . . . HORNS AND WHISTLES, VOICES: "HAPPY NEW YEAR." "HAPPY NEW YEAR!" . . . FADE INTO
SOUND OF AUTO APPROACHING, THEN CRASH . . .
A SCREAM . . . PAUSE . . . VOICES YELLING OFF-MIKE; "HEY, THAT CAR!"
"IT TURNED OVER!" . . . PEOPLE RUNNING . . .

We hear from various voices that a crowd has gathered. Bystanders pull a man from the crashed car. A police officer and a newspaper reporter arrive and an ambulance is called. The ambulance arrives with a doctor, who examines the man on the ground: "Officer, this man is *dead*." The man is only thirty-one years old and lives at 2114 Roosevelt. The police officer has found a Social Security card on him. The reporter becomes excited: "Say . . . if I'm not mistaken . . . the old age and survivors' insurance only took effect a couple of hours ago at midnight!" The reporter speeds around to talk to the sobbing widow. "He is dead . . . dead," she says. "He was a good husband too . . . he worked so hard . . . now . . . he's dead." She has seven children, the youngest just two months old. "With Ed gone, we'll starve," she cries. But the reporter has somehow already managed to speak to her husband's employer and has discovered that "he had enough time to his credit to earn him survivors' insurance under the Social Security Act. . . . The survivors' insurance went into effect at midnight. Your husband died just after it went into effect." The widow will get $45.54 a month until the children grow up. "It's a Godsend," she exclaims. "I can't believe it! It's a Godsend." This melodrama gets our attention. The episode then circles back to history. The narrator explains: "Even before the Depression years, there were a few pioneer voices crying in the wilderness that *great social risks* could not be met alone!" We hear some of those individuals explain their ideas, and we learn about old-age pensions. Finally, the commentator tells us that "the helping hand of Social Security reaches to the hut in the lonely bayou, or the cabin in the mountain . . . just as it does to the victims of the machine age, huddled in close quarters in our largest centers of industry. Perhaps, the job is not yet completed . . . perhaps it's only begun." But then the positive mood is interrupted for the dissonant chorus of the conclusion:

TAXPAYER: Yes, but . . . I'm the taxpayer . . . the man who pays and pays! And I think this is too much of a good thing! It's paternalism . . . the government playing nursemaid to the people! Keep that up, and no one will be able to stand on his feet!

WOMAN: Well I pay taxes too . . . and I don't agree with you. Americans banded together to set up and operate public schools. We've got as much reason to seek cooperative security from disease and poverty and unemployment as from anything else.

VOICE 1: The money would be better spent on national defense!

VOICE 2: This is national defense, isn't it?

VOICE 3: Rubbish! It's time this country started to economize!

VOICE 4: Well, what better way to economize than by saving human beings and protecting the family.

VOICE 5: Well . . . I'm a farm laborer . . . I don't get any insurance protection . . . yet . . . under the Social Security Act.

WOMAN 2: You're right . . . there's many things about it that needs to be improved.

ANNOUNCER: Well, it seems all American citizens are not always agreed . . . Most of the things we do are subjected to a lot of friendly discussion up and down this land of ours . . . In the United States, we sit down around the dining room table . . . or the conference table, and sort of argue out the pros and cons. And, sooner or later, we find the right answer through . . . DEMOCRACY IN ACTION.[87]

This kind of anonymous dissonant chorus became the preferred solution to the problem of the presentation of programs on divisive and partisan issues, with strong approval from Project leadership. Williams explained: "We must make it crystal clear that these programs are in no way forecasting the role of government in the future and that we recognize legitimate differences of opinion on the role of government in connection with these fields of activity. It is not enough simply to present this notion in the form of a commentator's speech. We must somehow demonstrate that there is a clash of opinion,—a genuine difference which we respect."[88] Of a December 1939 episode on Security for the Family, Boutwell noted that he "particularly liked the concluding statement. It succeeded in presenting our position of impartiality."[89]

Confirmation of how important the closing chorus had become to the "formula" for the series is found in the episode on the Arts in late August. The closing questions were inadvertently cut in production and Boutwell was agitated: "Those questions are extremely important to our formula and I wish you would instruct the production director at CBS that he can cut almost anything except the questions . . . You can't tell the story of Government and Art without telling the work of the WPA, and to many people's ears that sounds like propaganda. Hence the importance of the questions."[90] In the script we see these were not so much questions as statements about government from conflicting points of view:

> VOICE 1: Well, art is all right in its place—but the Government shouldn't have a hand in it.
> VOICE 2: Except, of course, in getting the right kind of architecture and art work on public buildings.
> VOICE 1: Sure—but Government aid to artists just fosters mediocrity. It stifles individual initiative.
> VOICE 3: Government aid encourages the arts—helps to bring out talent in our citizens that might not get a chance otherwise.[91]

We do not know what influenced Denison to adopt the dissonant chorus, but the chorus in modern drama has sometimes played exactly this role of articulating diversity rather than unanimity: "Choruses, ancient and modern, have a striking tendency to focus conceptions of political, artistic, and social existence, and thus serve as media for exploring similarity as well as difference, and for tracing continuity and rupture alike."[92] These choruses of voices with different and irreconcilable points of view expressed something important about New Deal nationalism and the conscientiously pluralist public sphere it was attempting to construct. Denison's device was a liberal chorus, dramatizing different viewpoints and the process of civilly sharing them. Modernist playwright Bertolt Brecht used choruses differently: "Brechtian choruses as socio-political agents are presented in a critical, even sinister light."[93] In DIA, the chorus is dissonant and no resolution is offered, except the onward journey of the American people using government to solve their problems, but the voices are generally benign in intention—each earnestly wants the best for the country; they simply differ on how to bring it about.

Conclusions

Democracy in Action was shaped by the Radio Project's accumulated experience and practiced artistry deriving from four years and thousands of hours of radio production. While educators grappled with the challenge of promoting democracy without producing government propaganda, practitioners experimented with new ways of dramatically representing democracy as a lived experience. Writers and producers took seriously an early set of goals for DIA, drafted by Boutwell: "Make each individual listener aware he participates in government all the time" and "show that in a democracy the individual takes part in a government that draws its power and authority from those participating."[94] The series exemplified a core concern of Commissioner Studebaker's Office of Education—adult education in and for democracy, the idea that democracy was a way of being in the world and of living for others as well as the self. As Studebaker explained to the American Adult Education Association in May 1940, "Democracy implies the development of that sympathetic understanding and altruistic spirit which contribute to the self-realization of each person."[95] An understanding of American democracy as always under construction, needing to be sustained in the lives and values of all Americans, was fundamental to Project thinking generally and to DIA in particular.

While other Project series utilized historical dramatizations to tell stories of national cooperation, unity, and tolerance, or fictional formats to model new modes of citizenship, DIA used a dissonant dramatized documentary format to perform the complexities and possibilities of government stewardship in a pluralist democracy. That the trajectory of DIA episodes was so often from an opening of sung choral unison to an ending that featured a spoken chorus of individual, assertive, conflicting voices tells us something about the Project's commitment to promoting participatory democracy, even as the New Deal cultural project at large was coming under increased attack. The trouble was that even that could be heard as partisan, as voices of dissent and disunity grew louder by the end of the decade.

6

Pleasantdale Folks

Social Security Soap

Pleasantdale Folks was an electrical transcription series of thirteen fifteen-minute episodes produced by the Radio Project in cooperation with the Social Security Board (SSB), WPA, and NBC. Beginning in January 1940, NBC offered the series on transcription disks to its affiliates at no cost and promoted it as a highly professional dramatization of Social Security that "station managers will welcome . . . as an interesting addition to their program schedules."[1] The Office of Education carefully tracked the number of stations airing the program and found that, by May 1940, the series had been booked by over half of the country's stations and was expected to air in 82 percent of broadcast cities.[2] As a recorded series, *Pleasantdale Folks* was able to reach a large national audience while also giving stations flexibility in when and how to air the show.

Pleasantdale Folks was a follow-up to an earlier four-part Social Security series, *January 1939!*, which presented the fictional character Joe Johnson as he lost his job, collected unemployment insurance, and ultimately returned to private employment.[3] Focusing on Joe Johnson's family and neighbors, *Pleasantdale Folks* expanded on the earlier fictional story to dramatize the new Social Security provisions being rolled out in 1939 and 1940. In late 1939, old-age insurance was extended to cover wage earners' dependents and survivors, and wives of insured workers were given one half of their husbands' benefits starting at age sixty-five. Monthly payments, however, did not begin until January 1940.[4] The federal government's share of state-level welfare provisions, including what was then called Aid to Dependent Children, increased from one-third to one-half, and aid to the blind and impoverished was expanded. But these provisions were not implemented in all states until mid-1940.[5] In addition, unemployment insurance was still being put into place in some states in early 1940.

Along with Joe Johnson, a machinist in his fifties, the Johnson family included "Mom," his "cheerful, plump, home-loving" wife; their daughter, Sue (twenty-four); and their son, Harvey (nineteen).[6] Although Joe's job remained secure, his children, relatives, and neighbors experienced various setbacks and layoffs in their jobs at the Pleasantdale ironworks, lumberyard, paper mill, and machine shop. Mom was a homemaker whose persona, as well as her name, was limited to the nurturing and caretaking activities of mother and wife. The drama focused mainly on Harvey and Sue, who were coming of age during the Depression. The first episode, for example, opened with Harvey's sense of humiliation at being unable to find a job after his first layoff. As Joe observed, "It's his first streak of bad luck and he takes it extra hard."[7] Much of the story focused on Sue's hesitancy about marrying her suitor, Ollie Larson, under the harsh and unstable economic conditions of the Depression years.

Like other Project series, *Pleasantdale Folks* was a governmental drama that aimed to normalize and naturalize the role of government in the everyday lives of Americans. It used the format of the dramatic serial or soap opera to highlight and explain the recent federal expansion of old-age insurance, unemployment insurance, and welfare coverage to the American public. Through the fictional Johnson family and community of Pleasantdale, the series showed how Social Security expansion could improve living standards and reduce economic insecurity for individuals, families, and communities. As the series' opening indicates, producers hoped that listeners would identify emotionally with the white, working-class Johnson family and therefore engage with the program's educational content: "Meet the Johnson Family of Pleasantdale: a typical American family in a typical American town. They should be as familiar to you as people in your own home, for they have the same problems, the same hopes, the same sorrows, and the same joys that every family knows."[8] Not surprisingly, *Pleasantdale Folks* did not present Social Security as an unprecedented government intervention in people's lives. Like other Project series, it aimed to counter the view that New Deal government activism was radical or extraordinary. Rather, the series presented New Deal social policies as continuing time-honored community traditions—but also as improving upon those traditions by allowing more independence for individuals and young families.

Unlike Project series examined so far, however, *Pleasantdale Folks* was originally conceived and prepared by an external agency—the Social Security Board's Information Service. The Project produced several shows of this collaborative kind, including series for the Department of Commerce, the Bureau of the Census, and other agencies and organizations.[9] As it amassed experience and success in radio production, the Project became in this way a resource and service provider for other government agencies. These shows were aired and promoted as Office of Education productions, and they sounded like other Project shows because they used the same directors, actors, and production practices, such as the use of the mixed chorus. These agency programs fit within the Project's objective of facilitating educational uses (broadly conceived) of commercial broadcasting and were an important aspect of what the Project did. Since the Project was not involved in researching or writing the scripts, we unfortunately lack the information on the production process that we have for most other shows. Neither the writing nor editing processes are mentioned in the Social Security Board documents that we consulted. However, we make up for this absence by closely analyzing the discourse of *Pleasantdale Folks* and comparing it with the Project's other major fictional program, *Wings for the Martins*.

We begin by comparing *Pleasantdale Folks* with *Wings for the Martins* in terms of audience orientation and genre. We also contextualize *Pleasantdale Folks* within the discourse of "preserving the American family" that shaped New Deal social policy. In particular, our analysis of *Pleasantdale Folks* explores the ways in which the dramatic dialogue focused on the need to "save" Harvey's respectable white masculinity while encouraging Susan to relinquish her economic independence. We take a closer look at the soap opera genre as it was developing in network radio at this time and investigate how the message of *Pleasantdale Folks* fitted within the generic expectations and practices of the soap opera. Finally, we draw conclusions about the role that fictional broadcasting genres like the soap opera and the sitcom played in fulfilling the mission of the Educational Radio Project.

Series Overview: From the Middle Class to the Folk

The fact that *Pleasantdale Folks* was produced as a transcription series rather than a live network broadcast *might* be viewed as a sign of the declining viability of cooperative New Deal–network radio productions by the end of 1939. There is evidence that the networks were significantly less accommodating to the Educational Radio Project and had less reason to be after Congress prohibited the use of most WPA funds for broadcasting.[10] However, memos from the SSB indicate that the project was indeed originally conceived as a transcription series. In September 1939 the SSB requested the Radio Project's help with the production of a series of radio transcriptions. Max Stern, director of the SSB Informational Service, wrote that his department had developed the concept of the program, commissioned the scripts, and planned to record transcriptions, but it needed actors, musicians, and other production support from the Office of Education.[11] Although the central component of Social Security was nationwide old-age insurance for (mostly industrial) workers, the SSB also worked in coordination with the states to provide unemployment compensation and aid to children and the blind. The SSB preferred to distribute *Pleasantdale Folks* as a transcription series to air the program on a state-by-state basis as individual states rolled out the new provisions. The transcription format also made it easier for the SSB to introduce and conclude its broadcasts with information by and about the state-level office that would be the main contact point for Social Security benefits.

Although both *Pleasantdale Folks* and *Wings for the Martins* claimed to represent the "typical" American family, the Martins and Johnsons were very different. The Martins were a middle-class nuclear family with four young children, while the Johnsons were a working-class family with two adult children still living at home but hoping to start families of their own. The first *Pleasantdale* episode began at the home of Joe Johnson as Harvey returned from an unsuccessful day of searching for work. He had registered for unemployment and expected his first insurance check within a week, but was nevertheless extremely bitter and demoralized. When his mother observed that he was not acting at all like himself, he snapped: "Shucks, Mom, what do you expect me to do, go around singin' songs?"[12] While Joe sympathized with Harvey's situation, Harvey's sister, Sue, expressed concern that he had started hanging out with the wrong crowd. At the end of the episode the cloud lifted, however, when the family learned that Harvey had after all gotten a job at the paper mill.

By focusing on young people who were not used to the layoffs and downturns that plagued industrial work, *Pleasantdale Folks* had the potential to speak to a broad range of listeners who faced unemployment and insecurity for the first time during the Depression years. Although the series focused on industrial workers as key beneficiaries of Social Security, it never articulated working-class solidarity or a working-class perspective on the Depression. Rather, through friends and acquaintances of the Johnsons, it showed the ravages of economic insecurity on all social groups, including small business owners and middle-class professionals who became impoverished in their old age. And as governmental radio, it dramatized not only the benign role of active government but also the knowledge and actions required of citizens. Overall, the program emphasized shared experiences across classes—"we're just Pleasantdale folks and need to stick together."[13]

In the second episode, Joe learned that his brother, Dick, had died after an illness, leaving behind a grieving widow, Mary, and several children. When the Johnsons went to console Mary, they discovered that Dick's ten-year-old daughter, Nancy, had run away because she was afraid of being sent to an orphans' home. Episodes two through five used Nancy's dramatic actions to explore the details of Social Security provisions. After she ran away to her neighbor Mrs. Jenkin's house, Nancy learned from the local doctor that welfare programs were in place to reassure the poorest citizens who did not need special care that "your place is in your own home."[14] When Nancy returned home in episode five, Dr. Henry and the family discussed Mary's survivor's benefits and explained the differences between social insurance and welfare, using people in the community as examples.

Episodes six through ten followed two parallel story lines: the fallout from a four-week layoff at the ironworks and Sue Johnson's concerns about starting a family of her own in such insecure times. These episodes both explained and promoted the benefits of unemployment insurance by "visiting" the many Pleasantdale families—friends and neighbors of the Johnsons—who had been affected by the layoff, to see how the promise of benefits lessened their fear and anxiety. These episodes also explored Sue's concerns about the difficulties that young married couples faced during the Depression. One of the central aims of the drama was to convince Sue that Social Security allowed her to plan for a household and family of her own and made it safe for her to marry her suitor, Ollie Larson.

In episodes eleven through thirteen we learn that Sue has agreed to marry Ollie and that they plan to honeymoon in Baltimore—to visit the Bureau of Old Age and Survivors' Insurance! Along with providing assurances about the security and accuracy of the Social Security system, these episodes framed the expanded insurance and welfare programs not as a profound change in the role of government in American life but simply as extensions of the traditional community spirit of self-help. This was a common trope in Project series—identifying New Deal initiatives as extensions of traditional American values. After family friend Dave Canfield completely lost his sight, Joe took up a collection for him at the shop and Dr. Henry helped Dave sign up for welfare benefits that would allow him to stay in his own home. As Dr. Henry opined, "As I look at it, this age is trying to do the same things that friends and neighbors used to do, but now people have to use the government to make it work." Even though economic aid now came from the government, "it's the same old helping hand for people in trouble."[15] *Pleasantdale Folks* advanced the view that social security and welfare programs helped maintain the community fabric by allowing economically disadvantaged Americans to continue to live in their own homes and contribute to their communities. At the same time, it touted the idea that these programs would liberate the younger generation from having to live with and help support their elderly parents. The series clearly forecasted the ways in which the Social Security program—through its old-age, unemployment, and survivor's benefits—promoted the nuclear family as a national norm during the twentieth century.

Pleasantdale Folks and the Soap Opera Genre

While *Wings* employed the family sitcom format to reach a middle-class audience, *Pleasantdale Folks* used the soap opera form to speak to a working-class audience. Both genres were still in formation in the 1930s and frequently blurred elements such as melodrama and comedy in the domestic setting.[16] However, the distinctions between domestic serials and domestic comedies were becoming solidified by the late 1930s. In particular, soap operas were oriented to a daytime audience and used a daily fifteen-minute "strip" format, whereas domestic comedies aired in the evenings with a weekly thirty-minute format. Domestic comedies typically opened with upbeat orchestral music, while most soap operas were introduced by weepy organ music. Instead of an organ, *Pleasantdale Folks* drew on the WPA chorus to provide a simple, homey, and sentimental opening theme (figure 14). Overall, daytime radio, and the soap opera in particular, was constructed by the networks as "lowbrow" and "feminine," while prime-time programming like the situation comedy was framed as "middlebrow" and "masculine." This was the case, Michele Hilmes points out, even though both daytime and nighttime radio audiences were predominantly female.[17]

During the Depression years, soap operas provided a model of how to represent lower-class families using strong female characters, folksy dialect, and homespun philosophies of courage and resilience.[18] It was also the case that the subject matter of *Pleasantdale Folks*—job loss, death, and disability—was less appropriate for a comic framework than the topic of parent education. Because *Pleasantdale Folks* dealt with the expansion of Social Security provisions to cover married women, widows, and mothers receiving aid for their children, it seems likely that the program specifically targeted women. As a short transcription series, *Pleasantdale Folks* could be slotted into the schedule wherever deemed best by the station—and it was. The series was broadcast at 7:00 P.M. in Sheboygan, Wisconsin, and 9:00 P.M. in Sayre, Pennsylvania, but it was aired at 9:00 A.M. in Jackson, Tennessee, and 11:15 A.M. in Santa Rosa, California. Nevertheless, whereas the middle-class family of *Wings* was associated with middlebrow comedies and male-led listening in the evening hours, the working-class family of *Pleasantdale Folks* was associated with the lowbrow cultural form of the melodrama that dominated daytime hours.[19]

Daytime serials also featured ongoing and unresolved narratives that included daily cliff hangers and "excessive" melodrama in both plot and performance, as opposed to sitcoms that resolved each "situation" encountered by the family on a weekly basis. As Robert C. Allen and other scholars have noted, the soap opera's open narrative defied expectations that drama should have a beginning, middle, and end, and instead seemed to be "composed of an indefinitely expandable middle."[20] As the program overview suggests, *Pleasantdale*

FIGURE 14 An Educational Radio Project mixed chorus at work. A similar chorus of WPA singers accompanied *Pleasantdale Folks* and other Project productions. (National Archives photo no. 12-E-32-2169. "Chorus—A mixed chorus of sixteen voices singing the thrilling theme opening of 'Brave New World,'" May 6, 1939, RG 12 Office of Education, Radio Project-WPA Photographs, 12-E-32, Box 39, RG 12 Office of Education, Still Picture Branch, National Archives, College Park, Maryland.)

Folks only partly conformed to the open narrative structure of the genre. Instead, it included some stories that extended across episodes (e.g., Nancy's experience of running away, Sue's ongoing reluctance to get married) as well as situations that were quickly resolved. Harvey's search for employment came to a happy ending in the first episode, and many of the problems facing other Pleasantdale folks were resolved in fifteen minutes. Given its need to cover specific information in a limited space of only thirteen episodes, it is not surprising that *Pleasantdale Folks* failed to develop the elongated, open narratives that were typical of most U.S. soap operas.

While the narrative structure of *Pleasantdale Folks* departed from the genre in some aspects, it closely emulated the way that soap operas interwove space and time into a web of interconnections between families, friends, and associates living in the same community. Although it centered on the Johnson family, it also brought in neighbors who were laid off or disabled, a friend working at a small grocery store, and an uncle who had died and left behind a grieving and destitute family. Using musical bridges or choral interludes, along with announcer descriptions, most episodes shifted scenes between individual homes and workplaces across Pleasantdale. This allowed listeners to "travel" around the community and "eavesdrop" on each family or group as it dealt with unemployment, disability, and other problems. A key aspect of this social webbing was to position the listener as part of a larger network of emotional connection. Listeners were welcomed into the unique spatial and affective community created in each soap opera. In the case of *Pleasantdale Folks*, the narrative networking of the community also portrayed the ways in which Social Security programs could be woven into local communities to strengthen them with an invisible safety net of government support.

Pleasantdale Folks was an early example of the educational use of soap operas—often called entertainment-education—that scholars and practitioners began developing globally in the 1970s and 1980s to promote literacy, health education, family planning, and other educational campaigns. Miguel Sabido, producer at commercial broadcaster Televisa in Mexico, was one of the first to develop the concept of entertainment-education programming in response to the international success and impact of the 1969 Peruvian soap opera (telenovela) *Simplemente Maria*. In the series, the heroine Maria transforms her life by attending night school and buying a sewing machine so that she can become a clothing designer, and this directly inspired thousands of Latin American viewers to take up similar educational and entrepreneurial activities.[21] This led Sabido to develop telenovelas that interwove specific educational campaigns into the love stories and rags-to-riches plots of the programs. The idea that soap opera audiences understood the shows as educational is much older than Sabido's efforts, however, and can be traced to Herta Herzog's early research on the "uses and gratifications" that women found in serialized programs.[22] Along with identifying with serial characters and becoming emotionally engaged in the stories, listeners reported that they found models of survival and success in soap operas to which they could adapt their own behavior. In sum, the decision to use the soap opera format to promote public education about Social Security reflected contemporary understandings of the didactic power of soap operas and foreshadowed the development of entertainment-education in the television era.

Pleasantdale Folks in the Context
of New Deal Social Policy

Pleasantdale Folks aimed to promote and help implement Social Security provisions that addressed the jarring social costs of the Great Depression through unemployment insurance, old-age insurance, and social welfare programs. One of the most disturbing, but perhaps least remembered, facts of the Great Depression was the suffering of vulnerable older Americans, some of whom were forced to rummage for food in garbage cans or quietly starve to death at home.[23] In 1933 Dr. Francis Townsend of California started a nationwide movement that proposed to give $200 per month to all Americans over the age of sixty, with the proviso that they spend the money monthly. Within two years, the Social Security Act's much less generous old-age insurance plan passed Congress with President Roosevelt's full support.[24]

While Social Security addressed the plight of impoverished older Americans, it was also an effort to target a larger perceived crisis of the American family.[25] At its worst, the Depression forced one out of five male wage earners onto federal relief roles and accelerated the entrance of women into the labor force. Young people aged eighteen to twenty-five were particularly hard hit by the economic crisis and eventually made up as much as one-third of the country's jobless (about 4 million in 1934). Under these conditions, young adults were forced to delay their marriages and prolong their economic and social dependence on parents and other relations.[26] In this environment, some observers expressed concern about the instability of the family and the possibility that an entire generation of Americans coming of age would lose faith in the traditional patriarchal family along with other social and economic institutions.[27]

Concerns about the fate of the "younger generation" were closely tied to fears about how working women might weaken the traditional family. The Great Depression put pressure on women to enter or remain in the workforce. At the same time, divorce rates increased, marriage rates plummeted, and birth rates declined.[28] Perhaps most significantly, public *perceptions* of a significant rise in female employment contributed to the environment of hostility against working women. Increases in female workforce participation were steeper after 1950, the decade often considered the heyday of (ultimately unsuccessful) ideological attempts at pushing women back into the home—but we can see a similar dynamic in the 1930s. Women in the workforce were in the Depression decade viewed by many as a threat to male power and identity as well as a danger to conventional patterns of child-rearing and home life.[29]

Elaine Tyler May argues that the Depression "opened the way for a new type of family based on shared bread winning and equality of the sexes," but simultaneously generated "nostalgia for a mythic past in which male breadwinners

provided a decent living and homemakers were freed from outside employment."[30] Palpable public concerns about the perceived negative social impacts
of working women inspired laws and regulations limiting women's opportunities in the workforce.[31] For example, the 1932 Economy Act included a provision aimed at dismissing married women from federal civil service jobs
(although the law technically dismissed "spouses" of government employees,
women were the intended targets). A number of states and localities specifically
discriminated against hiring married and unmarried women. Such policies
resembled the "back to the home" movements aimed at women in countries
like Italy and Germany.[32] As an analysis of *Pleasantdale Folks* makes clear, the
SSB positioned itself as a mechanism for countering the trend toward increased
labor-force participation by women, delayed marriages, and lower birth rates.[33]

This broad effort to "save" the American family from the ravages of the
Depression was aimed at particular kinds of families—namely, white working-
and middle-class families. For example, when Social Security provisions were
expanded in 1939 to cover the wives and dependents of male workers, nonwhite
women remained predominantly uninsured because it excluded domestic service.[34] As a number of scholars have noted, Social Security was one of several
New Deal policies that played a role in consolidating and institutionalizing
white privilege during the 1930s.[35] The Federal Housing Act of 1934, for example, channeled the majority of home loan money to white Americans. In addition, both the Wagner Act, which protected workers' rights to unionize, and
the Social Security Act, excluded farm workers and domestic workers—the
majority of whom were nonwhite.[36] Faced with the economic crisis of the
Depression, then, the New Deal state stepped in to protect the "wages of whiteness" at the direct expense of nonwhite Americans.[37]

The prerogatives of whiteness protected by Social Security, however, were
inextricably tied to the prerogatives of male privilege.[38] As Alice Kessler-Harris
argues, female independence threatened both manliness and whiteness: "Like
the wages of whiteness, the wages of a normative masculinity include a sense
of entitlement to particular kinds of jobs, skills, and economic security. And
as the concept of white privilege is imbued with gendered prerogatives, so the
concept of male privilege is imbued with racial license."[39] By maintaining gender privilege, men upheld racial boundaries. And women who challenged traditional gender roles were a threat to male prerogatives, "racial purity," and
white privilege. While Social Security insurance cut out most people of color,
it also excluded over 75 percent of female workers by failing to cover domes-
tics, agricultural laborers, educational workers, nonprofit workers, retail sales-
people, government office workers, and part-time laborers.[40] Exclusionary
boundaries of race and gender were intertwined. In addition, Social Security's
family provisions tied white men's citizenship rights to their roles as wage earners

and white women's rights to their roles as dependent wives and mothers. By institutionalizing white breadwinner husbands and homemaker wives, Social Security and other New Deal provisions promoted the white, patriarchal nuclear family as a national ideal.[41]

Saving Respectable White Masculinity and Promoting White Female Dependence

The stories of Sue and Harvey Johnson that anchored *Pleasantdale Folks* advanced a picture of the white nuclear family that prefigured the suburban archetype of postwar America. The program emphasized the ways in which the Depression threatened the strength and integrity of the nation not simply by crushing the domestic economy but by undermining "traditional" identities of white American men and women. As a male breadwinner coming of age during the Depression years, Harvey Johnson was the focus of the hopes and fears of the Johnson family. Harvey's situation was described as identical to those of "millions of young people just like him." Audience members were encouraged to identify with Harvey or to view him as a familiar sibling or son.[42] For example, when Harvey finally got a job after weeks of searching, the announcer concluded, "Harvey could think of just one thing: he wanted a job! That's what real security means to Harvey—and to all of us."[43] Throughout the series, listeners were asked to identify with the plight of the generation coming of age during the Depression and to see the importance of a social security system that "gives the young folks a better chance to make their own way, provide for young families of their own."[44] *Pleasantdale Folks* sought to reassure citizens that government activism was compatible with social and cultural traditionalism. In fact, it went even further—contrasting the dignified independence that government economic support provided compared with the potentially humiliating nature of dependence on family and friends.

Pleasantdale Folks showed how the loss of employment forced Harvey into a demoralizing cycle of searching for work and needing help from his parents. The economic downturn delayed independence from his family and literally transformed him from a cheerful, responsible, upright young man into a despondent, self-absorbed derelict. Harvey's inability to live up to respectable family norms signaled a crisis of both individual and national identity. After expressing his anger and frustration at having to rely on his parents for support, Harvey had the following exchange with his mother:

MOM: Why, Harvey! You know we don't begrudge it to ya'. In trouble a family always sticks together.

HARVEY: Yeah, I'm sticking alright. [Bitter; sighing][45]

Harvey turned the language of "sticking together" into an expression of being "stuck" in a position of dependence on his family. Later, Harvey refused to attend the Blakes' party, where he had promised to "sit next to Harry [Blake]'s younger sister," and Sue revealed to Mom that Harvey had been drinking and "hanging around with that poolroom gang all hours."[46] Instead of expressing virtuous masculinity through wholesome, family-oriented activities, a disenchanted Harvey sought the company of men outside respectable society. Governmental assistance was presented as more effective than "traditional" modes of self-help in addressing threats to Harvey's masculinity and to the nation as a whole. As the final episode pointed out, Harvey's newfound employment security had also restored his respectable masculine identity: his courtship of the reputable Peggy Morton appeared headed for marriage.[47]

Although it was hinted that Sue was employed in the service sector, it is significant that her work was never specifically mentioned. Like Social Security legislation itself, the program downplayed the role of white women in the paid labor force and attempted to persuade them that they could find security as homemakers.[48] Sue expressed vague uncertainty about marriage in the first episode, but it was not until the seventh episode that she articulated her feeling that marriage was no longer a secure, dependable institution given the economic crisis. Although she was economically dependent upon her family, that seemed more appealing to her than marriage, which appeared to be an unstable and even dangerous enterprise for women. When she learned that Harry Blake, her friend Jenny's husband, was one of the twenty men laid off at the Pleasantdale ironworks, she expressed grave concern about how the couple would suffer during the layoff. When Ollie Larson pointed out that because of unemployment insurance the Blakes would not go hungry, Sue retorted, "Oh, maybe not, but it'll make a lot of difference in the way they live. Half pay isn't full pay!"[49] She was particularly worried about Jenny, who would have to face mounting debts to the landlord, butcher, and grocer during the layoff.

The character of Ollie Larson played an interesting role in *Pleasantdale Folks*. With his strong Swedish accent and somewhat halting English, he stood out as a recent immigrant (he had come to the United States ten years earlier at the age of eighteen) who was not fully comfortable with American culture. Due to his Nordic heritage, however, he faced few ethnic barriers and was welcomed with open arms by the Johnson family and the other white working people of Pleasantdale. At the same time, his Swedish background was used to bolster the argument that government support for the unemployed, elderly, poor, and disabled was not an invention of New Deal radicals but a long-standing practice in many countries. Ollie reported that when he was a boy back in Sweden, his father received unemployment payments from his union when he lost his job and now he gets payments from the Swedish government. He also pointed out that part of the reason that he was able to emigrate to the United States was because he knew that his parents would be taken care of in their old age by a government pension. Ollie informed the Johnsons that this seemingly new American system of Social Security was commonplace in "Sweden, England, Switzerland, many countries."[50]

Along with normalizing the idea of Social Security and hence the New Deal, Ollie's main objective was to convince Sue that unemployment insurance and old-age insurance had restored some security to the American family. After explaining old-age insurance for wage earners and their wives, Ollie emphasizes that the plan not only made new marriages more secure but protected young families from the responsibilities of caring for the older generation. Ollie explained: "When your parents are old, Harvey, they won't have to come to you for support; they will not be a burden to you. That makes them free and it makes you and Susan free. If you want to marry you don't have to think, can my job take care of my family and a' old folks too?"[51] As public concern about the negative cultural consequences of delayed marriages grew in the late 1930s, the SSB positioned itself as a mechanism for countering this trend by promoting the independence and security of the nuclear family.[52]

While Ollie focused on male wage-earners, Mom brought up the situation of another Pleasantdale neighbor, Mattie Cole, who had been engaged to John Holden for eighteen years but could not marry him because of her responsibility to take care of her elderly parents. In Mom's words, "John can't afford to support them all, so four people have to suffer." The possibility that Mattie could marry John *and* keep her job to support her parents was not presented as an option because the formal employment of married women was not a part of the New Deal vision of family security. This view was reinforced by the following exchange:

SUE: Don't women get old age benefits, Dad?—I mean women who aren't married? [Timid]

JOE: Oh, yeah, sure they do if they work for 'em. Take Mattie Cole—she's been working at Woodrow's Store so she's insured like Harvey and me.

While Sue was reassured that Mattie would at least have security in her old age, Harvey chimed in that, "Ah, but if you're smart, though, Sue, you can get yourself fixed for old age by, by tyin' up with some nice young fella with a good job that's insured!" With a telling joke that romanticized female dependency, Harvey pointed to the government's role in providing both an institutional and an ideological path toward more "stable" gender relations in a nuclear family setting.[53]

Sue and Ollie's courtship ended with marriage and a honeymoon trip to the nation's capital and the offices of the Social Security Board—highlighting the government's ability to restore and reaffirm the sanctity of the family and strengthen the nation as a whole. As the announcer concluded, the Johnson family's discussion of Social Security benefits "put up a good argument for family life" and presented Social Security as a force that would help to preserve the American family. By the end of *Pleasantdale Folks*, the futures of Harvey and Sue were no longer imperiled by economic insecurity and Joe even declared that he envied the young people because they were able to take care of themselves and their families and they did not have to be afraid.[54] Governmental aid was presented as a continuation of community self-help, but also as an improvement on traditional practices that often made people feel compromised by family obligations or trapped at home well into adulthood. Through the characters of Mom and Sue, women were particular targets of this message. The program thus aimed to reassure women that their families were not defenseless against economic forces and to encourage them to give up the economic independence that many of them had sought during the Depression. In many ways, the discourse of *Pleasantdale Folks* was a preview of the post–World War II-era campaign that asked women to give up the economic independence they had gained through war work and relinquish their jobs to male breadwinners.

Selling New Deal Family Policy through the Soap Opera Genre

How well did the message of *Pleasantdale Folks* fit within the generic expectations and practices of the soap opera genre? In his comprehensive study of radio soap operas, J. Fred MacDonald lays out the "four cornerstones" of soap operas defined by ad executive Hubbell Robinson Jr. in 1940: (1) simple characterization; (2) understandable predicaments; (3) focus on female characters; and (4) philosophical relevance. While the first two elements are not unique to the soap opera, it is helpful to take a closer look at the ways in which *Pleasantdale Folks* addressed the generic expectations of female-centered stories and their philosophical relevance.

Although dramatic daytime serials sometimes had strong male lead characters during the 1930s and 1940s (*Just Plain Bill, Pepper Young's Family*, others) they tended to focus on women and issues of importance to women.[55] Soaps examined family relationships, including marriage and child-rearing, and explored power relations between men and women from a distinctly female perspective. Hilmes finds an apt characterization of soap operas in the fictional Lake Wobegon's claim to be a place where, "all the women were strong and all the men were good-looking." Men tended to be weak in comparison to strong female leads; indeed, men were often represented as "unstable, disabled, or criminal" to create a more even playing field of power relations between men and women in dramatic serials.[56]

In *Pleasantdale Folks* the male characters fared better than their commercial counterparts, although their authority was at times ambiguous and blunted, largely due to the difficulties they faced in coping with the ongoing economic crisis. Harvey Johnson, for example, reacted emotionally and irresponsibly when he had difficulty finding a job in the first episode, although he was able to regain his respectability over the course of the series. Similarly, when Joe Johnson began to break down in sobs over his brother Dick's death, he was quickly admonished by Dr. Henry and the family to "pull himself together" to be a responsible caretaker of Dick's widow and children.[57] Ollie Larson was a constant source of support for the Johnsons and other Pleasantdale families, as well as being a font of authoritative information about Social Security. When he was promoted to foreman at the lumberyard, Ollie became the only *Pleasantdale Folks* character to experience upward mobility. However, his masculine authority was somewhat dulled by his use of Swedish dialect, which in the context of commercial radio was often used to signal ineptitude and ignorance. Although the leading men of *Pleasantdale Folks* faced some challenges to their traditional masculinity, they retained their male prerogatives as principal breadwinners and present (and future) heads of household. Dr. Henry played the role of a trusted although somewhat ancillary authority, just as doctors, lawyers, and judges often did in soap operas of the 1930s and 1940s.[58] His authority came from his position of knowledge and power in the community, as well as from his new role as a bridge and mediator between the community and government authorities.

While female characters were central to the drama in *Pleasantdale Folks* (for example, Sue, Nancy, Mom, and Mrs. Jenkins), they did not attain the status of heroes (or villains) that many female characters gained in daytime serials. Like commercial serials, *Pleasantdale Folks* validated the importance of domestic issues such as marriage and child-rearing that were often the most important aspects of women's lives. At the same time, however, it reinforced the idea that women were limited to the domestic sphere. *Pleasantdale Folks* provided a space for Sue Johnson to complain about the indignities suffered by dependent, married women during the Depression, while ultimately encouraging her to embrace that dependence herself. As Terry Lovell argued in her analysis of the British serial *Coronation Street*, soaps provide "a context in which women can ambiguously express both good-humoured acceptance of their oppression and recognition of that oppression and some equally good-humoured protest against it."[59] While Sue reflected on gender inequalities, she ultimately accepted the need for women to do their part in supporting the New Deal vision of the normative white American family based on working men and homemaker women.

The "philosophical relevance" of soap operas is an important component of daytime serials in the 1930s that has received relatively little attention.

MacDonald discusses the role of folk wisdom and homespun philosophies in radio soap operas in giving listeners a sense of edification and moral direction. Christian-inspired aphorisms and folk wisdom such as "the meek shall inherit the earth" and "virtue is its own reward" were common themes of Depression-era serials.[60] It was also very common for serials and other shows oriented to women to offer expressions such as "life is beautiful" and "there's always tomorrow" as themes to help people maintain hope during hard times. *Pleasantdale Folks* also emphasized a combination of "pulling oneself together" and "everyone sticking together" to make the program relevant to the struggles of listeners. But while the series started with these Christian-inspired folk philosophies, it converted them into a new kind of New Deal folk wisdom. For example, Dr. Henry and the program announcer played important roles in connecting ideas like "everyone needs a helping hand" and "we take care of our own" to the growing role of government agencies in everyday life. Social Security was not just an example of lending a hand when things got tough; it transformed that helping hand from an obligation to a right because it now came from government. The language of expanded rights was essential to the New Deal folk philosophy of *Pleasantdale Folks*. At the end of each episode, the announcer often added New Deal aphorisms to the show's vocabulary, emphasizing the active role of the government and articulating new rights such as the "right to work." Through the webbed interconnections of the soap opera, then, *Pleasantdale Folks* incorporated New Deal ideas about government activism and social security into the folk philosophy that made the genre edifying and relevant to many listeners.

Conclusions

In contrast to the dramatized documentary format that predominated in Project radio productions, *Pleasantdale Folks* used the fictional format of the soap opera to promote specific New Deal solutions to the Depression crisis and ameliorate its negative impact on American families. As in the case of *Wings for the Martins*, the fictional series provided listeners with specific practical and moral lessons that they could emulate and enact in their own lives. *Pleasantdale Folks* aimed directly to influence listeners by modeling particular attitudes and behaviors in relation to government policies—pointing toward the entertainment-education strategy that would emerge in the late twentieth century. The success of these models depended on the ability of listeners to see themselves or their loved ones in the characters of Sue and Harvey and learn, as they did, how to make sense of the changing relationships between work, community, citizenship, and government.

As a genre, soap operas have traditionally provided space for women to acknowledge, protest, and negotiate the limitations placed on them by patriarchal social relations. In the case of *Pleasantdale Folks*, the social conservatism of the soap opera genre and the social conservatism of New Deal family policy fitted neatly together. While reckoning with the bonds of domesticity, the soap opera also provided a format for framing New Deal family policy as part of the long-standing tradition of "lending a helping hand." At the same time, *Pleasantdale Folks* presented Social Security and other family social provisions as a right of citizenship rather than a weighty obligation.

While fictional series like *Wings for the Martins* and *Pleasantdale Folks* differed greatly from the Educational Radio Project's dramatized documentary programs in form and content, they were fundamentally similar in combining drama and documentation as a means of citizenship education. Whereas shows like *Americans All, Immigrants All* began with real historical documents and dramatized them to build audience identification, *Pleasantdale Folks* and *Wings* began with dramatic genres that would engage audiences and inserted models of citizenship into them that the series creators hoped would inspire real changes in American families and communities. While the dramatized documentary situated the listener inside a patriotic pageant of national citizenship, the New Deal soap opera located listeners in intimate relationships that taught the meaning of citizenship at the level of individual, family, and community. Our analysis of *Pleasantdale Folks* reveals the close connections between broadcast representations of the American family and the project of citizenship education that preoccupied both government agencies and corporate advertisers during the interwar period. In sum, our examination of New Deal radio offers a new perspective on how different program genres were being explored, tested, and transformed under the political, cultural, and industrial pressures of the 1930s.

Conclusion

The story of the end of the Project in 1940 underlines the tentative and fleeting nature of New Deal radio's intervention in commercial broadcasting. Despite the hopes of Studebaker and others that educational radio production could become a permanent part of the Office of Education's work, this was, after all, always an "emergency" project, funded on temporary money. There is no question that the networks felt coerced into working with the FREC and Studebaker, who NBC's John Royal considered a "dangerous" man.[1] While CBS was somewhat more welcoming of the educational experiment, both networks kept Project series, to some degree, at arm's length. Except for Sunday afternoon, which was considered a high-quality weekend time slot, most Project programs were broadcast on weekdays outside of prime time—either before 7:00 P.M. or after 10:00 P.M. Eastern. Although some Project programs reached large national audiences, the majority of network radio listeners still encountered advertising-sponsored programming rather than educational fare when they tuned in.

At the same time, this was a period when national networks had Educational Departments and understood the need to produce program content that at least appeared to serve the "public interest." The Radio Project staff worked directly with their educational counterparts at the networks—Edward R. Murrow, Franklin Dunham, Walter Preston—to produce programs that would fulfill this need. In this sense, it is possible to view the Project as providing a government subsidy for the production of the public service and educational programs that broadcasters were required by law to provide. On the other hand, one can also argue that government-commercial partnerships like the Radio Project turned commercial networks into quasi-public broadcasters, with surprisingly little disruption or conflict. In both cases, the end result was the same: commercial networks devoted millions of dollars of airtime to educational radio series that addressed the meaning of citizenship and democracy during a time of national and global political upheaval.

We conclude our study by taking a closer look at the political changes that led to the ending of funding for the Educational Radio Project and the consequences for the Office of Education and its personnel. We then explore the implications of our study in three main areas. First, we contend that our investigation of government-industry cooperation in radio supports the argument that U.S. network broadcasting in the 1930s was not only shaped by commercialism but also by a "civic paradigm" that emphasized active citizenship.[2] Second, our study shows that dramatized documentary programming played a bigger role in U.S. network radio than previously acknowledged—and that this mode of documentary deserves closer aesthetic and historical investigation. Finally, our research demonstrates that commercial networks played a significant, but largely unrecognized, role in enabling New Deal political and cultural projects. In particular, our work indicates that New Deal agencies, commercial networks, and their staffs created thoughtful and timely radio series designed to teach listeners that government could be a positive and constructive presence in U.S. society and in individual American's lives.

The End of the Educational Radio Project

The Radio Project fell victim to the changed balance of power between New Deal Democrats, conservative Democrats, and Republicans after the 1938 elections. Roosevelt's attempt at that election to "purge" conservative Democrats in Congress and replace them with New Deal–aligned liberals was an almost complete failure—the result was a "conservative triumph" that "intensified the liberal-conservative split within the Democratic party."[3] The Democrats lost seventy-two House seats and seven Senate seats and thus faced both reduced numbers and a reenergized conservative bloc. Conservative Democrats and Republicans assailed the budget proposal in 1939, shaving $150 million off the amount requested for the WPA in committee, based on allegations of political influence on WPA spending and a perception that relief money was being disproportionately spent in urban areas.[4] Representative Clifton A. Woodrum of Virginia, of the House Appropriations committee, said the bill would "dress up and clean up" the administration of relief.[5] An attempt in April, at the request of the president, to add $150 million to the WPA budget was lost.[6] New Deal radio projects were fundamentally dependent on WPA funding and could not function without the radio performers, production workers, and support staff hired through the WPA.

Governmental reorganizations also affected the Project. In July 1939, the Office of Education was transferred from the Department of the Interior to the new Federal Security Agency. Around the same time, the National Emergency Council became the Office of Government Reports and the Council's film and radio activities were moved into the Office of Education.[7] Studebaker was excited by the change—he wrote to Roosevelt: "I am sure that in making this transfer you had in mind the protection of the right of the citizen to impartially disseminated knowledge of the workings of his society and his Government."[8] The Film Service distributed acclaimed documentary films such as *The Plow that Broke the Plains* and *The River*. The Radio Division of the National Emergency Council was established by Executive Director Lowell Mellett from July 1938. It produced a series titled *United States Government Reports* that was by mid-1939 being broadcast on 175 stations.[9] Unfortunately, these bureaucratic recombinations led to misunderstandings about which agencies had produced which programs, which in turn accounted for some congressional hostility toward the Office of Education's Radio Project. Some conservatives attacked the Office for films that were actually produced by the National Emergency Council, such as *The Fight for Life*, which they perceived as the beginning of a campaign for "socialized medicine." Jeanette Sayre reported: "It was said that these organizations [the American Medical Association and the American Dental Association] influenced anti-New Deal Democrats to oppose funds for the Film Service, and also, while they were at it, for the Radio Service."[10]

A political battle over the Office of Education's radio and film projects played out in Appropriations committee hearings in 1940. Anti–New Deal criticisms focused on the potential danger of government propaganda, allegations of communist influence in the WPA, and the desire to rein in relief spending at a time when jobs were beginning to open in defense industries. In addition, conservatives voiced states' rights concerns about the federal government delivering education to citizens directly, when the Office of Education was only permitted by its original legislation to assist the states to improve education. The House Appropriations committee eliminated the Radio Division and the Film Service from the budget on the technical grounds that no legislative authorization for the work existed, but also because of concerns about federal control. Butler Hare from South Carolina expressed this clearly: "For instance, you take *Democracy in Action*. That is educational to the public, to my children and your children, and to our grandchildren. The point is that we could substitute any other subject for 'Democracy in Action.' You could have some communistic doctrine disseminated in the same way. We could have some religious doctrine disseminated in the same way. There will be nothing, as I understand it, to prevent your Office of Education from disseminating that kind of information. The only thing would be the exercise of your discretion and your judgment."[11] The Senate Appropriations Committee upheld the House committee's decision. In the Senate hearings, Democrat Senator Kenneth McKellar from Tennessee said, "You know it as well as I do, that there is not the slightest basis for education in our Federal Constitution and the only way that we can do this is to set up an organization to help the States."[12] Studebaker specifically sought funds to "continue *Democracy in Action* in cooperation with CBS to help citizens through educational programs by radio to know more about the work of Congress, the executive agencies, and our courts."[13] Studebaker wanted to move from emergency funding to a regular appropriation for the radio service: "We claim that [radio] work comes within the legitimate functions of education on a permanent basis."[14] But the committee was in no mood to agree.

In the summer of 1940, Studebaker and others in the Office of Education battled to keep the Radio Project alive. They tried via Eleanor Roosevelt to get the president to intervene, as she was known to be supportive of the work of Rachel DuBois and that of the Radio Project. When that did not produce results, Studebaker repitched the radio production program as a part of the national defense buildup.[15] By July a plan authored by Boutwell was circulating in government agencies. Headed "Use of Radio for National Defense," a colorful brochure outlined several possible new radio series—"United We Stand," "This Hemisphere of Freedom," "American Family Hour," and "Health Is Wealth"—that the Office could undertake to support the defense effort. Notably, all these programs appear to be renewals or extensions of programs previously produced by the Radio Project. The document offered the Project's accumulated experience to the nation in its hour of need: "The plan can apply six years successful experience—of the Government's only complete radio producing group—the Radio Division of the Office of Education—immediately to the service of national defense." But an attached August note in the Social Security Administration files copy of the plan says that the plan was "washed up" and had been turned down by the president.[16] Although a Radio Division was authorized in 1941, its activities were limited to helping schools and universities improve techniques of broadcasting through activities such as the Script Exchange.[17] As the House Appropriations committee report concluded, "the radio unit is, in effect, a library service."[18]

The end of funding to the Educational Radio Project was part of a broader shift in Congress against government broadcasting. The radio activities of the Office of Education were curtailed by a provision in the Emergency Relief Appropriation Act for 1941 that limited WPA expenditure on radio broadcasting to $100,000.[19] Requests to the WPA for $60,000 to continue the efforts of the Office in promoting education by radio were unsuccessful.[20] By the 1941–1942 financial year, the radio activities of the Office were mostly on a war footing—the transcription service had become *Transcriptions for Victory*.[21] The Office did produce one more major network series—*Freedom's People*, on African American history and culture, the story of which is well told in Barbara

Savage's *Broadcasting Freedom: Radio, War, and the Politics of Race 1938–1948*. *Freedom's People* was pitched to NBC by Office of Education adult education specialist Ambrose Caliver as part of an effort to promote national unity and improve race relations on the eve of U.S. entry into World War II. Because the Office no longer had funds for production, Caliver garnered external funding from the Rosenwald Fund and the Southern Education Foundation.[22] *Freedom's People* was the final Office of Education production that made use of the radio techniques, skills, and talents developed by the Radio Project over its short life. As Sayre summarized, "Under the circumstances, the Office of Education felt that its experiment in the dramatic-narrative technique had been highly successful."[23]

Several of the men who played prominent roles in the Project, not surprisingly, went on to hybrid careers in commercial and educational media and public relations. In 1945 Bill Boutwell began working for Scholastic Magazines, where he was an editorial vice president until 1971; he then founded an educational publishing consultancy firm and died in 1977.[24] John Studebaker resigned from the Office of Education in 1948 to become vice president and chair of the editorial board of Scholastic Magazines, working there with Boutwell until 1968. He died in 1989, aged 102.[25] Chester S. Williams worked in educational and informational capacities for the United Nations and the U.S. State Department between 1943 and 1950, and then served as deputy director in the Office of Public Information, U.S. Mission to the United Nations, until 1952. For the rest of the 1950s and until his retirement in 1968, he undertook public relations work for businesses and nonprofit agencies; he died in 1992.[26] Only Philip Cohen took a primarily commercial trajectory. After heading up the Office of War Information's American broadcasting station in Europe during World War II, he worked in radio production for advertising agencies after the war and became director of advertising for the American Tobacco Company from 1964 to 1976; he died in 1992.[27]

Most of the women who were in middle age when they contributed to the Project had long careers at the Office of Education or moved on to university positions. Bess Goodykoontz and Effie Geneva Bathurst, two Iowans who supervised *Wings for the Martins*, are good examples. Before retiring in 1962, Goodykoontz spent thirty-four years at the Office of Education in roles ranging from assistant and associate commissioner of education to director of international education relations. Bathurst, who also became active in international education, left the Office to become a professor of education at Dakota State University (formerly General Beadle State College).[28] Laura Vitray, who joined the Project after a successful career as a newspaper editor, went on to become editor of *United Nations World* magazine in the 1940s and then of *American Girl* magazine in the 1950s; she died in 1963.[29] Like the Project leaders, she moved between work in public service and commercial media.

Most of the young women who joined the Project as writers and researchers right out of college continued writing activities of various kinds. Selma Goldstone (Hirsh), who worked on *Democracy in Action* scripts, published a book on the origins of prejudice and went on to an almost forty-year career with the American Jewish Committee.[30] Jane Ashman, who wrote scripts for *Americans All, Immigrants All* and *Gallant American Women*, worked for NBC and Mutual radio networks in the 1940s before moving to television. Her television writing included contributions to *Good Neighbors* (1948) and *Stand by for Crime* (1949)—a show that allowed viewers to guess the solution to the crime before it was revealed. In 1949, with Ralph W. Ferrin, she created Ashman-Ferrin Productions, described by Ryan Ellett as "a Chicago-based television production company that did not leave much of an imprint on the burgeoning industry."[31] Although Ashman does not appear to have found success as a television writer, it is notable that Ferrin went on to a long television career as assistant director and production manager for many popular series from *Ozzie and Harriet* to *Dynasty*.[32]

The Civic Paradigm of U.S. Network Radio

The creation of the FREC in 1935—and the cooperative broadcasting arrangements between the networks and the Educational Radio Project (and many other government agencies) that emerged from it—encouraged the production of innovative programming that served civic rather than commercial ends. Although this government-sponsored hybrid of entertainment and educational programming was limited in terms of its marginal position in the network schedule and its short life span, it had a regular presence in broadcasting during a formative period of program development and network expansion in the late 1930s. The radio productions of New Deal agencies augmented the educational and cultural programs already being produced by the networks and lent authority to the idea that network radio *should* be educational and civic-minded. The Educational Radio Project and the Radio Division of the Federal Theatre Project alone engaged hundreds of radio producers, writers, and actors in a national project to use commercial broadcasting techniques to stimulate democratic thought and action. Radio played a central role in the modern process of state- and nation-building that emerged following World War I, and U.S. network radio was no exception. As we discussed in chapter 1, the United States resembled Latin American countries such as Mexico and Argentina in drawing on government-commercial partnerships to produce dramatized radio documentaries celebrating national history and culture.[33]

By looking at both the documentary and fiction programs developed by the Project, our study denaturalizes the distinctions between fiction and nonfiction and reveals the shared methods between "didactic" programming for civic and commercial ends. This is particularly evident in the few Project programs that focused on the American family. *Wings for the Martins*, for example, contributed to the development of the sitcom as a space for citizenship education, which would become a central component of Cold War television sitcoms. The working-class-focused *Pleasantdale Folks*, alternatively, showed a family struggling to live up to a nuclear family "ideal" that offered support to white male workers at the expense of racial minorities and women. These fictional shows indicate how closely interconnected traditions of moral education and entertainment have been in U.S. media history. Our study of New Deal radio suggests that late 1930s network radio deserves further investigation as a site where genre formation, government activism, and educational idealism came together to develop and exploit the pedagogic possibilities of entertainment formats.

The Role of Documentary in U.S. Radio History

By bringing the Radio Project into focus, our study also draws attention to the little-studied genre of the dramatized documentary. Along with well-remembered and long-running shows like *March of Time* and *Cavalcade of America*, network radio carried scores of dramatized documentaries on crime, sports, education, and other topics. Although there have been some important studies of radio docudramas, the longer historical trajectory of documentary production in U.S. broadcasting has not been adequately investigated.[34] What were the continuities between prewar and postwar radio documentaries? How should we understand the emergence of dramatized documentary in radio in the 1930s through the mid-1940s and its resurgence in television in the early 1970s? Industrial, creative, and cultural links between these two moments in broadcasting history warrant investigation, as do the points of continuity and discontinuity between radio documentary and the documentary impulse shaping podcast production—particularly the popular "true crime" genre. Our understanding of radio history would benefit from a closer investigation of the complex negotiation between dramatization and documentation in broadcast programming.

We characterize the majority of the output of the Radio Project as governmental dramatized documentary—programs that offered a vision of how government could better the lives of its citizens, and how citizens could contribute to the democratic life of their country. From *Brave New World* to *Democracy in Action*, Office of Education writers, producers, and actors creatively elaborated on this format, interweaving dramatization, invented dialogue, music, and narration to represent facts and explain government in an emotional and believable way. Although the Radio Project was influenced by a transnational documentary movement—and particularly by experimentation at the BBC—it adopted and adapted a distinctly American approach to dramatizing the real.

This mode of dramatized documentary was originally developed by commercial media and public relations practitioners to reconstruct and reimagine reality through a corporate lens. While broadcasters in the United Kingdom and Canada were quicker to incorporate actuality documentary, U.S. radio networks were pioneers in programming that blurred documentary and drama to appeal to a mass audience.

New Deal Radio: Reimaging Government and Citizenship

This book has focused closely on the Educational Radio Project. If we think, however, of these shows alongside the content produced by the Radio Division of the Federal Theatre Project and all the other government agencies that went on the air in this period, it amounts to a really considerable sustained experiment with a distinctively American mode of public broadcasting, built on and out of what Goodman has described as "the endemic creative tension between American radio's entertainment and its educational and civic purposes."[35] The Educational Radio Project produced radio shows with high civic ambition but also with considerable expenditure of time, effort, and money on giving that civic material the form and sound of entertainment programming. Sometimes these radio series translated the political project of the New Deal into the popular cultural forms and genres that were emerging in the commercial radio industry and did so with skill and panache—we have seen this in *Brave New World*'s dramatization of the Good Neighbor Policy and in the performance of the positive impact of Social Security in *Pleasantdale Folks*. At other times though they developed sophisticated mechanisms to do the opposite—to distance the authorial voice of the program from New Deal perspectives. For example, we identified the use of dissonant choruses to dramatize political debate in *Democracy in Action*. The late Project shows we have written about in this book were fascinating attempts to produce governmental dramatized documentary radio in a fraught political culture—to demonstrate that government radio need not be propaganda for the current regime but could more disinterestedly enhance democracy by using radio to increase citizen awareness and appreciation of the democratic process and showing people that government could be a positive and constructive presence in their lives. Bill Boutwell was no radical, but he had become convinced by 1939 that the continuing commercialization of the American airwaves was bad for democracy: "Broadcasters have sabotaged many efforts for public use of radio for public purposes. Commercialization tends to force all programs to common denominator levels thus preventing the increase of choices (which is the essence of democracy). Commercialization tends to prevent experimentation in programming and this too runs counter to democratic practice."[36] By modeling an educational and public-minded mode of media production, the Project did—as we saw in chapter 2—reinforce concerns among some Americans that commercial broadcasting was not adequately performing its civic role. The Project's public-private partnership, its skill in dramatizing history and the political process, the sheer hard work it put into selling democracy and active citizenship to the people, made real an alternative way of doing things, showed that it could be done.

The Educational Radio Project and its ethos evokes something very distant from our present moment. Critical as we might be of some aspects of what they produced, we can recognize the value of having government make the case for practices and values such as pluralism, inclusion, and democratic participation through cultural forms likely to reach the people far more effectively than mere political rhetoric. Jill Lepore, looking back on the 1930s from 2020, observed that "the last time democracy nearly died," Americans "tried to fix it."[37] This book has documented both some of the energy and creativity that agencies of the U.S. government brought to that task in the late 1930s and the complex and conscious modernity of their deployment of the still-new mass medium of radio.

Acknowledgments

The idea for this book grew from a conference panel in 2015, and we have worked on it off and on ever since—from Melbourne, Australia and Iowa City, USA, respectively. We spent time separately in Washington, D.C., doing research and have only twice (briefly) been in the same city at the same time—there is much talk about distant reading these days, but this shows that distant writing is also possible. Substantial work on the book was undertaken during 2020, so this was also in some ways a lockdown project. Our weekly Zoom calls through parts of 2020 helped set writing and revision deadlines, but more importantly allowed the ideas in the book to evolve through ongoing discussions. One of the frustrations of the research was how seldom we could match scripts and audio, but some of our most interesting conversations toward the end were about the sound of the shows. This is then a collaboratively written book. The introduction, chapter 1, and conclusion were fully jointly written; the other chapters initially had a lead author but were extensively revised as we edited and discussed them together. We thank our editor at Rutgers University Press, Nicole Solano, who was very supportive of us and our project during the challenging times of the pandemic—this book would not have been possible without Nicole and team.

David thanks Joy for those conversations and for committing to this project and keeping it going when the goal of a book was by no means assured. I want to thank archivists, especially Lisa Gervais at the Archives and Special Collections of the Queen's University Library in Ontario, Canada and John Vallier at the Milo Ryan Phonoarchive at the library of the University of Washington in Seattle, both of whom kindly made digitized material available to me in 2019. Josh Shepperd organized panels at two conferences that heard early drafts of some of this material; he has our thanks for that and for the energy and enthusiasm he gives to the radio history community. I thank the Faculty of Arts at the University of Melbourne for the 2016 sabbatical that allowed some extended time in the National Archives in College Park and for the small research grant that enabled a final research trip to the United States in February 2020, just ahead of the pandemic. I also thank my family—Julie and our daughters Clara and Eva.

Joy thanks David for suggesting this collaboration in the first place and for always appearing confident that two strangers from different disciplines located at opposite ends of the globe could write a book together. I learned a lot from his archival work and really enjoyed the process of writing with him. I would like to acknowledge support from the Department of Communication Studies at the University of Iowa, which funded my research trips to archives—trips I was fortunate enough to complete before pandemic-related closures. Special thanks to the archive staff of the Wisconsin Historical Society. I also benefited from my dear friend and organizer of virtual writing groups Nora Patterson, who helped me get the writing done and feel connected in a time of isolation. Kathy Battles, Al Martin, and other friends and colleagues made our virtual meetings both fun and productive. Finally, my family has been understanding and supportive of all the time I've devoted to this work. Thanks to Alma González-Hayes, Jesús González-Hayes, Barbara Fenton, Mya Hayes, Jacqui Michel, and Miles Hayes. One last word of acknowledgment goes out to all the women radio scholars who have inspired me and made my work possible. To the pioneers of the 1930s and 1940s, including Jeanette Sayre (who comes up frequently in this book), Herta Herzog, and Hazel Gaudet, and to the scholars who have shaped the contemporary field of radio studies, including Michele Hilmes, Susan Douglas, and Barbara Savage—thank you.

Notes

Introduction

1 "Radio Experts Help U.S. Office of Education," *Washington Post*, March 21, 1937, TR 5.
2 See, for example, Robert W. McChesney, *Telecommunications, Mass Media, and Democracy: The Battle for the Control of U.S. Broadcasting, 1928–1935* (New York: Oxford University Press, 1993); Douglas B. Craig, *Fireside Politics: Radio and Political Culture in the United States, 1920–1940* (Baltimore: Johns Hopkins University Press, 2000); Hugh Richard Slotten, *Radio's Hidden Voice: The Origins of Public Broadcasting in the United States* (Urbana: University of Illinois Press, 2009).
3 Jeanette Sayre, *An Analysis of the Radiobroadcasting Activities of Federal Agencies* (Cambridge, MA: Littauer Center, Harvard University, 1941), 23; John Frazier, "Uncle Sam Speaks," *Washington Evening Star*, March 7, 1936, 7.
4 "Interior Department's Costly Layout for Radio," *Racine Journal Times*, September 16, 1938, 21.
5 "Visions School Operating 1000 Radio Stations," *Burlington Free Press*, December 7, 1938, 4.
6 "Work of Office of Education Division Is Expanded," *Broadcasting*, October 1, 1938, 34.
7 James D. Strong to Maria M. Proffitt, December 17, 1936, and J. W. Studebaker to Alva B. Adams, June 21, 1940, both Box 1, Entry 172, RG 12 Office of Education, National Archives, College Park, Maryland.
8 "Programs Produced During the Fiscal Year 1940," Box 1, Entry 182, RG 12; Lamar Kelley, "Say Air Education Has Big Following," *New York Times*, July 11, 1937, 71.
9 "US Office of Education Is Jostled by Committee When Seeking Air Funds," *Variety*, March 27, 1940, 31.
10 Alexander Russo, *Points on the Dial: Golden Age Radio Beyond the Networks* (Durham NC: Duke University Press, 2010), 110–113. Russo identifies the growing use of transcription disks during the 1930s as means of circulating national radio content to local stations without using national networks. NBC also started a transcription service for its affiliates.

11   "Programs Produced During the Fiscal Year 1940," Box 1, Entry 182, RG 12;
     "Office of Education Designated to Direct Five Projects," December 23, 1935, Box
     16, Entry 175, RG 12.

12   Office of Education Press Release, July 25, 1938, Box 10, Entry 175, RG 12; Boutwell
     Memo, November 7, 1939, Box 5, Entry 187, RG 12. By mid-1938, 130,000 copies of
     scripts had been shared with 3,000 educational organizations; by late 1939 there
     were nearly 500 different scripts in the library.

13   James T. Patterson, *Congressional Conservatism and the New Deal: The Growth of the
     Conservative Coalition in Congress, 1933–1939* (Westport, CT: Greenwood Press, 1981
     [1967]); Leo Ribuffo, *The Old Christian Right: The Protestant Far Right from the
     Great Depression to the Cold War* (Philadelphia: Temple University Press, 1983). The
     Project triggered the old republican fear that the use of government resources to
     produce propaganda and patronage would help keep one party in power indefinitely.

14   Frazier, "Uncle Sam Speaks," 7.

15   "Federal Government Big User of Air Time," *Variety*, February 12, 1936, 1.

16   "Studebaker's Funds Crisis," *Variety*, April 3, 1940, 4.

17   Slotten, *Radio's Hidden Voice*; James A. Brown, "Struggle against Commercialism:
     The 1934 'Harney Lobby' for Nonprofit Frequency Allocations," *Journal of
     Broadcasting and Electronic Media* 33, no. 3 (Summer 1989): 273–291; Josh Shepperd,
     "Infrastructure in the Air: The Office of Education and the Development of
     Public Broadcasting in the United States, 1934–1944," *Critical Studies in Mass
     Communication* 31, no. 3 (2014): 230–243.

18   William D. Boutwell, "SI had Early Role in Saving Broadcast Channels for
     Public," *Smithsonian Torch* 76–1 (1976): 6.

19   Barbara Savage offers an illuminating study of *Americans All, Immigrants All* and
     Freedom's People in her book *Broadcasting Freedom: Radio, War, and the Politics of
     Race, 1938–1948*, and Emily Westkaemper has written about *Gallant American
     Women* in her *Selling Women's History: Packaging Feminism in Twentieth-Century
     American Popular Culture*.

20   Brian Winston, *Claiming the Real: The Griersonian Documentary and its
     Legitimations* (London: British Film Institute, 1995), 103; Bill Nichols, *Introduc-
     tion to Documentary* (Bloomington: Indiana University Press, 2017); Holly
     Rogers, ed., *Music and Sound in Documentary Film* (New York: Routledge, 2015).

21   Matthew C. Ehrlich, *Radio Utopia: Postwar Audio Documentary in the Public
     Interest* (Urbana: University of Illinois Press, 2011).

22   Kathleen Battles, *Calling All Cars: Radio Dragnets and the Technology of Policing*
     (Minneapolis: University of Minnesota Press, 2010); Cynthia Meyers, "The March
     of Time Radio Docudrama: Time Magazine, BBDO, and Radio Sponsors,
     1931–39," *American Journalism* 35, no. 4 (Fall 2018): 420–443.

23   Sayre, *Radiobroadcasting Activities of Federal Agencies*, 84.

24   "Name Members of Staff for Educational Radio Project" Press Release, Febru-
     ary 5, 1936, Box 16, Entry 175, RG 12. These staff members included Maurice
     Lowell, production director from NBC's Chicago Division; James D. Strong,
     former CCC camp broadcaster who headed the Radio Workshop; and B. P.
     Brodinsky, a former CCC camp educational director with an MA from the
     University of Pennsylvania who served as director of station and listener relations.

25   Emily Westkaemper, *Selling Women's History: Packaging Feminism in Twentieth-
     Century American Popular Culture* (New Brunswick, NJ: Rutgers University
     Press, 2017), 101.

26   Sayre, *Radiobroadcasting Activities of Federal Agencies*; Allison L. Rowland and
     Peter Simonson, "The Founding Mothers of Communication Research: Toward a
     History of a Gendered Assemblage," *Critical Studies in Media Communication* 31,
     no. 1 (2014): 3–26. Sayre is unfortunately not accounted for in recent attempts to
     include women in the history of communication research.

27   John Studebaker to Franklin Roosevelt, September 26, 1938, PPF 2896, Frank-
     lin D. Roosevelt Library, Hyde Park, New York.

28   "Studebaker Warns of a Dictatorship," *New York Times*, June 2, 1935, 1.

29   "Radio 'Projector' with Feat of Much Work Defended by Boss," *Washington Post*,
     March 18, 1936, X3.

30   William Boutwell, "The Educational Radio Project of the Office of Education,"
     presented to second National Conference of Educational Broadcasters, Chicago,
     1937, Box 53, NBC Records, Wisconsin Historical Society, Madison, Wisconsin.

31   Chester S. Williams to Mrs. Johanne Hawley, November 22, 1972, Folder 5, Box 1,
     Chester S. Williams Papers, Special Collections, University of Oregon Library,
     Eugene, Oregon.

32   "Radio 'Projector' with Feat," X3.

33   "Rudolf Schramm," *New York Times*, April 11, 1981, 47; *Nanook of the North*
     (1922), Full Cast and Crew, Music by Rudolf Schramm (1947), https://www.imdb
     .com/title/tt0013427/.

34   Frances M. Seeber, "Eleanor Roosevelt and Women in the New Deal: A Network
     of Friends," *Presidential Studies Quarterly* 20, no. 4 (1990): 707–717.

35   "Selma G. Hirsh, 92, Humanitarian," *New York Times*, February 25, 2010, A31.
     Goldstone Hirsh (1917–2010) went on to a long forty-year career with the
     American Jewish Committee and published a book on the origins of prejudice.

36   Laura Vitray, "Author Page," Amazon.com, accessed July 14, 2020, https://www
     .amazon.com/LauraVitray/e/B001KDV0WS%3Fref=dbs_a_mng_rwt_scns_share.

37   Rachel Davis DuBois and Corann Okorodudu, *All This and Something More:
     Pioneering in Intercultural Education, an Autobiography* (Bryn Mawr, PA:
     Dorrance, 1984).

38   Katherine M. Marino, "Transnational Pan-American Feminism: The Friendship
     of Bertha Lutz and Mary Wilhelmine Williams, 1926–1944," *Journal of Women's
     History* 26, no. 2 (2014): 63–87; "Seckler-Hudson, Cateryn" in John Stewart
     Bowman, ed. *The Cambridge Dictionary of American Biography* (New York:
     Cambridge University Press, 1995), 657.

39   Jonathan M. Schoenwald, "Brunauer, Esther (1901–1959), international affairs
     specialist and State Department official," *American National Biography*, Febru-
     ary 1, 2000. https://doi.org/10.1093/anb/9780198606697.article.0700039.

40   Boutwell to Dunham, September 9, 1937, Folder 17 FREC, Box 53, National
     Broadcasting Company (NBC) Records.

41   Kate Dossett, "Gender and the Dies Committee Hearings on the Federal Theatre
     Project," *Journal of American Studies* 47, no. 4 (2013): 995.

42   José Luis Ortiz Garza, *Mexico en Guerra* (Mexico City: Planeta, 1989).

43   Joy Elizabeth Hayes, *Radio Nation: Communication, Popular Culture, and
     Nationalism in Mexico, 1920–1950* (Tucson: University of Arizona Press, 2000);
     Elizabeth Fox and Sylvio R. Waisbord, eds., *Latin Politics, Global Media* (Austin:
     University of Texas Press, 2002).

44   Ian Aitken, *The Documentary Film Movement: An Anthology* (Edinburgh: Edin-
     burgh University Press, 1998), 1–68; Zoë Druick and Jonathan Kahana, "New Deal

Documentary and the North Atlantic Welfare State," in *The Documentary Film Book*, ed. Brian Wilson (Basingstoke: Palgrave Macmillan, 2013), 153–158.

45   Druick and Kahana, "New Deal Documentary," 153.

46   Zoë Druick, *Projecting Canada: Government Policy and Documentary Film at the National Film Board* (Montreal: McGill-Queen's University Press, 2007), 16–17, 23.

47   David Goodman, *Radio's Civic Ambition: American Broadcasting and Democracy in the 1930s* (New York: Oxford University Press, 2011).

48   Michele Hilmes, "NBC and the Network Idea: Defining the American System," in *NBC: America's Network*, ed. Michele Hilmes and Michael Henry (Berkeley: University of California Press, 2007), 7–24; Goodman, *Radio's Civic Ambition*.

49   Michele Hilmes, *Network Nations: A Transnational History of British and American Broadcasting* (New York: Routledge, 2011), 4.

50   Sayre, *Radiobroadcasting Activities of Federal Agencies*, 71–72.

51   "Summary of the Two Day Session of the Federal Radio Education Committee," February 16 and 17, 1936, Box 45, NBC Records.

52   "Radio Teachers Study Faults," *New York Herald Tribune*, July 26, 1936, 16.

53   Erik Barnouw, *History of Broadcasting in the United States, Volume II, The Golden Web, 1933 to 1953* (New York: Oxford University Press, 1985), 26–27.

54   McChesney, *Telecommunications, Mass Media, and Democracy*, 232–233.

55   Eugene E. Leach, "Tuning Out Education: The Cooperation Doctrine in Radio, 1922–38," *Current* (August 1983): 2.

56   Leach, "Tuning Out Education," 2.

57   John S. Studebaker, "Radio in the Service of Education," Speech to National Conference on Educational Broadcasting, December 10, 1936, 3, Box 45, NBC Records.

58   "Office of Education," *Kansas City Star*, October 31, 1929, 34.

59   Howard A. Dawson, "Federal Government and Education," *Journal of Educational Sociology* 12, no. 4 (1938): 229.

60   "Hutchins Sees Need for Federal Aid in Education," *Mason City Globe Gazette*, March 14, 1934, 6.

61   Martha H. Swain, "Harrison Education Bills, 1936–1941," *Mississippi Quarterly* 31, no. 1 (1977): 119–131.

62   Quoted in Dawson, "Federal Government and Education," 231; "Urges Schools to Fight for Federal Funds," *Chicago Defender*, March 26, 1938, 4.

63   Swain, "Harrison Education Bills," 128.

64   "Federal Funds for Education," *New York Herald Tribune*, May 17, 1938, 13.

65   "Rift on School Aid," *New York Times*, September 4, 1938, 22.

66   Bailey to H. C. Perry, June 8, 1937, Bailey Papers Box 176, quoted in Swain, "Harrison Education Bills," 125; "Bill for Federal Aid to Education full of Loopholes," *Atlanta Daily World*, January 13, 1937, 1.

67   Evan Roberts quoted in Sayre, *Radiobroadcasting Activities of Federal Agencies*, 113.

68   Cynthia Meyers, *Word from Our Sponsor: Admen, Advertising, and the Golden Age of Radio* (New York: Fordham University Press, 2014); Anna McCarthy, *The Citizen Machine: Governing by Television in 1950s America* (New York: New Press, 2010).

69   Bill Boutwell to Franklin Dunham, n.d. [1937], Box 53, NBC Records.

70   Boutwell, "The Educational Radio Project of the Office of Education," Chicago, 1937, Box 53, NBC Records.

71   "Democracy in Action, Script #17," Box 2, Entry 174, RG 12.

72 Arvind Singhal, Michael J. Cody, Everett M. Rogers and Miguel Sabido, eds., *Entertainment-Education and Social Change: History, Research, and Practice* (New York: Routledge, 2003).

Chapter 1   An American Documentary Tradition

1 Angela G. Ray, *The Lyceum and Public Culture in the Nineteenth Century United States* (East Lansing: Michigan State University Press, 2005).

2 Neil Harris, *Humbug: The Art of P.T. Barnum* (Chicago: University of Chicago Press, 1981).

3 John E. Tapia, *Circuit Chautauqua: From Rural Education to Popular Entertainment in Early Twentieth Century America* (Jefferson, NC: McFarland, 1997).

4 Emily Rosenberg, *Spreading the American Dream: American Economic and Cultural Expansion, 1890–1945* (New York: Macmillan, 1982); Joy S. Kasson, *Buffalo Bill's Wild West: Celebrity, Memory and Popular History* (New York: Hill and Wang, 2000), 5.

5 Anthony G. Picciano and Joel Spring, *The Great American Education-Industrial Complex: Ideology, Technology, and Profit* (London: Taylor & Francis Group, 2013), 149. Beard resigned from her role as adviser to the series *Gallant American Women* after hearing the broadcast of episode two about women and peace because, against her advice, it had ended with an evocation of the statue of Christ the Redeemer in the Andes. Beard understood this as a contest between the needs of drama and those of documentary: "I must try to maintain my honesty of mind above the exactions of 'drama' as drama is conceived by others," she wrote, making it clear that she thought this episode was "not documentary according to the pretensions of the whole program."

6 Derek Paget, *No Other Way to Tell It: Docudrama on Film and Television*, 3rd edition (Manchester: Manchester University Press, 2016), 19, 119–121. He describes "docudrama" as a combination of didactic, persuasive, documentary, and representational modes of communication.

7 Suruchi Sood, Tiffany Menard, and Kim Witte, "The Theory Behind Entertainment-Education," in *Entertainment-Education and Social Change: History, Research, and Practice,* ed. Arvind Singhal, Michael J. Cody, Everett M. Rogers, and Miguel Sabido (Mahwah, N.J.: Lawrence Erlbaum Associates, 2004), 117–145. These fictional programs aimed directly to influence listeners by modeling particular attitudes and behaviors in relation to new educational practices and government policies. They resembled the educational soap operas—sometimes called entertainment-education—which have become globally ubiquitous as means of promoting literacy, family planning, and other pro-social practices and attitudes.

8 The OED says that "docudrama" came into use in North American English in the 1960s.

9 Paget, *No Other Way to Tell It*; Janet Staiger and Horace Newcomb, "Docudrama," in *Encyclopedia of Television*, 2nd edition, ed. Newcomb (Chicago: Fitzroy Dearborn, 2004), 737–740; Elaine Rapping, *The Movie of the Week: Private Stories, Public Events* (Minneapolis: University of Minnesota Press, 1992); Derek Paget and Steven N. Lipkin, "'Movie-of-the-Week' Docudrama, 'Historical-Event' Television, and the Steven Spielberg Series *Band of Brothers*," *New Review of Film and Television Studies* 7, no. 1 (2009), 93–107; Andrew Crisell, *An Introductory History of British Broadcasting,* (London: Psychology Press, 2002), 41.

10 Ehrlich, *Radio Utopia*, 5; Bluem, *Documentary in American Television*.

11 Paddy Scannell, "Radio Documentary from Profession to Apparatus," in *Prix Italia: The Quest for Radio Quality: The Documentary* (1996), 33–40.

12 Crisell, *Introductory History*, 41.

13 Paddy Scannell, "'The Stuff of Radio': Developments in Radio Features and Documentaries Before the War," in *Documentary and the Mass Media*, ed. John Corner (London: Edward Arnold, 1986), 2.

14 Paget, *No Other Way to Tell It*, 42, 46; David Hendy, "Afterword: Radio Modernisms: Features, Cultures and the BBC," *Media History* 24, no. 2 (2018), 284.

15 Scannell, "'Stuff of Radio'"; Crisell, *Introductory History*. After BBC management banished Harding to Manchester because of his radical views, the city's North Region Office became home to a flourishing documentary production program between 1935 and 1939.

16 Tim Crook, *Radio Drama: Theory and Practice* (New York: Routledge, 1999), 203–204. Crook notes that, unlike other features from the early 1930s, a recording of *Crisis in Spain* survives at the BBC because it was reproduced in the late 1930s as a training exercise. It was played to him by former BBC features producer Bennett Maxwell.

17 Peter M. Lewis, "'A Claim to Be Heard': Voices of Ordinary People in BBC Radio Features," *Revue Française de Civilisation Britannique* 26, no. 1 (2020): 2. To prepare for the subsequent program on *Coal* in 1938, Bridson spent a month living and working with miners.

18 Scannell, "'Stuff of Radio,'" 5, 17.

19 Kate Whitehead, *The Third Programme: A Literary History* (Oxford: Clarendon Press, 1988), 110.

20 John Grierson, "The Documentary Idea" (1942) in *The Documentary Film Movement: An Anthology*, ed. Ian Aitken (Edinburgh: Edinburgh University Press, 1998), 106.

21 Quoted in Kathryn Elder, "The Legacy of John Grierson," *Journal of Canadian Studies* 21, no. 4 (1986–1987): 153–154.

22 Winston, *Claiming the Real*, 99.

23 Victor Pickard, "Communication's Forgotten Narratives: The Lost History of Charles Siepmann and Critical Policy Research," *Critical Studies in Media Communication* 33, no. 4 (October 2016): 346–357.

24 Charles A. Siepmann, "Can Radio Educate?," *Journal of Educational Sociology* 14, no. 6 (1941): 350.

25 "Capital Is White Spot," *Sacramento Bee*, February 27, 1936, 1.

26 "Auto Accident Broadcast Set," *Miami Tribune*, September 1, 1937, 31.

27 "Air Drama to Reenact Gainesville Disaster," *Atlanta Constitution*, April 17, 1936, 7.

28 "Ryan Wins Police Hero Award," *Philadelphia Inquirer*, January 24, 1940, 1.

29 "Crime Story on Radio," *Pittsburgh Sun-Telegraph*, June 11, 1936, 2.

30 "Judge Delays Poulnot Case," *Tampa Times*, June 13, 1936, 8.

31 "Warden Shuts Murderers Off Radio Drama," *Stockton Independent*, April 23, 1936, 2.

32 "Martin Durkin Bad Man," *Jacksonville Daily Journal*, August 18, 1937, 1. See also objections to crime dramatizations discussed in Elena Razlagova, *The Listener's Voice: Early Radio and the American Public* (Philadelphia: University of Pennsylvania Press, 2011).

33 Bill Wilson, "Goin' Places with Bill," *Amarillo Globe-Times*, January 3, 1939, 7.

34 John Dunning, *On the Air: The Encyclopedia of Old-Time Radio* (New York: Oxford University Press, 1998), 30, 182.

35 Dunning, *On the Air.*

36 Battles, *Calling All Cars*, 52, 61.

37 George Creel, *How We Advertised America* (New York: Harper & Brothers, 1920), 4; Stuart Ewen, *PR: A Social History of Spin* (New York: Basic Books, 1996); Roland Marchand, *Creating the Corporate Soul: The Rise of Public Relations and Corporate Imagery in American Big Business* (Berkeley: University of California Press, 1998), 220–223.

38 *The March of Time*, CBS, January 18, 1937.

39 Lawrence Lichty and Thomas W. Bohn, "Radio's 'March of Time': Dramatized News," *Journalism Quarterly* 51, no. 3 (1974): 459; Meyers, "The March of Time Radio Docudrama," 433.

40 Jack C. Ellis, *The Documentary Idea: A Critical History of English-Language Documentary Film and Video* (Englewood Cliffs, NJ: Prentice Hall, 1989); *The March of Time*, CBS, April 4, 1935. *March of Time* claimed to bring listeners "a new kind of reporting of the news—the re-enacting of memorable scenes from the news of the week." Actors played the roles of ordinary people and heads of state, with appropriate national accents, while music swelled in the background to enhance the drama of events.

41 John Marshall diary, September 11, 1936, Rockefeller Archive Center, https://dimes.rockarch.org/objects/arwAbRYFfDCYtAgkNaYM5A/view.

42 Dunning, *On the Air*; Meyers, *A Word from Our Sponsor.*

43 Meyers, *Word from Our Sponsor*, 182.

44 Meyers, *Word from Our Sponsor*, 180–181; Ian Tyrrell, *Historians in Public: The Practice of American History, 1890–1970* (Chicago: University of Chicago Press, 2005), 105.

45 Meyers, *Word from Our Sponsor*, 182.

46 Tyrrell, *Historians in Public*, 105.

47 Rudolph Arnheim, *Radio: An Art of Sound* (London: Faber and Faber, 1936), 135–142; Michel Chion, *Sound: An Acoulogical Treatise* (Durham, NC: Duke University Press, 2016), 134, 148–149.

48 Battles, *Calling All Cars*; Neil Verma, *Theater of the Mind: Imagination, Aesthetics, and American Radio Drama* (Chicago: University of Chicago Press, 2012).

49 National Association of Broadcasters, *How to Use Radio in the Classroom* (Washington, DC: National Association of Broadcasters, 1939), 2.

50 Edgar E. Willis, "The Relative Effectiveness of Three Forms of Radio Presentation in Influencing Attitudes," *Speech Monographs* 7, no. 1 (December 1940): 42–44.

51 Donnasue Lohmeyer and Ralph H. Ojemann, "The Effectiveness of Selected Methods of Radio Education at the School Level," *Journal of Experimental Education* 9, no. 2 (1940): 119–120.

52 Talia Brenner, "Radio's Democratic Promise: Aspirations for Historical Radio Dramas, 1930–1943" (Senior thesis, AB, Brown University, 2019), 4.

53 Brenner, "Radio's Democratic Promise," 5.

54 Arnold Muller, "Adventures in the Library," *Green Bay Press-Gazette*, December 28, 1939, 6.

55 A search of Google Books Ngram of American books shows negligible use of the phrase *radio documentary* before 1940 but a very steep rise thereafter.

56 "Wireless Notes and Programmes," *Guardian*, June 1, 1939, 2.

57 Quoted in John K. Hutchens, "Toward a Better World," *New York Times*, March 7, 1943, X9.

58 William Stott, *Documentary Expression and Thirties America* (Chicago: University of Chicago Press, 1986 [1973]), 86.

59 Stott, *Documentary Expression*, 12, 14.

60 Office of Education to Burgess Meredith, January 17, 1938, Box 8, Entry 170, RG 12 Office of Education, National Archives, College Park, Maryland.

61 Chester S. Williams to Studebaker, February 9, 1939, Box 3, Entry 174, RG 12.

62 Typescript "Prospectus: Of the People," Box 2, Entry 174, RG 12.

63 Laura Vitray to Merrill Denison, May 2, 1939, Box 6, Entry 187, RG 12.

64 Mary Beard to Boutwell, November 14, 1939, Box 1, Entry 170, RG 12.

65 Seldes to Boutwell, January 12, 1939, Box 9, Entry 170, RG 12.

66 The reference is to the Federal Theatre Project's 1938 Living Newspaper play about housing problems in New York, *One Third of a Nation*, which drew conservative ire in Congress. The Federal Theatre Project became a particular target of Representative Martin Dies, chair of the House Special Committee on Un-American Activities, and lost funding in 1939.

67 Dated February 21, 1939, Box 1, Entry 174, RG 12.

68 Boutwell to Cohen, February 5, 1939, Box 6, Entry 170, RG 12.

69 Scannell, "Radio Documentary from Profession to Apparatus," 35.

70 David Hogarth, "The Other Documentary Tradition: Early Radio Documentaries in Canada," *Historical Journal of Film, Radio and Television* 21, no. 2 (2001): 125–126.

71 Hogarth, "Other Documentary Tradition," 125.

72 Hogarth, "Other Documentary Tradition," 125.

73 Cohen to Boutwell, June 2, 1938, Box 5, Entry 170, RG 12.

74 Boutwell to Sterling Fisher, October 8, 1938, Box 3, Entry 170, RG 12.

75 Philip Cohen, "Documentary Radio," *Education by Radio* 9, no. 3 (May 1939): 1.

76 "Documentary Programs," *Education on the Air: Yearbook of the Institute for Education by Radio* (Columbus: Ohio State University, 1941), 245–246.

77 Hilmes, *Network Nations*, 128–131.

78 Saul Carson, "Notes Toward an Examination of Radio Documentary," *Hollywood Quarterly* 4, no. 1 (1949): 69; Erik Barnouw, *Radio Drama in Action: Twenty-Five Plays of a Changing World* (New York: Farrar & Rinehart, 1945), 49. In relation to *Rebirth in Barrow's Inlet*, Erik Barnouw observed that "programs of this type, using people, not actors, had been tried by the British Broadcasting Company, but were almost unknown in the United States." Our evaluation of the available recording of the broadcast, however, indicates that it was a dramatized documentary using actors rather than real people.

79 Cohen to Boutwell, February 23, 1939, Box 6, Entry 170, RG 12.

80 Charles T. Harrell, "The Library of Congress Radio Research Project," *ALA Bulletin* 35 (1941), 448–452; Hilmes, *Network Nations*, 131.

81 Available on the Library of Congress website, After the Day of Infamy: "Man-on-the-Street" Interviews Following the Attack on Pearl Harbor, https://www.loc.gov/collections/interviews-following-the-attack-on-pearl-harbor/.

82 Druick, *Projecting Canada*, 4; Michel Foucault, *The Foucault Effect: Studies in Governmentality* (Chicago: University of Chicago Press, 1991).

83 Druick, *Projecting Canada*, 23; Lars Weckbecker, "Re-Forming Vision: On the Governmentality of Griersonian Documentary Film," *Studies in Documentary Film* 9, no. 2 (2015): 174, 176; Rob Aitken, "'An Instrument for Reaching into Experience': Progressive Film at the Rockefeller Boards, 1934–1945," *Journal of Historical Sociology* 30, no. 2 (2017): 288, 285.

84 Aitken, "'Instrument for Reaching into Experience,'" 285–288.

85 "Notes on the Report," 3–4, 12, 20, G 4 14 7, John Grierson Archive, University of Stirling, Stirling, Scotland.

86 Document 84, part 4, p. 39, Folder 4, Box 4, Commission on Freedom of the Press Records 1944–1946, University of Chicago Library, Chicago, Illinois.

87 Hayes, *Radio Nation*, 66–67.

88 Renfro Cole Norris, "A History of 'La Hora Nacional': Government Broadcasting via Privately Owned Radio Stations in Mexico" (PhD diss., University of Michigan, 1963), 13.

89 Sonia Robles, "Shaping Mexico Lindo: Radio, Music, and Gender in Greater Mexico, 1923–1946" (PhD diss., Michigan State University, 2012).

90 Christine Ehrick, *Radio and the Gendered Soundscape: Women and Broadcasting in Argentina and Uruguay, 1930–1950* (New York: Cambridge University Press, 2015), 117–118; Nathan Widener, "Perón's Political Radio Melodrama: Peronism and Radio Culture: 1920–1955," (Master's thesis, Appalachian State University, 2014), 41.

91 Ehrick, *Radio and the Gendered Soundscape*, 118.

92 Hilmes, *Network Nations*, 122.

Chapter 2   *Brave New World*

1 Earle McGill, *Radio Directing* (New York: McGraw-Hill, 1940), 227–268; Justus D. Doenecke and John E. Wilz, *From Isolation to War: 1931–1941* (New York: John Wiley & Sons, 2015), 199–204. McGill included an annotated production script for the episode in his book and observed that the broadcast on peace had a striking timeliness—airing right before Christmas on December 20, 1937, just a week after the unprovoked sinking of the USS *Panay* by Japanese fighters in China. Although the Panay incident was not long remembered, it dovetailed with a surge of anti-war isolationism in the United States in late 1937 and early 1938.

2 McGill, *Radio Directing*, 260–261.

3 McGill, *Radio Directing*, 258.

4 McGill, *Radio Directing*, 268; Cohen to Boutwell, December 14, 1937, Box 5, Entry 170, RG 12 Office of Education, National Archives, College Park, Maryland.

5 On listener reciprocity, see Razlogova, *The Listener's Voice* and Joy Elizabeth Hayes, "Did Herbert Hoover Broadcast the First Fireside Chat? Rethinking the Origins of Roosevelt's Radio Genius," *Journal of Radio Studies* 7, no. 1 (2000): 76–92.

6 "Conquerors of A New World" Script, p. 3, Box 1, Entry 187, RG 12.

7 Amy Spellacy, "Mapping the Metaphor of the Good Neighbor: Geography, Globalism, and Pan-Americanism during the 1940s," *American Studies* 47, no. 2

(2006): 40; George Black, *The Good Neighbor: How the United States Wrote the History of Central America and the Caribbean* (New York: Pantheon Books, 1988); Fred Fejes, *Imperialism, Media, and the Good Neighbor: New Deal Foreign Policy and United States Shortwave Broadcasting to Latin America* (Norwood, NJ: Ablex, 1986); David Green, *The Containment of Latin America: A History of the Myths and Realities of the Good Neighbor Policy* (Chicago: Quadrangle Books, 1971).

8 Solana Larsen, "The Anti-immigration Movement: From Shovels to Suits," *NACLA Report on the Americas* 40, no. 3 (2007): 14–18; Ernesto Castañeda, *Building Walls: Excluding Latin People in the United States* (Lanham, MD: Rowman & Littlefield, 2019).

9 Boutwell, "The Educational Radio Project of the Office of Education." The series was also beamed to Latin America on CBS's shortwave service.

10 Studebaker to W. P. Williamson Jr., October 22, 1937, Box 1, Entry 187, RG 12; "Brave New World," *Education by Radio* 7, no. 11 (1937): 54. A letter from Commissioner Studebaker to a radio station manager stated that "every library will have displays and every superintendent and principal of every school in your community will be contacted by me and urged to promote listening."

11 "Work of Office of Education Division Is Expanded by Additional WPA Grant," *Broadcasting, Broadcast Advertising* 15, no. 7 (1938): 34.

12 Studebaker quoted in William D. Boutwell, "New History Plays Devised for Radio," *New York Times*, October 31, 1937, 51.

13 Pennee Bender, "Film as an Instrument of the Good Neighbor Policy, 1930s–1950s" (PhD diss., New York University, 2002), 23, 45.

14 Mary Wilhelmine Williams, "The College Course in Hispanic American History," *Hispanic American Historical Review* (1919): 415.

15 Fejes, *Imperialism, Media and the Good Neighbor*; Hayes, *Radio Nation*.

16 *Brave New World* Poster, File 19-85 Closed, January 1929–December 1937, Box 125, RG 173 FCC, National Archives, College Park, Maryland.

17 Brave New World Transcriptions on File, June 4, 1938, Box 1, Entry 174, RG 12. The final list of episodes produced was almost the same as the proposed list shown on the *Brave New World* poster, except that one episode was eliminated and two were moved to accommodate script revisions.

18 Boutwell to Dunham, September 9, 1937, Folder 17 "Federal Radio Education Committee," Box 53, NBC Records, 1921–1976, Wisconsin Historical Society, Madison, Wisconsin.

19 The total budget for *Brave New World* included $38,900 for supervisory salaries, $3,155 for nonrelief staff, $14,344 for WPA relief staff, a printing budget of almost $10,000, and over $6,000 for supplies, materials, and transportation expenses. Pan American Budget (Breakdown), May 19, 1937, Box 1, Entry 174, RG 12.

20 Edgar P. Sneed, "Inman, Samuel Guy," *Handbook of Texas Online*, November 9, 2020, https://tshaonline.org/handbook/entries/inman-samuel-guy.

21 Boutwell to Dunham, September 9, 1937, Folder 17, Box 53, NBC Records.

22 Clifford B. Casey, "The Creation and Development of the Pan American Union," *Hispanic American Historical Review* 13, no. 4 (1933): 437–456.

23 Richard Cándida Smith, *Improvised Continent: Pan-Americanism and Cultural Exchange* (Philadelphia: University of Pennsylvania Press, 2017).

24 Bender, "Film as Instrument."

25 Fejes, *Imperialism, Media and the Good Neighbor*, 14–16; Rosenberg, *Spreading the American Dream*.

26 Bryce Wood, *The Making of the Good Neighbor Policy* (New York: Columbia University Press, 1961); Rosenberg, *Spreading the American Dream*; Alan McPherson, "Herbert Hoover, Occupation Withdrawal, and the Good Neighbor Policy," *Presidential Studies Quarterly* 44, no. 4 (2014): 623–639.

27 Ellis W. Hawley, "Herbert Hoover, the Commerce Secretariat, and the Vision of an 'Associative State,' 1921–1928," *Journal of American History* 61, no. 1 (1974): 116–140.

28 Rosenberg, *Spreading the American Dream*; James Schwoch, *The American Radio Industry and Its Latin American Activities, 1900–1939* (Urbana: University of Illinois Press, 1990); Black, *The Good Neighbor*.

29 Bender, "Film as Instrument," 26.

30 Robert David Johnson, "Anti-Imperialism and the Good Neighbour Policy: Ernest Gruening and Puerto Rican Affairs, 1924–1939," *Journal of Latin American Studies* 29, no. 1 (1997): 89–94.

31 Green, *Containment of Latin America*; Fejes, *Imperialism, Media and the Good Neighbor*.

32 Johnson, "Anti-Imperialism," 89, 92.

33 United States Department of State, *Inter-American Cultural Relations* (Washington, DC: GPO, 1939), 3–5.

34 Bryce Wood cited in Bender, "Film as Instrument," 23, 29; Johnson, "Anti-Imperialism," 101.

35 Johnson, "Anti-Imperialism," 89.

36 Johnson, "Anti-Imperialism."

37 Bender, "Film as Instrument," 42.

38 Bender, "Film as Instrument," 23, 45.

39 Spellacy, "Mapping the Metaphor," 42.

40 Williams on Program 13, "Ariel and the Latin American Idealists," January 16, 1938, Box 1, Entry 174, RG 12.

41 Boutwell, "Educational Radio Project of the Office of Education."

42 Boutwell, "Educational Radio Project of the Office of Education."

43 Cohen to Boutwell, December 14, 1937, Box 5, Entry 170, RG 12.

44 "Rudolf Schramm," *New York Times*, April 11, 1981, 47; Jay Carr, Nanook of the North, *Turner Classic Movies*, http://www.tcm.com/this-month/article /296740%7C0/Nanook-of-the-North.html. Schramm was music director for more than 15,000 network radio programs and composed eighty-six film scores, including the 1947 musical score for the landmark documentary *Nanook of the North* (1922).

45 Scannell, "'The Stuff of Radio,'" 1–26; Ellis, *The Documentary Idea*.

46 Rogers, *Music and Sound in Documentary Film*, 12.

47 *Cavalcade of America*, "Railroad Builders," CBS, April 15, 1936. Music included a special overture inspired by three popular railroad songs and composed by "distinguished conductor" and composer Harold Levey.

48 Michael Billig, *Banal Nationalism* (New York: Sage, 1995).

49 "Conquerors of A New World" Script, p. 3, Box 1, Entry 187, RG 12.

50 Bender, "Film as Instrument," 248–249; and Hayes, *Radio Nation*. Bender observes that the World War II propaganda office aimed at Latin America, the

Office of the Coordinator of Inter-American Affairs (OCIAA), recycled New Deal rhetoric that focused on "inter-American unity, stability, and similarities to life in the US."

51 "Writer Bares Red Past," *Kansas City Times*, August 20, 1952, 14.

52 "Conquerors of A New World" Script, p. 23, Box 1, Entry 187, RG 12.

53 "The Damon and Pythias of the Revolution" Script, Box 47, The Papers of Samuel Guy Inman, Manuscript Division, Library of Congress, Washington, D.C.

54 "The Schoolmaster President," December 27, 1937, Audio Recording 12-24, RG 12 Office of Education, Motion Pictures, Sound and Video Branch, National Archives, College Park, Maryland.

55 Although Juarez was represented as a brave and talented statesman, the moniker "Little Indian" indicates that cultural and racial bias persisted along with the primarily positive and progressive view of Latin America.

56 Memo from Wm. D. Boutwell, December 14, 1937, p. 1, Box 1, Entry 174, RG 12.

57 Memo from Wm. D. Boutwell, December 14, 1937, pp. 1, 3, Box 1, Entry 174, RG 12.

58 Boutwell to Studebaker, December 6, 1937, Box 1, Entry 174, RG 12. Boutwell frequently asserted that too much history would turn off radio listeners.

59 Notes on Caribbean Cruise by Boutwell (likely December 1937), Box 1, Entry 174, RG 12.

60 "The Beloved Ruler of Brazil," January 3, 1938, Audio Recording 12-25, RG 12, Motion Pictures, Sound, and Video Branch.

61 Brave New World, n.d., p. 1, Box 1, Entry 174, RG 12.

62 Brave New World, n.d., p. 4, Box 1, Entry 174, RG 12.

63 Boutwell to Studebaker, December 6, 1937, Box 1, Entry 174, RG 12. A proposed episode, "A Caribbean Pilgrim," which aimed to dramatize "the struggle to find a satisfactory basis of political and economic freedom in the Caribbean," was removed entirely from the production schedule.

64 Memo from Boutwell, April 5, 1938, Box 1, Entry 174, RG 12.

65 "*Ariel* and Latin America Idealists" Script, p. 2, Box 1, Entry 174, RG 12.

66 "*Ariel* and Latin America Idealists" Script, p. 3, Box 1, Entry 174, RG 12.

67 "*Ariel* and Latin America Idealists" Script, p. 20, Box 1, Entry 174, RG 12.

68 "Ariel and Latin-American Idealists" Memo from Boutwell, January 10, 1938, p. 1, Box 1, Entry 174, RG 12.

69 William F. Montavon to Studebaker, February 4, 1938, p. 1, Box 1, Entry 174, RG 12.

70 Memo regarding script on "Ariel and Latin-American Idealists" as revised . . . from C. F. Klinefelter to Shannon Allen, January 15, 1938, p. 2, Box 1, Entry 174, RG 12.

71 Williams on Program 13, "Ariel and the Latin American Idealists," January 16, 1938, Box 1, Entry 174, RG 12.

72 Williams on Program 13, "Ariel and the Latin American Idealists," January 16, 1938, Box 1, Entry 174, RG 12; Marino, "Transnational Pan-American Feminism: The Friendship of Bertha Lutz and Mary Wilhelmine Williams, 1926–1944," 63–87.

73 Memo from Boutwell to Studebaker, December 6, 1937, Box 1, Entry 174, RG 12.

74 Bender, "Film as Instrument," 42.

75 "Letters from Listeners Explode a Radio Myth," *New York Times*, April 11, 1937, 12X.

76 Boutwell, "Educational Radio Project of the Office of Education," 23.

77 Sayre, *An Analysis of the Radiobroadcasting Activities of Federal Agencies*.

78 This regional categorization, based on U.S. Department of Agriculture regional zones, is as follows: Pacific West 16% = WA, OR, ID, CA, NV, UT, AZ; Plains 9% = MT, ND, SD, WY, NE, CO, KS, NM, OK, TX; Midwest 28% = MN, WI, MI, IA, IL, IN, OH, MO, KY; Southeast 5% = AR, TN, NC, LA, MS, AL, GA, SC, FL; Northeast 34% = ME, VT, NH, NY, MA, CT, RI, PA, NJ, WV, VA, DC, DE, MD; Canada 7%; Unknown 1%.

79 Boutwell form letter, Box 3, Entry 187, RG 12.

80 V. Cirigliano, February 22, 1938, Box 3.

81 R. Wiley, March 1, 1938, Box 3; E. Duncan, February 22, 1938, Box 2. Another rural writer was interested in "colonization" in the Argentine.

82 L. Greenhill, n.d., Box 2.

83 E. MacDonald, March 8, 1938, Box 2.

84 C. Martin, March 7, 1938, Box 2.

85 A. Nonnenberg, May 3, 1938, Box 3; A. Helfand, May 3, 1938, Box 3. See also S. MacAluse, February 21, 1938, Box 3.

86 See letters from M. Johnston, J. Bluestein, and J. O'Hearne, March 8, 1938, Box 2.

87 L. Farnum, March 7, 1938, Box 2.

88 J. Bluestein, March 8, 1938, Box 2.

89 L. Ashton, March 8, 1938, Box 2.

90 E. Cohen, March 7, 1938, Box 2.

91 L. Grackolski, n.d., Box 3.

92 L. Schott, February 21, 1938, Box 3; S. Smith, May 2, 1938, Box 2; G. Clark, December 21, 1937, Box 2; J. DeMille, May 3, 1938, Box 3.

93 Cohen to Boutwell, December 14, 1937, Box 5, Entry 170, RG 12.

94 Q. Taylor, February 22, 1938; L. Schott, February 21, 1938; and Filipponi, February 22, 1938, Box 3.

95 J. O'Hearne, March 8, 1938, Box 2.

96 A. Helfand, May 3, 1938, Box 3.

97 B. Hepburn, March 10, 1938, Box 2.

98 R. Irwin, March 12, 1938, Box 2.

99 A. Estey, March 8, 1938, Box 2.

100 D. Walther, May 3, 1938; F. Schlegel, May 2, 1938, Box 3.

101 Slotten, *Radio's Hidden Voice*; Brown, "Struggle against Commercialism:" 273–291; Shepperd, "Infrastructure in the Air," 1–14.

Chapter 3   *Americans All, Immigrants All*

1 "Report by Commissioner of Education J.W. Studebaker," June 2, 1939, Box 1, Entry 172, RG 12 Office of Education, National Archives, College Park, Maryland.

2 Diana Selig, *Americans All: The Cultural Gifts Movement* (Cambridge, MA: Harvard University Press, 2008), 245.

3 Boutwell to Murrow, November 22, 1938, Box 3, Entry 170, RG 12.

4 Boutwell to Fisher, December 20, 1938, Box 3, Entry 170, RG 12.

5 Boutwell Memo, November 21, 1938, Box 3, Entry 170, RG 12.

6 Boutwell to Sterling Fisher, November 21, 1938, Box 3, Entry 170, RG 12.

7 Boutwell to Cohen, October 11, 1938, Box 5, Entry 170, RG 12.

8 Boutwell to Cohen, November 14, 1938, Box 5, Entry 170, RG 12.

9 Minutes of planning meeting, September 28, 1938, Box 1, Entry 174, RG 12.

10 Boutwell to William Robson, February 16, 1939, Box 4, Entry 170, RG 12.

11 Studebaker to Boutwell, January 3, 1939, Box 9, Entry 170, RG 12; Boutwell to Cohen, January 18, 1939, Box 4, Entry 170, RG 12.

12 "New York City Happy Hunting Ground of Dialecticians," *Pensacola News Journal*, April 9, 1939, 18.

13 Michael G. Kammen, *The Lively Arts: Gilbert Seldes and the Transformation of Cultural Criticism in the United States* (New York: Oxford University Press, 1996), 15.

14 "Airlines," *San Diego Union*, January 28, 1935, 6.

15 Quoted in Barbara Dianne Savage, *Broadcasting Freedom: Radio, War, and the Politics of Race, 1938–1948* (Chapel Hill: University of North Carolina Press, 1999), 26.

16 Philip Leonard Green to DuBois, July 29, 1938, Box 22, DuBois Papers, Immigration Research History Center, University of Minnesota Library, Minneapolis, Minnesota.

17 Seldes to Boutwell, January 12, 1939, Box 9, Entry 170, RG 12.

18 Jane Ashman, application for employment, Box 1, Entry 170, RG 12.

19 Jane Ashman to Margaret Cuthbert, November 28, 1939, Box 1, Entry 170, RG 12.

20 Jane Ashman to William Boutwell, November 18, 1939, Box 1, Entry 170, RG 12.

21 Jane Ashman to William Boutwell, September 24, 1939, Box 1, Entry 170, RG 12.

22 Boutwell to Nat T. Frame, March 21, 1939, Box 4, Entry 170, RG 12.

23 Studebaker to Thad Holt, Manager WAPI, Birmingham AL, n.d. [Sept/Oct 1938?], Box 1, Entry 175, RG 12.

24 Boutwell to Ed Kirby, December 3, 1938, Box 3, Entry 170, RG 12.

25 Memo to Radio Division, January 30, 1939, Box 1, Entry 175, RG 12.

26 "Report by Commissioner of Education J.R. Studebaker on the Educational Radio Project," n.d., Box 1, Entry 172, RG 12.

27 Boutwell to Ralph Beals, December 13, 1937, Box 3, Entry 170, RG 12.

28 Radio Division of the Office of Education, "Prospectus for Americans All, Immigrants All," November 1938, Box 1, Entry 175, RG 12.

29 Cohen to Boutwell, January 17, 1939, Box 6, Entry 170, RG 12. Subsequently, the publicity work was taken on by Ben Brodinsky.

30 Studebaker Memo, October 29, 1938, Box 1, Entry 174, RG 12.

31 Minutes of planning meeting, September 28, 1938, Box 1, Entry 174, RG 12.

32 "Uncle Sam Schoolmaster," *Radio Guide*, December 10, 1938, 3.

33 "Fight Due in Congress on Help to Jews," *Waterloo Courier*, November 20, 1938, 1.

34 Edward Ashley Bayne to Jeanette Sayre, February 16, 1939, Box 26, DuBois Papers.

35 Jeanette Sayre to Edward Ashley Bayne, February 18, 1939, Box 26, DuBois Papers.

36 Boutwell to Murrow, September 24, 1938, Box 3, Entry 170, RG 12.

37 Studebaker to Adamic, September 14, 1938, Box 1, Entry 172, RG 12.

38 Rachel Davis DuBois to William Boutwell, January, 10, 1939, Box 1, Entry 174, RG 12.

39 Seldes to Boutwell, January 12, 1939, Box 9, Entry 170, RG 12.

40 Zoe Burkholder, *Color in the Classroom: How American Schools Taught Race, 1900–1954* (New York: Oxford University Press, 2011), 27.

41 Commissioner of Education Memo, September 30, 1939, Box 1, Entry 172, RG 12.

42 Rachel Davis DuBois, "Adventures in Intercultural Education" (PhD diss., New York University, 1940), 2, 4.

43 Rachel Davis DuBois Memo, September 26, 1938, Box 22, DuBois Papers.

44 Rachel Davis DuBois to Studebaker, "Tentative Suggestions for Radio series," Box 22, DuBois Papers.

45 Rachel Davis DuBois, "How the Work Developed," typed ms, Box 12, DuBois Papers.

46 DuBois, "Adventures in Intercultural Education," 67; Rosenberg, *Intercultural Education, Folklore, and the Pedagogical Thought of Rachel Davis DuBois*, 77.

47 Selig, *Americans All*, 78.

48 Selig, *Americans All*, 102–103.

49 Charles Hight, "All Cultures Matter: Rachel Davis Dubois, The Intercultural Education and Group Conversation Methods" (PhD diss., Georgia State University, 2020), 42.

50 Interview with Rachel Davis DuBois, November 17, 1984, in George Attwood Crispin, "Rachel Davis DuBois: Founder of the Group Conversation as an Adult Educational Facilitator for Reducing Intercultural Strife" (D. Ed. diss., Temple University, 1987), 280.

51 Rachel Davis DuBois and Corann Okorodudu, *All This and Something More: Pioneering in Intercultural Education, an Autobiography* (Bryn Mawr, PA: Dorrance, 1984), 83–86.

52 Michele Hilmes, "Invisible Men: Amos 'n Andy and the Roots of Broadcast Discourse," *Critical Studies in Media Communication* 10, no. 4 (1993): 303. See also Joy Elizabeth Hayes, "White Noise: Performing the White, Middle-Class Family on 1930s Radio," *Cinema Journal* 51, no. 3 (2012): 97–118.

53 "Plan Tolerance Course in Public Schools," *Brooklyn Daily Eagle*, December 22, 1938, 22.

54 "Plan Tolerance Course in Public Schools," *Brooklyn Daily Eagle*, December 22, 1938, 22; "New York Praised for Tolerance Aid," *New York Times*, January 2, 1939, 24.

55 "Tolerance Courses Urged in School," *New York Times*, December 9, 1938, 27.

56 "Schools Ordered to Teach 'Tolerance,'" *New York Times*, December 22, 1938, 9.

57 Rachel Davis Dubois to Studebaker, January 21, 1939, Box 1, Entry 174, RG 12.

58 "New York Praised for Tolerance Aid," *New York Times*, January 2, 1939, 24; Studebaker Press Release, January 5, 1939, Box 1, Entry 175, RG 12.

59 DuBois, "Adventures in Intercultural Education," 25, 27.

60 Rachel Davis Dubois, "Sharing Culture Values," *Journal of Educational Sociology* 12, no. 8 (1939): 482.

61 Selig, *Americans All*, 187.

62 See Burkholder, *Color in the Classroom*, 21; Selig, *Americans All*, 69.

63 Rachel Davis-DuBois Memo, September 26, 1938, Box 22, DuBois Papers.

64 Burkholder, *Color in the Classroom*, 68, 70, 88.

65 See Peter Mandler, *Return from the Natives: How Margaret Mead Won the Second World War and Lost the Cold War* (New Haven, CT: Yale University Press, 2013).

66 Selig, *Americans All*, 243.

67 Seldes to Boutwell, January 12, 1939, Box 9, Entry 170, RG 12.

68 J. Morris Jones, *Americans All, Immigrants All: A Handbook for Listeners* (Washington D.C.: Federal Radio Education Committee, 1939), 11.

69 AAIA script #16, Box 32, Columbia Broadcasting System Radio Scripts, Manuscript Division, Library of Congress, Washington, D.C.

70 Prospectus for American All, Immigrants All, November 1938, Box 1, Entry 175, RG 12.

71 Selig, *Americans All*, 13.

72 Harold Rugg, *Our Country and Our People: An Introduction to American Civilization* (Boston: Ginn and Company, 1938), 34.

73 Prospectus for American All, Immigrants All, November 1938, Box 1, Entry 175, RG 12.
74 Pamphlet of activities relating to episode 1, Box 1, Entry 175, RG 12.
75 Philip Leonard Green to Rachel Davis DuBois, August 18, 1938, Box 22, DuBois Papers.
76 Minutes of meeting, September 28, 1938, Box 1, Entry 174, RG 12.
77 Savage, *Broadcasting Freedom*, 25–26.
78 Kammen, *Lively Arts*, 262.
79 Gilbert Seldes, "General Statement on Approach to Writing of Script for Immigrants All, Americans All," Box 1, Entry 174, RG 12.
80 Rachel Davis Dubois, radio talk on WEVD, July 26, 1938, Box 1, Entry 174, RG 12.
81 W.E.B. Du Bois, "Criticism of Americans All—Immigrants All, ca. November 30, 1938," W.E.B. Du Bois Papers (MS 312), Special Collections and University Archives, University of Massachusetts Amherst Libraries, Amherst, MA. http://credo.library.umass.edu/view/full/mums312-b085-i018.
82 Minutes, September 28, 1938, Box 1, Entry 174, RG 12.
83 Nicholas V. Montalto, "The Forgotten Dream: A History of the Intercultural Education Movement, 1924–1941" (PhD diss., University of Minnesota, 1977), 180.
84 DuBois and Okororudu, *All This and Something More*, 87.
85 Mrs. A. H. Sulzberger to A. Derounian, February 24, 1939, Box 3, DuBois Papers.
86 Chester S. Williams to Studebaker, February 23, 1939, Box 1, Entry 174, RG 12.
87 Boutwell to Studebaker, February 9, 1939, Box 1, Entry 174, RG 12.
88 Selig, *Americans All*, 235–236.
89 Selig, *Americans All*, 248.
90 Selig, *Americans All*, 249.
91 Quoted in Selig, *Americans All*, 251.
92 Selig, *Americans All*, 254–255.
93 DuBois and Okorodudu, *All This and Something More*, 95.
94 Rachel Davis DuBois to Louis Adamic, June 30, 1938, Box 3, DuBois Papers.
95 DuBois, "Adventures in Intercultural Education," 22.
96 See Selig, *Americans All*; Robert L. Fleegler, *Ellis Island Nation: Immigration Policy and American Identity in the Twentieth Century* (Philadelphia: University of Pennsylvania Press, 2015).
97 Boutwell to Seldes, October 17, 1938, Box 3, Entry 170, RG 12.
98 Seldes, "General Statement on Approach to Writing of Script for Immigrants All, Americans All," Box 1, Entry 174, RG 12.
99 Boutwell Memo, November 21, 1938, Box 3, Entry 170, RG 12; Neil Verma, "Radio's 'Oblong Blur': Notes on the Corwinesque," *Sounding Out!* (blog), June 25, 2012. http://soundstudiesblog.com/2012/06/25/6606/. Neil Verma describes this technique as "kaleidosonic radio" in which "we segue from place to place, experiencing shallow scenes as if from a series of fixed apertures, thereby giving time periods expressive existence."
100 Vitray to Boutwell and Green, December 9, 1938, Box 1, Entry 174, RG 12.
101 Ashman to Cuthbert, November 28, 1939, Box 1, Entry 170, RG 12.
102 Boutwell to Seldes, Cohen, and McGill, November 21, 1938, Box 1, Entry 174, RG 12.
103 Boutwell to Seldes, January 13, 1939, Box 9, Entry 170, RG 12.
104 Kammen, *Lively Arts*, 262.

105 Paul Lazarsfeld, *Radio and the Printed Page: An Introduction to the Study of Radio and Its Role in the Communication of Ideas* (New York: Duell, Sloan & Pearce, 1940), 134.

106 Nicholas V. Montalto, "The Intercultural Education Movement, 1924–41," in *American Education and the European Immigrant: 1840–1940*, ed. Bernard J. Weiss (Urbana: University of Illinois Press, 1982), 153.

107 Rachel Davis DuBois to Boutwell, January 10, 1939, Box 1, Entry 174, RG 12.

108 Boutwell to Sterling Fisher, October 14, 1939, Box 1, Entry 174, RG 12.

109 Cohen to Boutwell, February 23, 1939, Box 6, Entry 170, RG 12.

110 Cohen to Boutwell, July 28, 1939, Box 1, Entry 174, RG 12.

111 Sterling Fisher to Boutwell, October 19, 1939, Box 1, Entry 174, RG 12.

112 Stewart G. Cole to Boutwell, September 19, 1940, Box 1, Entry 174, RG 12.

113 Boutwell to Cole, June 26, 1940, Box 1, Entry 174, RG 12.

114 Jill Lepore, "The Last Time Democracy Almost Died," *New Yorker*, February 3, 2020, https://www.newyorker.com/magazine/2020/02/03/the-last-time -democracy-almost-died.

Chapter 4 *Wings for the Martins*

1 Herta Herzog, "On Borrowed Experience: An Analysis of Listening to Daytime Sketches," in *Mass Communication and American Social Thought: Key Texts, 1919–1968*, ed. John Durham Peters and Peter Simonson (Lanham, MD: Rowman & Littlefield, 2004), 154.

2 John Studebaker to Lenox Lohr, November 8, 1938, Folder 53, Box 65, NBC Records, 1921–1976, Wisconsin Historical Society, Madison, Wisconsin.

3 Frank R. McNinch to Studebaker, October 31, 1938, Folder 53, Box 65, NBC Records.

4 NBC Press Release, "Problems of Average Parents Theme of New NBC Series," November 2, 1938, Folder 53, Box 65, NBC Records.

5 Angell Letter, December 7, 1938 (note that it was sent to the U.S. Department of Education List and the NBC "institutional list"), Folder 53, Box 65, NBC Records.

6 Angell to K. H. Berkeley, September 19, 1938, Folder 10 US Department of Interior, Box 65, NBC Records.

7 John W. Boyer, *The University of Chicago: A History* (Chicago: University of Chicago Press, 2015), 528.

8 Michele Hilmes, *Radio Voices: American Broadcasting, 1922–1952* (Minneapolis: University of Minnesota Press, 1997); Goodman, *Radio's Civic Ambition*.

9 Franklin Dunham to John Royal, July 30, 1936, Folder 6, Box 92, NBC Records.

10 "Tune In . . . Wings for the Martins" Pamphlet, n.d., Folder Wings for the Martins, Box 6, Entry 182, RG 12.

11 Comments on Wings for the Martins Broadcasts, n.d., Folder Wings for the Martins Notes and Comments, Box 5, Entry 182, RG 12.

12 Edith Allen to Studebaker, March 11, 1939, Folder Wings for the Martins, Box 6, Entry 182, RG 12.

13 "Nightwork" Script, n.d., Folder Wings for the Martins—Scripts, Box 6, Entry 174, RG 12.

14 Mary [Julia] Grant, "Modernizing Motherhood: Child Study Clubs and the Parent Education Movement, 1915–1940" (PhD diss., Boston University, 1992), 26, 252.

15 Ann Johnson and Elizabeth Johnston, "Up the Years with the Bettersons: Gender and Parent Education in Interwar America," *History of Psychology* 18, no. 3 (2015): 258.

16 Wings for the Martins Titles and Problems—Annotated, n.d., p. 7, Folder Wings for the Martins—Planning, Box 6, Entry 174, RG 12.

17 Julia Grant, "A 'Real Boy' and Not a Sissy: Gender, Childhood, and Masculinity, 1890–1940," *Journal of Social History* 37, no. 4 (2004): 829–851.

18 "He Didn't Make the Team" Script, April 12, 1939, Folder Wings for the Martins—Scripts, Box 6, Entry 174, RG 12.

19 Johnson and Johnston, "Up the Years with the Bettersons," 265; Grant, "A 'Real Boy' and Not a Sissy"; Ralph LaRossa, *The Modernization of Fatherhood: A Social and Political History* (Chicago: University of Chicago Press, 1997).

20 Wings for the Martins Press Release, October 28, 1938, Folder Wings for the Martins—Planning, Box 6, Entry 174, RG 12.

21 Grant, "Modernizing Motherhood," vi.

22 Clifford John Doerksen, *American Babel: Rogue Radio Broadcasters of the Jazz Age* (Philadelphia: University of Pennsylvania Press, 2005).

23 Grant, "Modernizing Motherhood," vi.

24 Grant, "Modernizing Motherhood," 70; Maxine L. Margolis, *Mothers and Such: Views of American Women and Why They Changed* (Berkeley: University of California Press, 1984); LaRossa, *The Modernization of Fatherhood*.

25 Lawrence K. Frank, "The Beginnings of Child Development and Family Life Education in the Twentieth Century," *Merrill-Palmer Quarterly of Behavior and Development* 8, no. 4 (1962): 207–227.

26 Johnson and Johnston, "Up the Years with the Bettersons," 252.

27 Elizabeth Lomax, "The Laura Spelman Rockefeller Memorial: Some of Its Contributions to Early Research in Child Development," *Journal of the History of the Behavioral Sciences* 13, no. 3 (1977): 283–293.

28 Lomax, "Laura Spelman Rockefeller Memorial," 284; Grant, "Modernizing Motherhood," 53.

29 Paul E. Blackwood, "Later Leaders in Education: Bess Goodykoontz: 1894–1990," *Childhood Education* 67, no. 4 (1991): 265–270.

30 Frances M. Seeber, "Eleanor Roosevelt and Women in the New Deal: A Network of Friends," *Presidential Studies Quarterly* 20, no. 4 (1990): 707–717.

31 Blackwood, "Later Leaders in Education: Bess Goodykoontz," 267. Goodykoontz became director of the Division of Elementary Education (1946–1949) and associate commissioner of education (1949–1952). Between 1952 and her retirement in 1962, she took a position in International Education, first as director of comparative education and then as director of the International Education Relations branch.

32 Effie G. Bathurst, WorldCat Identities, http://worldcat.org/identities/lccn -n85120208/, accessed January 3, 2020.

33 Lisa J. McClure, "Helen K. Mackintosh: Expanding the Concept of Our World," in *Missing Chapters: Ten Pioneering Women in NCTE and English Education*, ed. Jeanne Marcum Gerlach and Virginia R. Monseau (National Council of Teachers of English, 1991), 186–201.

34 "P.T.A. Will Hear Dr. Mary D. Davis: Chevy Chase Group's First Night Meeting to Be Held Wed," *Washington Post*, October 9, 1932, 3.

35 "Elise H. Martens," *Washington Post*, March 22, 1961, B6.

36 Blackwood, "Later Leaders in Education," 266.

37 Melissa A. Milkie and Kathleen E. Denny, "Changes in the Cultural Model of Father Involvement: Descriptions of Benefits to Fathers, Children, and Mothers in Parents' Magazine, 1926–2006," *Journal of Family Issues* 35, no. 2 (2014): 248.

38 Steven Schlossman, "Perils of Popularization: The Founding of Parents' Magazine," *Monographs of the Society for Research in Child Development* 50, no. 4–5 (1986): 66.

39 Milkie and Denny, "Changes in the Cultural Model of Father Involvement," 235. The percentage of articles touting the benefits of parenting for fathers dropped to 40 percent by 1965, rose to 80 percent by 1975, and dropped to 40 percent by 2006.

40 Grant, "Modernizing Motherhood," 45.

41 Johnson and Johnston, "Up the Years with the Bettersons," 255–256.

42 Johnson and Johnston, "Up the Years with the Bettersons," 256.

43 Bathurst to Cohen, December 10, 1938, Box 5, Entry 170, RG 12.

44 Cohen to Boutwell, December 15, 1938, Box 5, Entry 170, RG 12.

45 Boutwell to Cohen, February 9, 1939, Box 4, Entry 170, RG 12.

46 Pauline Gibson to Bill Boutwell, February 7, 1939, Folder Gilsdorf, Box 7, Entry 170, RG 12.

47 Miss Bathurst to Miss Vitray and Mr. Boutwell, April 10, 1939, Folder Laura Vitray, Box 11, Entry 170, RG 12.

48 Pauline Gibson to Bill Boutwell, February 7, 1939, Folder Gilsdorf, Box 7, Entry 170, RG 12.

49 Gibson to Boutwell, February 7, 1939.

50 Gibson to Boutwell, February 7, 1939.

51 *Wings for the Martins* Scripts, Folder Research Materials, Box 5, Entry 182, RG 12.

52 Gibson to Boutwell, February 7, 1939.

53 *Wings for the Martins*, Audio Recordings 106–240 to 106–251, Smithsonian Institution Records, Motion Pictures, Sound and Video Branch, National Archives, College Park, Maryland.

54 Steven Mintz and Susan Kellogg, *Domestic Revolutions: A Social History of American Family Life* (New York: Free Press; Collier Macmillan, 1988).

55 Ralph LaRossa et al., "The Fluctuating Image of the 20th Century American Father," *Journal of Marriage and Family* 53, no. 4 (1991): 987–997; John Demos, "The Changing Faces of Fatherhood," in *Father and Child: Developmental and Clinical Perspectives*, ed. Stanley H. Cath, Alan R. Gurwitt, and John Munder Ross (Boston: Little, Brown, 1982), 425–450.

56 LaRossa et al., "20th Century American Father;" 992; Randal D. Day and Wade C. Mackey, "Role Image of the American Father: An Examination of a Media Myth," *Journal of Comparative Family Studies* 17, no. 3 (1986): 371–388.

57 Susan J. Douglas, *Listening In: Radio and the American Imagination* (New York: Times Books, 1999); Margaret T. McFadden, "'America's Boy Friend Who Can't Get a Date': Gender, Race, and the Cultural Work of the Jack Benny Program, 1932–1946," *Journal of American History* 80, no. 1 (1993): 113–134.

58 Hayes, "White Noise," 97–118.

59 Miss Bathurst to Miss Vitray and Mr. Boutwell, April 10, 1939, Folder Laura Vitray, Box 11, Entry 170, RG 12.

60 Dunning, *On the Air*, 516.

61 Nina C. Leibman, *Living Room Lectures: The Fifties Family in Film and Television* (Austin: University of Texas Press, 1995); Mary R. Desjardins, *Father Knows Best*

(Detroit: Wayne State University Press, 2015), 5–6; Horace Newcomb, *TV: The Most Popular Art* (New York: Anchor Books, 1974), 55.

62 George Lipsitz, "The Meaning of Memory: Family, Class, and Ethnicity in Early Network Television Programs," *Camera Obscura* 6, no. 1 (1988): 78–116; Lynn Spigel, *Make Room for TV: Television and the Family Ideal in Postwar America* (Chicago: University of Chicago Press, 1992), 173; Ella Taylor, *Prime-Time Families: Television Culture in Postwar America* (Berkeley: University of California Press, 1989); David Marc, "Origins of the Genre: In Search of the Radio Sitcom," in *The Sitcom Reader America Viewed and Skewed*, ed. Mary M. Dalton and Laura R. Linder (Albany: State University of New York Press, 2005), 21. Marc goes so far as to suggest that the twenty-five-year life of network radio was "perhaps too short to fully realize any genres of its own." By this logic, the twenty-five-year life of television's classic network system was also, perhaps, too short to shape its own genres.

Chapter 5 *Democracy in Action*

1 Boutwell to Sterling Fisher, September 22, 1939, Box 4, Entry 174, RG 12 Office of Education, National Archives, College Park, Maryland.
2 Memo, November 18, 1938, Box 3, Entry 174, RG 12.
3 Cohen to Boutwell, June 5, 1939, Box 6, Entry 170, RG 12.
4 Gerd Horten, *Radio Goes to War: The Cultural Politics of Propaganda during World War II* (Berkeley: University of California Press, 2003), 19.
5 Chester S. Williams to Boutwell, November 23, 1938, Box 3, Entry 174, RG 12.
6 Minutes of meeting, November 19, 1938, Box 7, Entry 170, RG 12.
7 Wilson to Boutwell, February 14, 1939, Box 3, Entry 174, RG 12.
8 Minutes of meeting, November 19, 1938, Box 7, Entry 170, RG 12.
9 Democracy in Action Script #1, May 14, 1939, Columbia Broadcasting System Radio Scripts, Manuscripts Division, Library of Congress, Washington, D.C.
10 "Security Today and Tomorrow," DIA broadcast January 28, 1940, audio recordings from the Milo Ryan Phonoarchive at the library of the University of Washington, Seattle.
11 Williams to Boutwell, November 23, 1938, Box 3, Entry 174, RG 12; Cohen to Boutwell, August 11, 1938, Box 5, Entry 170, RG 12.
12 "Work of Office of Education Division Is Expanded by Additional WPA Grant," *Broadcasting, Broadcast Advertising* 15, no. 7 (1938): 34.
13 Boutwell to Studebaker, October 5, 1938, Box 3, Entry 174, RG 12.
14 Boutwell to Cohen, October 30, 1938, Box 5, Entry 170, RG 12.
15 Boutwell to Studebaker, October 5, 1938, Box 3, Entry 174, RG 12.
16 Allan Wilson to Boutwell, February 14, 1939, Box 3, Entry 174, RG 12.
17 Boutwell to Cohen, March 15, 1939, Box 6, Entry 170, RG 12.
18 Robert W. Rydell, "Introduction," in *Designing Tomorrow: America's World's Fairs of the 1930s*, ed. Robert W. Rydell and Laura Burd Schiavo (New Haven, CT: Yale University Press, 2010), 14.
19 Boutwell to Fisher, July 14, 1939, Box 4, Entry 174, RG 12.
20 Boutwell to Fisher, July 14, 1939, Box 4, Entry 174, RG 12.
21 Denison to Boutwell, April 4, 1939, Box 2, Entry 174, RG 12.
22 Denison to Boutwell, April 10, 1939, File 5, Box 33, Merrill Denison Fonds, Queens University Archives, Kingston, Ontario.

23 Boutwell to Cohen, April 8, 1939, Box 6, Entry 170, RG 12.

24 "Proposed Titles: CBS Series, Sundays 2 P.M.," File 5, Box 33, Denison Fonds.

25 Denison to Boutwell, April 10, 1939, File 5, Box 33, Denison Fonds.

26 Cohen to Boutwell, April 21, 1939, Box 6, Entry 170, RG 12.

27 Studebaker to Theodore Hayes, May 9, 1939, Box 2, Entry 174, RG 12.

28 Denison to Boutwell, July 19, 1939, Box 6, Entry 170, RG 12.

29 Cohen to Boutwell, August 13, 1939, Box 6, Entry 170, RG 12.

30 Boutwell to Denison, July 13, 1939, Box 4, Entry 174, RG 12.

31 Denison to Boutwell, July 19, 1939, Box 6, Entry 170, RG 12.

32 Hudson and Marshall to Williams, July 10, 1939, Box 6, Entry 170, RG 12.

33 Studebaker Memo, May 3, 1939, File 5, Box 33, Denison Fonds.

34 Denison to Williams, May 26, 1939, Box 7, Entry 174, RG 12.

35 Williams to Denison, May 9, 1939, File 5, Box 33, Denison Fonds.

36 Cohen to Boutwell, May 15, 1939, Box 6, Entry 170, RG 12.

37 Denison to Williams, June 7, 1939, Box 6, Entry 170, RG 12.

38 Williams to Denison, June 9, 1939, Box 7, Entry 174, RG 12.

39 Cohen to Williams, June 6, 1939, Box 7, Entry 174, RG 12.

40 Williams to Cohen, June 9, 1939, Box 2, Entry 174, RG 12.

41 Belmont Farley to Boutwell, April 24, 1939, File 5, Box 33, Denison Fonds.

42 Denison to Williams, May 26, 1939, Box 7, Entry 174, RG 12.

43 C. F. Klinefelter to Denison, July 13, 1939, File 5, Box 33, Denison Fonds.

44 C. F. Klinefelter to Merrill Denison August 16, 1939, Box 7, Entry 170, RG 12.

45 Boutwell to Sterling Fisher, July 28, 1939; Williams to Cohen July 6, 1939, Box 7, Entry 174, RG 12.

46 Denison to Boutwell, October 18, 1939, Box 6, Entry 170, RG 12.

47 Boutwell to Cohen, June 11, 1937, Box 5, Entry 170, RG 12.

48 Boutwell to Cohen, June 3, 1937, Box 5, Entry 170, RG 12.

49 Boutwell to Cohen, October 15, 1937, Box 5, Entry 170, RG 12.

50 *School Life* 25, no. 1 (October 1939): 28.

51 Columbia Broadcasting System Radio Scripts, Box 35, LOC.

52 Williams to Boutwell, May 1, 1939, Box 2, Entry 174, RG 12.

53 Williams to Denison, May 16, 1939, Box 7, Entry 174, RG 12.

54 Denison to Williams, June 7, 1939, Box 6, Entry 170, RG 12.

55 Vitray Memo on Script #2 Democracy in Action, Box 7, Entry 174, RG 12.

56 Denison to Boutwell, April 10, 1939, File 5, Box 33, Denison Fonds.

57 Marco Duranti, "Utopia, Nostalgia and World War at the 1939–40 New York World's Fair," *Journal of Contemporary History* 41, no. 4 (2006): 666.

58 Denison to Williams, July 12, 1939, Box 7, Entry 174, RG 12.

59 Democracy in Action Script, August 27, 1939, Box 35, CBS Radio Scripts, LOC.

60 Democracy in Action Script, June 11, 1939, Box 35, CBS Radio Scripts, LOC.

61 Ben Gross, "Listening In," *Daily News*, June 12, 1939, 32.

62 Democracy in Action Script, May 28, 1939, Box 35, CBS Radio Scripts, LOC.

63 Vitray Memo to Denison on DIA Script #3, Box 7, Entry 174, RG 12.

64 Boutwell Memo, November 21, 1938, Box 3, Entry 174, RG 12.

65 Boutwell to Williams, May 1, 1939, Box 2, Entry 174, RG 12.

66 Boutwell to Williams, June 5, 1939, Box 7, Entry 174, RG 12.

67 Boutwell to Denison, n.d., Denison papers, File 5, Box 33.

68 Laura Vitray to Denison, May 3, 1939, File 5, Box 33, Denison Fonds.

69 Democracy in Action Script, August 27, 1939, Box 35, CBS Radio Scripts, LOC.

70   Boutwell to Studebaker, February 3, 1939, Box 3, Entry 174, RG 12.
71   Williams to Studebaker, February 9, 1939, Box 3, Entry 174, RG 12.
72   Boutwell to Williams, February 7, 1939, Box 3, Entry 174, RG 12.
73   Boutwell Memo October 30, 1939, Box 2, Entry 174, RG 12.
74   Boutwell Memo January 2, 1940, Box 2, Entry 174, RG 12.
75   Boutwell Memo January 17, 1940, Box 2, Entry 174, RG 12.
76   Denison to Williams, May 16, 1939, Box 7, Entry 174, RG 12.
77   Wylie to Boutwell, June 15, 1939, Box 2, Entry 174, RG 12.
78   Wylie to Fisher (CBS), September 19, 1939, Box 2, Entry 174, RG 12.
79   Williams to Boutwell, August 10, 1939, Box 7, Entry 174, RG 12.
80   Boutwell to Schramm, August 29, 1939, Box 4, Entry 170, RG 12.
81   Boutwell Memo, March 25, 1940, Box 2, Entry 174, RG 12.
82   Boutwell to Schramm, August 29, 1939, Box 4, Entry 170, RG 12.
83   McGill, *Radio Directing*, 261.
84   Irve Tunick, draft of "Of the People," n.d., Box 4, Entry 170, RG 12.
85   Democracy in Action, Script #2, May 21, 1939, Box 35, CBS Rdio Scripts, LOC.
86   Democracy in Action, Script #3, May 28, 1939, Box 35, CBS Rdio Scripts, LOC.
87   Democracy in Action Script, January 28, 1940, Box 36, CBS Rdio Scripts, LOC.
88   Williams to Denison, May 10, 1939, Box 4, Entry 170, RG 12.
89   Boutwell Memo, December 26, 1939, Box 4, Entry 170, RG 12.
90   Boutwell to Cohen, August 27, 1939, Box 5, Entry 170, RG 12.
91   Democracy in Action script, August 27, 1939, "Arts," Box 35, CBS Rdio Scripts, LOC.
92   Joshua Billings, Felix Budelmann, and Fiona Macintosh, eds., "Introduction," in *Choruses, Ancient and Modern*, ed. Joshua Billings, Felix Budelmann, and Fiona Macintosh (Oxford: Oxford University Press, 2013), 2.
93   Martin Revermann, "Brechtian Chorality," in *Choruses, Ancient and Modern*, 166.
94   Boutwell to Marshall and Hudson, February 24, 1939, Box 3, Entry 174, RG 12.
95   Studebaker, "Twentieth Century Approaches in the Use of Communication," address to AAEA conference, May 22, 1940, Box 8, Entry 187, RG 12.

Chapter 6   *Pleasantdale Folks*

1   Max Stern to Oscar M. Powell with attached NBC Bulletin, January 11, 1940, Folder 062.1, Box 156, Office of the Commissioner Executive Files Unit 1935–1940, RG 47 Social Security Administration, National Archives, College Park, Maryland.
2   The report stated that 300 sets of transcriptions were allotted for distribution to stations. Out of 736 total stations, 427 booked the series, and 411 of those stations (96 percent) had broadcast the series as of early May 1940. These stations covered nearly 82 percent of U.S. cities. Robert Huse to Oscar M. Powell with attached Progress Report, May 8, 1940, Folder 062.1, Box 156, RG 47.
3   *January 1939!* Promotional Material, Folder 062.11, Box 156, RG 47.
4   Lois Scharf, *To Work and to Wed: Female Employment, Feminism, and the Great Depression* (Westport, CT: Greenwood Press, 1980), 128.
5   Ann Shola Orloff, "The Political Origins of America's Belated Welfare State" in *The Politics of Social Policy in the United States*, ed. Margaret Weir, Ann Shola Orloff and Theda Skocpol (Princeton, NJ: Princeton University Press, 1988), 76–79.

6 *Pleasantdale Folks*, Episode 1, audio recordings 196-29 SSB, Social Security Board Records, Motion Pictures, Sound and Video Branch, National Archives, College Park, Maryland. Recordings of all episodes are from this collection. All quotes are from transcriptions made from these recordings.

7 *Pleasantdale Folks*, Episode 1.

8 *Pleasantdale Folks*, Episode 1.

9 Sayre, *An Analysis of the Radiobroadcasting Activities of Federal Agencies*, 83.

10 Phil Cohen to William Boutwell, April 13, 1939, Folder Cohen, Phil January 1, 1939–August 31, 1939, Box 6, E 170, RG 12; Boutwell to John Studebaker, File 1939—Boutwell Correspondence, June–December, Box 4, E 170, RG 12.

11 Max Stern to Oscar M. Powell, September 26, 1939, Folder 062.1, Box 156, Office of the Commissioner, RG 47.

12 *Pleasantdale Folks*, Episode 1.

13 *Pleasantdale Folks*, Episode 8.

14 *Pleasantdale Folks*, Episode 4.

15 *Pleasantdale Folks*, Episode 10.

16 While genres have a readily identifiable style and structure, they are never entirely fixed. As cultural and industrial products they are "constituted by media practices and subject to ongoing change and definition." Jason Mittel, *Genre and Television: From Cop Shows to Cartoons in American Culture* (New York: Routledge, 2004), 1.

17 Hilmes, *Radio Voices*, 165–182.

18 J. Fred MacDonald, "Soap Operas as a Social Force" in *Don't Touch That Dial!: Radio Programming in American Life, 1920–1960* (Chicago: Nelson-Hall, 1979), 231–280.

19 Hilmes, *Radio Voices*; MacDonald, "Soap Operas."

20 Dennis Porter cited in Robert C. Allen, *Speaking of Soap Operas* (Chapel Hill: University of North Carolina Press, 1985), 13. See also Martha Nochimson, *No End to Her: Soap Opera and the Female Subject* (Berkeley: University of California Press, 1992); Tania Modleski, *Loving with a Vengeance: Mass Produced Fantasies for Women*, 2nd edition (New York: Routledge, 2008).

21 Alvind Singhal, Rafael Obregon, and Everett M. Rogers, "Reconstructing the Story of *Simplemente Maria*, the Most Popular Telenovela in Latin America of All Time," *International Communication Gazette* 54, no. 1 (1995): 1–15; Sood, Menard, and Witte, "The Theory Behind Entertainment-Education," 117–145.

22 Herzog, "On Borrowed Experience," 139–157.

23 Alan Brinkley, *Voices of Protest: Huey Long, Father Coughlin, and the Great Depression* (New York: Vintage, 2011), 222.

24 Edwin Amenta, *When Movements Matter: The Townsend Plan and the Rise of Social Security* (Princeton, NJ: Princeton University Press, 2006); Frances Perkins, *The Roosevelt I Knew* (New York: Penguin, 2011 [1946]).

25 Richard A. Reiman, *The New Deal and American Youth: Ideas and Ideals in a Depression Decade* (Athens: University of Georgia Press, 1992); Elaine Tyler May, *Homeward Bound: American Families in the Cold War Era* (New York: Basic Books, 2008).

26 Ruth Milkman, "Women's Work and Economic Crisis: Some Lessons of the Great Depression," in *On Gender, Labor, and Inequality* (Urbana: University of Illinois Press, 2016), 13–46; Reiman, *New Deal and American Youth*.

27 Reiman, *New Deal and American Youth*; May, *Homeward Bound*, 40.

28 Michael A. Bernstein, "Why the Great Depression Was Great," in *The Rise and Fall of the New Deal Order, 1930–1980*, ed. Steve Fraser and Gary Gerstle (Princeton, NJ: Princeton University Press, 1989), 41; May, *Homeward Bound*, 40, 48.

29 Barbara Melosh, *Engendering Culture: Manhood and Womanhood in New Deal Art and Theater* (Washington, DC: Smithsonian Institution Press, 1991), 2, 16, 30; Scharf, *To Work and to Wed*, 43–44.

30 May, *Homeward Bound*, 38.

31 Claudia Goldin, "The Quiet Revolution That Transformed Women's Employment, Education, and Family," *American Economic Review* 96, no. 2 (2006): 5; Scharf, *To Work and to Wed*, 52.

32 John McGuire, "'The Most Unjust Piece of Legislation': Section 213 of the Economy Act of 1932 and Feminism During the New Deal," *Journal of Policy History* 20, no. 4 (2008): 516–541; Victoria De Grazia, *How Fascism Ruled Women, Italy, 1922–1945* (Berkeley: University of California Press, 1992).

33 May, *Homeward Bound*, 40; Melosh, *Engendering Culture*, 157.

34 Gwendolyn Mink, *The Wages of Motherhood: Inequality in the Welfare State, 1917–1942* (Ithaca: Cornell University Press, 1995), 136–139.

35 George Lipsitz, *The Possessive Investment in Whiteness: How White People Profit from Identity Politics* (Philadelphia: Temple University Press, 2018), 3; Mary Poole, *The Segregated Origins of Social Security: African Americans and the Welfare State* (Chapel Hill: University of North Carolina Press, 2006); Alice Kessler-Harris, *Gendering Labor History* (Urbana: University of Illinois Press, 2007).

36 George Lipsitz, "The Possessive Investment in Whiteness: Racialized Social Democracy and the 'White' Problem in American Studies," *American Quarterly* 47, no. 3 (1995): 372.

37 Such racially exclusionary policies can be traced, in part, to the New Deal's dependence on southern Democrats. See Ira Katznelson, *Fear Itself: The New Deal and the Origins of Our Time* (New York: W. W. Norton & Company, 2013).

38 Lipsitz overlooks the long-standing scholarship on the gendered nature of New Deal social policy, including Steven Mintz and Susan Kellogg, *Domestic Revolutions: A Social History of American Family Life* (New York: Free Press; Collier Macmillan, 1988); Winifred D. Wandersee, *Women's Work and Family Values, 1920–1940* (Cambridge, MA: Harvard University Press, 1981); Scharf, *To Work and to Wed*; Mink, *Wages of Motherhood*; Kessler-Harris, *Gendering Labor History*.

39 Kessler-Harris, *Gendering Labor History*, 279.

40 Alice Kessler-Harris, "In the Nation's Image: The Gendered Limits of Social Citizenship in the Depression Era," *Journal of American History* 86, no. 3 (1999): 1251–1279.

41 Stephanie Coontz, *The Way We Never Were: American Families and the Nostalgia Trap* (New York: Basic Books, 1992); Linda Gordon, *Women, the State, and Welfare* (Madison: University of Wisconsin Press, 1990); Mintz and Kellogg, *Domestic Revolutions*.

42 *Pleasantdale Folks*, Episode 7.

43 *Pleasantdale Folks*, Episode 1.

44 *Pleasantdale Folks*, Episode 7.

45 *Pleasantdale Folks*, Episode 1.

46 *Pleasantdale Folks*, Episode 1.

47 *Pleasantdale Folks*, Episode 13.

48 May, *Homeward Bound*, 47.
49 *Pleasantdale Folks*, Episode 7.
50 *Pleasantdale Folks*, Episode 7.
51 *Pleasantdale Folks*, Episode 7.
52 May, *Homeward Bound*, 40; Melosh, *Engendering Culture*, 157.
53 *Pleasantdale Folks*, Episode 7.
54 *Pleasantdale Folks*, Episode 13.
55 MacDonald, "Soap Operas," 243; Hilmes, *Radio Voices*, 170–172.
56 Hilmes, *Radio Voices*, 171.
57 *Pleasantdale Folks*, Episode 2.
58 MacDonald, "Soap Operas," 243.
59 Lovell, "Ideology and *Coronation Street*," in *Coronation Street*, ed. Richard Dyer (London: British Film Institute, 1981), 50–51.
60 MacDonald, "Soap Operas," 241.

Conclusion

1 Royal Memo to Patterson, May 3, 1935, Folder 69, Box 41, NBC Records, 1921–1976, Wisconsin Historical Society, Madison, Wisconsin.
2 Goodman, *Radio's Civic Ambition*.
3 Patterson, *Congressional Conservatism and the New Deal*, 284–285.
4 James E. Sargent, "Woodrum's Economy Bloc: The Attack on Roosevelt's WPA, 1937–1939," *Virginia Magazine of History and Biography* 93, no. 2 (1985): 195.
5 *Albuquerque Journal*, June 16, 1939, 16; Sargent, "Woodrum's Economy Bloc," 175, 200–201. Republicans and conservative Democrats combined calls for economy with claims about the subversive influence of the Workers Alliance of America, the WPA workers union. In March 1939 the House approved a resolution from the Rules Committee for an investigation of the WPA, and Woodrum launched it in April. In 1939 the Federal Theatre Radio Division was shut down.
6 Patterson, *Congressional Conservatism*, 294–296, 304.
7 *Annual Report of the Commissioner of Education for the Fiscal Year Ended June 30, 1940* (Washington: GPO, 1941), 97.
8 Studebaker to Roosevelt, May 22, 1939, PPF 2896, Roosevelt Presidential Library, Hyde Park, New York.
9 Mordecai Lee, *The First Presidential Communications Agency: FDR's Office of Government Reports* (Albany: State University of New York Press, 2005), 27, 43. Scripts of basic questions and answers were sent to local stations to present a summary of the work of a particular federal agency by interviewing local agency staff. After transfer to the Office of Education, *United States Government Reports* became, at Roosevelt's suggestion, national rather than local in focus, and programs were distributed on transcription disks.
10 Sayre, *An Analysis of the Radiobroadcasting Activities of Federal Agencies*, 75; "Bob Berger Unaffected," *Variety*, January 24, 1940, 26. Funding for the radio operations of the Office of Government Reports was also cut in early 1940; *Variety* quoted Republican senator Everett Dirksen as saying its transcription programs were "claptrap and tommyrot" and the organization "nothing but a political bureau."
11 *Hearings before the Subcommittee of the Committee on Appropriations, House of Representatives, on the Department of Labor—Federal Security Agency Appropriation Bill for 1941*, United States Senate, 76th Congress, 3rd session, 277–278.

12 *Hearings Before the Subcommittee of the Committee on Appropriations on HR 9007*, United States Senate, 76th Congress, 3rd Session, 230.

13 *Hearings Before the Subcommittee of the Committee on Appropriations on HR 9007*, United States Senate, 76th Congress, 3rd Session, 232, 240.

14 *Hearings Before the Subcommittee of the Committee on Appropriations on HR 9007*, United States Senate, 76th Congress, 3rd Session, 240.

15 Savage, *Broadcasting Freedom*, 55; Eva von Baum Hansl to Boutwell, May 22, 1940, Box 7, Entry 170, RG 12 Office of Education, National Archives, College Park, Maryland. Hansl, who had collaborated on *Gallant American Women*, offered in May to rally "friends of our program" in the states of the key senators to write in support of the Project.

16 Memo to Paul McNutt, "Use of Radio for National Defense," Folder 062.1, Box 156, RG 47 Social Security Administration, National Archives, College Park, Maryland.

17 United States House of Representatives, *Hearings Before the Subcommittee of the Committee on Department of Labor—Federal Security Agency Appropriation Bill for 1942* (Washington: GPO, 1941), 76–78.

18 "Receives Appropriation for Radio," *School Life* (October 1941): 4.

19 Sayre, *Radiobroadcasting Activities of Federal Agencies*, 77.

20 *Annual Report of the Commissioner of Education for the Fiscal Year Ended June 30, 1940* (Washington: GPO, 1941), 93.

21 *Annual Reports of the United States Office of Education for the fiscal year 1941–42, 1942–43* (Washington: GPO, 1943), 82.

22 Savage, *Broadcasting Freedom*.

23 Sayre, *Radiobroadcasting Activities of Federal Agencies*, 78.

24 "William D. Boutwell Dies, Consultant to Publishers," *Washington Post*, March 8, 1977, C3.

25 "John Studebaker, 102, ex-educator," *New York Times*, July 29, 1989, B17.

26 Finding Aid for the Chester S. Williams Papers, University of Oregon Libraries, http://archiveswest.orbiscascade.org/ark:/80444/xv67041.

27 "Philip H. Cohen, 80, Radio-TV Producer with Ad Agencies," *New York Times*, July 17, 1992, A22.

28 Blackwood, "Later Leaders in Education: Bess Goodykoontz: 1894–1990," 267; "Dr Effie G. Bathurst, BA '21," *Alumnus* 55, no. 4 (December 1970).

29 "Laura Vitray Dies at 70," *Washington Post*, February 5, 1963, B3.

30 "Selma G. Hirsh, 92, Humanitarian," *New York Times*, February 25, 2010, A31.

31 Ryan Ellett, *Radio Drama and Comedy Writers, 1928–1962* (Jefferson, NC: McFarland, 2017), 20.

32 Ralph Ferrin, https://www.imdb.com/name/nm0274845/.

33 Hayes, *Radio Nation*; Robles, "Shaping Mexico Lindo"; Ehrick, *Radio and the Gendered Soundscape*.

34 Battles, *Calling All Cars*; Lichty and Bohn, "Radio's 'March of Time': Dramatized News"; Meyers, "The March of Time Radio Docudrama."

35 Goodman, *Radio's Civic Ambition*, xv.

36 Boutwell to Kenneth Jones, November 24, 1939, Box 4, Entry 170, RG 12.

37 Lepore, "The Last Time Democracy Almost Died."

Bibliography

Primary Sources

ARCHIVES

Columbia Broadcasting System Radio Scripts. Manuscript Division, Library of Congress.

Commission on Freedom of the Press Records 1944–1946. Special Collections, University of Chicago Library.

Denison, Merrill Fonds. Queens University Archives, Kingston, Ontario.

DuBois, Rachel Davis Papers. Immigration Research History Center, University of Minnesota Library, Minneapolis.

Federal Communications Commission (FCC) Records, Record Group 173. National Archives, College Park, Maryland.

Grierson, John Archive. University of Stirling, Scotland.

Inman, Samuel Guy Papers. Manuscript Division, Library of Congress.

National Broadcasting Company (NBC) Records, 1921–1976. Wisconsin Historical Society, Madison.

Office of Education Records, Record Group 12. National Archives, College Park, Maryland.

Office of Education Records, Record Group 12. Radio Project-WPA Photographs, 12-E-32, Box 39. Still Pictures Branch, National Archives, College Park, Maryland.

Roosevelt, Franklin D. President's Personal File (PPF 2896). Franklin D. Roosevelt Presidential Library, Hyde Park, New York.

Social Security Administration Records, Record Group 47, National Archives, College Park, Maryland.

Williams, Chester S. Papers, Special Collections, University of Oregon Library, Eugene.

BROADCAST RECORDINGS

Americans All, Immigrants All. Episodes 2–26. https://www.wnyc.org/series /americans-all-immigrants-all/1.

Brave New World. "The Beloved Ruler of Brazil" and "The Schoolmaster President." Audio Recordings 12-24 and 12-25, Office of Education Records. Motion Pictures, Sound and Video Branch, National Archives, College Park, Maryland.

Cavalcade of America. "Railroad Builders," CBS, April 14, 1936. https://archive.org
/details/COA_OTRR_Cert_CD1/Calv360415028RailroadBuilders.mp3.

Democracy in Action. Audio recordings from the Milo Ryan Phonoarchive at the
library of the University of Washington, Seattle.

The March of Time. CBS, April 4, 1935.

The March of Time. CBS, January 18, 1937.

Pleasantdale Folks. Audio recordings 196–29 SSB, Social Security Board Records.
Motion Pictures, Sound and Video Branch, National Archives, College Park.

Wings for the Martins. Audio Recordings 106–240 to 106–251, Smithsonian Institution Records. Motion Pictures, Sound and Video Branch. National Archives,
College Park, Maryland.

Secondary Sources

Aitken, Ian. *The Documentary Film Movement: An Anthology*. Edinburgh: Edinburgh
University Press, 1998.

Aitken, Rob. "'An Instrument for Reaching into Experience': Progressive Film at the
Rockefeller Boards, 1934–1945." *Journal of Historical Sociology* 30, no. 2 (2017):
284–314.

Allen, Robert C. *Speaking of Soap Operas*. Chapel Hill: University of North Carolina
Press, 1985.

Amenta, Edwin. *When Movements Matter: The Townsend Plan and the Rise of Social
Security*. Princeton, NJ: Princeton University Press, 2006.

Arnheim, Rudolf. *Radio: An Art of Sound*. London: Faber and Faber, 1936.

Barnouw, Erik. *A History of Broadcasting in the United States, Volume II, The Golden
Web, 1933 to 1953*. New York: Oxford University Press, 1985.

———. *Radio Drama in Action: Twenty-Five Plays of a Changing World*. New York:
Farrar & Rinehart, 1945.

Bathurst, Effie G. WorldCat Identities. Accessed January 3, 2020, http://worldcat.org
/identities/lccn-n85120208/.

Battles, Kathleen. *Calling All Cars: Radio Dragnets and the Technology of Policing*.
Minneapolis: University of Minnesota Press, 2010.

Bender, Pennee. "Film as an Instrument of the Good Neighbor Policy, 1930s–1950s."
PhD diss., New York University, 2002.

Bernstein, Michael A. "Why the Great Depression Was Great: Toward a New
Understanding of the Interwar Economic Crisis in the US." In *The Rise and Fall of
the New Deal Order, 1930–1980*, edited by Steve Fraser and Gary Gerstle, 32–54.
Princeton, NJ: Princeton University Press, 1989.

Billig, Michael. *Banal Nationalism*. New York: Sage, 1995.

Billings, Joshua, Felix Budelmann, and Fiona Macintosh, eds. "Introduction." In
Choruses, Ancient and Modern, edited by Joshua Billings, Felix Budelmann, and
Fiona Macintosh, 1–11. Oxford: Oxford University Press, 2013.

Black, George. *The Good Neighbor: How the United States Wrote the History of Central
America and the Caribbean*. New York: Pantheon Books, 1988.

Blackwood, Paul E. "Later Leaders in Education: Bess Goodykoontz: 1894–1990."
Childhood Education 67, no. 4 (1991): 265–270.

Bluem, A. William. *Documentary in American Television*. New York: Hastings, 1965.

Boutwell, William D. "The Educational Radio Project of the Office of Education."

Presented at the National Conference on Educational Broadcasting, Chicago, November 29, 1937.

———. "Letters from Listeners Explode a Radio Myth." *New York Times*, April 11, 1937.

———. "New History Plays Devised for Radio." *New York Times*, October 31, 1937, 51.

———. "SI Had Early Role in Saving Broadcast Channels for Public," *Smithsonian Torch* No. 76–1 (January 1976): 6.

Boyer, John W. *The University of Chicago: A History.* Chicago: University of Chicago Press, 2015.

"Brave New World." *Education by Radio* 7, no. 11 (1937): 54.

Brenner, Talia. "Radio's Democratic Promise: Aspirations for Historical Radio Dramas, 1930–1943." Senior thesis (AB), Brown University, 2019.

Brinkley, Alan. *Voices of Protest: Huey Long, Father Coughlin, and the Great Depression.* New York: Vintage, 2011.

Brown, James A. "Struggle against Commercialism: The 1934 'Harney Lobby' for Nonprofit Frequency Allocations." *Journal of Broadcasting & Electronic Media* 33, no. 3 (Summer 1989): 273–291.

Burkholder, Zoë. *Color in the Classroom: How American Schools Taught Race, 1900–1954.* New York: Oxford University Press, 2011.

Cándida Smith, Richard. *Improvised Continent: Pan-Americanism and Cultural Exchange.* Philadelphia: University of Pennsylvania Press, 2017.

Carson, Saul. "Notes Toward an Examination of Radio Documentary," *Hollywood Quarterly* 4, no. 1 (1949): 69–74.

Casey, Clifford B. "The Creation and Development of the Pan American Union." *Hispanic American Historical Review* 13, no. 4 (1933): 437–456.

Castañeda, Ernesto. *Building Walls: Excluding Latin People in the United States.* Lanham, MD: Rowman & Littlefield, 2019.

Chion, Michel. *Sound: An Acoulogical Treatise.* Durham, NC: Duke University Press, 2016.

Cohen, Philip. "Documentary Radio," *Education by Radio* 9, no. 3 (May 1939): 1.

Coontz, Stephanie. *The Way We Never Were: American Families and the Nostalgia Trap.* New York: Basic Books, 1992.

Craig, Douglas B. *Fireside Politics: Radio and Political Culture in the United States, 1920–1940.* Baltimore: Johns Hopkins University Press, 2000.

Creel, George. *How We Advertised America.* New York: Harper & Brothers, 1920.

Crisell, Andrew. *An Introductory History of British Broadcasting.* London: Psychology Press, 2002.

Crispin, George Atwood. "Rachel Davis Dubois: Founder of the Group Conversation as an Adult Educational Facilitator for Reducing Intercultural Strife." D. Ed. diss., Temple University, 1987.

Crook, Tim. *Radio Drama: Theory and Practice.* New York: Routledge, 1999.

Dawson, Howard A. "The Federal Government and Education." *Journal of Educational Sociology* 12, no. 4 (1938): 226–243.

Day, Randal D., and Wade C. Mackey. "Role Image of the American Father: An Examination of a Media Myth." *Journal of Comparative Family Studies* 17, no. 3 (1986): 371–388.

De Grazia, Victoria. *How Fascism Ruled Women: Italy, 1922–1945.* Berkeley: University of California Press, 1992.

Demos, John. "The Changing Faces of Fatherhood." In *Father and Child: Developmental and Clinical Perspectives*, edited by Stanley H. Cath, Alan R. Gurwitt, and John Munder Ross, 425–450. Boston: Little, Brown, 1982.

Desjardins, Mary R. *Father Knows Best*. Detroit: Wayne State University Press, 2015.

"Documentary Programs." *Education on the Air: Yearbook of the Institute for Education by Radio*. Columbus: Ohio State University, 1941, 245–246.

Doenecke, Justus D., and John E. Wilz. *From Isolation to War: 1931–1941*. New York: John Wiley & Sons, 2015.

Doerksen, Clifford John. *American Babel: Rogue Radio Broadcasters of the Jazz Age*. Philadelphia: University of Pennsylvania Press, 2005.

Dossett, Kate. "Gender and the Dies Committee Hearings on the Federal Theatre Project." *Journal of American Studies* 47, no. 4 (2013): 993–1017.

Douglas, Susan J. *Listening In: Radio and the American Imagination*. New York: Times Books, 1999.

Druick, Zoë. *Projecting Canada: Government Policy and Documentary Film at the National Film Board*. Montreal: McGill-Queen's University Press, 2007.

Druick, Zoë, and Jonathan Kahana. "New Deal Documentary and the North Atlantic Welfare State." In *The Documentary Film Book*, edited by Brian Wilson, 153–159. Basingstoke: Palgrave Macmillan, 2013.

DuBois, Rachel Davis. "Adventures in Intercultural Education." PhD diss., New York University, 1940.

———. "Sharing Culture Values." *Journal of Educational Sociology* 12, no. 8 (1939): 482–486.

DuBois, Rachel Davis, and Corann Okorodudu. *All This and Something More: Pioneering in Intercultural Education, an Autobiography*. Bryn Mawr, PA: Dorrance, 1984.

Dunning, John. *On the Air: The Encyclopedia of Old-Time Radio*. New York: Oxford University Press, 1998.

Duranti, Marco. "Utopia, Nostalgia and World War at the 1939–40 New York World's Fair." *Journal of Contemporary History* 41, no. 4 (2006): 663–683.

Ehrick, Christine. *Radio and the Gendered Soundscape: Women and Broadcasting in Argentina and Uruguay, 1930–1950*. New York: Cambridge University Press, 2015.

Ehrlich, Matthew C. *Radio Utopia: Postwar Audio Documentary in the Public Interest*. Urbana: University of Illinois Press, 2011.

Elder, Kathryn. "The Legacy of John Grierson." *Journal of Canadian Studies* 21, no. 4 (1986–1987): 153–154.

Ellett, Ryan. *Radio Drama and Comedy Writers, 1928–1962*. Jefferson, NC: McFarland, 2017.

Ellis, Jack C. *The Documentary Idea: A Critical History of English-Language Documentary Film and Video*. Englewood Cliffs, NJ: Prentice Hall, 1989.

Ewen, Stuart. *PR: A Social History of Spin*. New York: Basic Books, 1996.

Fejes, Fred. *Imperialism, Media, and the Good Neighbor: New Deal Foreign Policy and United States Shortwave Broadcasting to Latin America*. Norwood, NJ: Ablex, 1986.

Fleegler, Robert L. *Ellis Island Nation: Immigration Policy and American Identity in the Twentieth Century*. Philadelphia: University of Pennsylvania Press, 2015.

Foucault, Michel. *The Foucault Effect: Studies in Governmentality*. Chicago: University of Chicago Press, 1991.

Fox, Elizabeth, and Silvio R. Waisbord, eds. *Latin Politics, Global Media*. Austin: University of Texas Press, 2002.

Frank, Lawrence K. "The Beginnings of Child Development and Family Life Education in the Twentieth Century." *Merrill-Palmer Quarterly of Behavior and Development* 8, no. 4 (1962): 207–227.

Goldin, Claudia. "The Quiet Revolution That Transformed Women's Employment, Education, and Family." *American Economic Review* 96, no. 2 (2006): 1–21.

Goodman, David. *Radio's Civic Ambition: American Broadcasting and Democracy in the 1930s*. New York: Oxford University Press, 2011.

Gordon, Linda. *Women, the State, and Welfare*. Madison: University of Wisconsin Press, 1990.

Grant, Julia. "A 'Real Boy' and Not a Sissy: Gender, Childhood, and Masculinity, 1890–1940." *Journal of Social History* 37, no. 4 (2004): 829–851.

Grant, Mary [Julia]. "Modernizing Motherhood: Child Study Clubs and the Parent Education Movement, 1915–1940." PhD diss., Boston University, 1992.

Green, David. *The Containment of Latin America: A History of the Myths and Realities of the Good Neighbor Policy*. Chicago: Quadrangle Books, 1971.

Grierson, John. "The Documentary Idea." In *The Documentary Film Movement: An Anthology*, edited by Ian Aitken, 103–114. Edinburgh: Edinburgh University Press, 1998 [1942].

Harrell, Charles T. "The Library of Congress Radio Research Project," *ALA Bulletin* 35 (1941): 448–452.

Harris, Neil. *Humbug: The Art of P.T. Barnum*. Chicago: University of Chicago Press, 1981.

Hawley, Ellis W. "Herbert Hoover, the Commerce Secretariat, and the Vision of an 'Associative State,' 1921–1928." *Journal of American History* 61, no. 1 (1974): 116–140.

Hayes, Joy Elizabeth. "Did Herbert Hoover Broadcast the First Fireside Chat? Rethinking the Origins of Roosevelt's Radio Genius." *Journal of Radio Studies* 7, no. 1 (2000): 76–92.

———. *Radio Nation: Communication, Popular Culture, and Nationalism in Mexico, 1920–1950*. Tucson: University of Arizona Press, 2000.

———. "White Noise: Performing the White, Middle-Class Family on 1930s Radio." *Cinema Journal* 51, no. 3 (2012): 97–118.

Hendy, David. "Afterword: Radio Modernisms: Features, Cultures and the BBC." *Media History* 24, no. 2 (2018): 283–287.

Herzog, Herta. "On Borrowed Experience: An Analysis of Listening to Daytime Sketches." In *Mass Communication and American Social Thought: Key Texts, 1919–1968*, edited by John Durham Peters and Peter Simonson, 139–157. Lanham, MD: Rowman & Littlefield, 2004.

Hight, Charles. "All Cultures Matter: Rachel Davis DuBois, the Intercultural Education and Group Conversation Methods." PhD diss., Georgia State University, 2020.

Hilmes, Michele. "Invisible Men: Amos 'n Andy and the Roots of Broadcast Discourse." *Critical Studies in Media Communication* 10, no. 4 (1993): 301–321.

———. "NBC and the Network Idea: Defining the American System." In *NBC: America's Network*, edited by Michele Hilmes and Michael Henry, 7–24. Berkeley: University of California Press, 2007.

——— . *Network Nations: A Transnational History of British and American Broadcasting*. New York: Routledge, 2011.

——— . *Radio Voices: American Broadcasting, 1922–1952*. Minneapolis: University of Minnesota Press, 1997.

Hogarth, David. "The Other Documentary Tradition: Early Radio Documentaries in Canada." *Historical Journal of Film, Radio and Television* 21, no. 2 (2001): 123–135.

Horten, Gerd. *Radio Goes to War: The Cultural Politics of Propaganda during World War II*. Berkeley: University of California Press, 2003.

Johnson, Ann, and Elizabeth Johnston. "Up the Years with the Bettersons: Gender and Parent Education in Interwar America." *History of Psychology* 18, no. 3 (2015): 252–269.

Johnson, Robert David. "Anti-Imperialism and the Good Neighbour Policy: Ernest Gruening and Puerto Rican Affairs, 1934–1939." *Journal of Latin American Studies* 29, no. 1 (1997): 89–110.

Jones, J. Morris. *Americans All, Immigrants All: A Handbook for Listeners*. Washington D.C.: Federal Radio Education Committee, 1939.

Kammen, Michael G. *The Lively Arts: Gilbert Seldes and the Transformation of Cultural Criticism in the United States*. New York: Oxford University Press, 1996.

Kasson, Joy S. *Buffalo Bill's Wild West: Celebrity, Memory and Popular History*. New York: Hill and Wang, 2000.

Katznelson, Ira. *Fear Itself: The New Deal and the Origins of Our Time*. New York: W. W. Norton & Company, 2013.

Kessler-Harris, Alice. *Gendering Labor History*. Urbana: University of Illinois Press, 2007.

——— . "In the Nation's Image: The Gendered Limits of Social Citizenship in the Depression Era." *Journal of American History* 86, no. 3 (1999): 1251–1279.

LaRossa, Ralph. *The Modernization of Fatherhood: A Social and Political History*. Chicago: University of Chicago Press, 1997.

LaRossa, Ralph, Betty Anne Gordon, Ronald Jay Wilson, Annette Bairan, and Charles Jaret. "The Fluctuating Image of the 20th Century American Father." *Journal of Marriage and Family* 53, no. 4 (1991): 987–997.

Larsen, Solana. "The Anti-immigration Movement: From Shovels to Suits." *NACLA Report on the Americas* 40, no. 3 (2007): 14–18.

Lazarsfeld, Paul Felix. *Radio and the Printed Page: An Introduction to the Study of Radio and Its Role in the Communication of Ideas*. New York: Duell, Sloan & Pearce, 1940.

Leach, Eugene E. "Tuning Out Education: The Cooperation Doctrine in Radio, 1922–38." *Current* (August 1983): 1–19.

Lee, Mordecai. *The First Presidential Communications Agency: FDR's Office of Government Reports*. Albany: State University of New York Press, 2005.

Leibman, Nina C. *Living Room Lectures: The Fifties Family in Film and Television*. Austin: University of Texas Press, 1995.

Lepore, Jill. "The Last Time Democracy Almost Died," *New Yorker*, February 3, 2020, https://www.newyorker.com/magazine/2020/02/03/the-last-time-democracy -almost-died.

Lewis, Peter M. "'A Claim to Be Heard': Voices of Ordinary People in BBC Radio Features." *Revue Française de Civilisation Britannique*. 26, no. 1 (2021): 1–13.

Lichty, Lawrence, and Thomas W. Bohn. "Radio's 'March of Time': Dramatized News." *Journalism Quarterly* 51, no. 3 (1974): 458–462.

Lipsitz, George. "The Meaning of Memory: Family, Class and Ethnicity in Early Network Television Programs." *Camera Obscura* 6, no. 1 (1988): 78–116.

———. *The Possessive Investment in Whiteness: How White People Profit from Identity Politics*. Philadelphia: Temple University Press, 2018.

———. "The Possessive Investment in Whiteness: Racialized Social Democracy and the "White" Problem in American Studies." *American Quarterly* 47, no. 3 (1995): 369–387.

Lohmeyer, Donnasue, and Ralph H. Ojemann. "The Effectiveness of Selected Methods of Radio Education at the School Level." *Journal of Experimental Education* 9, no. 2 (1940): 119–120.

Lomax, Elizabeth. "The Laura Spelman Rockefeller Memorial: Some of Its Contributions to Early Research in Child Development." *Journal of the History of the Behavioral Sciences* 13, no. 3 (1977): 283–293.

Lovell, Terry. "Ideology and *Coronation Street*." In *Coronation Street*, edited by Richard Dyer, 40–52. London: British Film Institute, 1981.

MacDonald, J. Fred. "Soap Operas as a Social Force." In *Don't Touch That Dial!: Radio Programming in American Life, 1920–1960*. Chicago: Nelson-Hall, 1979, 231–280.

Mandler, Peter. *Return from the Natives: How Margaret Mead Won the Second World War and Lost the Cold War*. New Haven, CT: Yale University Press, 2013.

Marc, David. "Origins of the Genre: In Search of the Radio Sitcom." In *The Sitcom Reader America Viewed and Skewed*, edited by Mary M. Dalton and Laura R. Linder, 15–24. Albany: State University of New York Press, 2005.

Marchand, Roland. *Creating the Corporate Soul: The Rise of Public Relations and Corporate Imagery in American Big Business*. Berkeley: University of California Press, 1998.

Margolis, Maxine L. *Mothers and Such: Views of American Women and Why They Changed*. Berkeley: University of California Press, 1984.

Marino, Katherine M. "Transnational Pan-American Feminism: The Friendship of Bertha Lutz and Mary Wilhelmine Williams, 1926–1944." *Journal of Women's History* 26, no. 2 (2014): 63–87.

May, Elaine Tyler. *Homeward Bound: American Families in the Cold War Era*. New York: Basic Books, 2008.

McCarthy, Anna. *The Citizen Machine: Governing by Television in 1950s America*. New York: New Press, 2010.

McChesney, Robert W. *Telecommunications, Mass Media, and Democracy: The Battle for the Control of U.S. Broadcasting, 1928–1935*. New York: Oxford University Press, 1993.

McClure, Lisa J. "Helen K. Mackintosh: Expanding the Concept of Our World." In *Missing Chapters: Ten Pioneering Women in NCTE and English Education*, edited by Jeanne Marcum Gerlach and Virginia R. Monseau, 186–201. National Council of Teachers of English, 1991.

McFadden, Margaret T. "'America's Boy Friend Who Can't Get a Date': Gender, Race, and the Cultural Work of the Jack Benny Program, 1932–1946." *Journal of American History* 80, no. 1 (1993): 113–134.

McGill, Earle. *Radio Directing*. New York: McGraw-Hill, 1940.

McGuire, John. "'The Most Unjust Piece of Legislation': Section 213 of the Economy Act of 1932 and Feminism During the New Deal." *Journal of Policy History* 20, no. 4 (2008): 516–541.

McPherson, Alan. "Herbert Hoover, Occupation Withdrawal, and the Good Neighbor Policy." *Presidential Studies Quarterly* 44, no. 4 (2014): 623–639.

Melosh, Barbara. *Engendering Culture: Manhood and Womanhood in New Deal Public Art and Theater.* Washington, DC: Smithsonian Institution Press, 1991.

Meyers, Cynthia B. "The March of Time Radio Docudrama: Time Magazine, BBDO, and Radio Sponsors, 1931–39." *American Journalism* 35, no. 4 (Fall 2018): 420–443.

———. *A Word from Our Sponsor Admen, Advertising, and the Golden Age of Radio.* New York: Fordham University Press, 2014.

Milkie, Melissa A., and Kathleen E. Denny. "Changes in the Cultural Model of Father Involvement: Descriptions of Benefits to Fathers, Children, and Mothers in Parents' Magazine, 1926–2006." *Journal of Family Issues* 35, no. 2 (2014): 223–253.

Milkman, Ruth. "Women's Work and Economic Crisis: Some Lessons of the Great Depression." In *On Gender, Labor, and Inequality.* Urbana: University of Illinois Press, 2016, 13–46.

Mink, Gwendolyn. *The Wages of Motherhood: Inequality in the Welfare State, 1917–1942.* Ithaca: Cornell University Press, 1995.

Mintz, Steven, and Susan Kellogg. *Domestic Revolutions: A Social History of American Family Life.* New York: Free Press; Collier Macmillan, 1988.

Mittell, Jason. *Genre and Television: From Cop Shows to Cartoons in American Culture.* New York: Routledge, 2004.

Modleski, Tania. *Loving with a Vengeance: Mass-Produced Fantasies for Women.* Second edition. New York: Routledge, 2008.

Montalto, Nicholas V. "The Forgotten Dream: A History of the Intercultural Education Movement, 1924–1941." PhD diss., University of Minnesota, 1977.

———. "The Intercultural Education Movement, 1924–41." In *American Education and the European Immigrant: 1840–1940,* edited by Bernard J. Weiss, 142–160. Urbana: University of Illinois Press, 1982.

National Association of Broadcasters. *How to Use Radio in the Classroom.* Washington, DC: National Association of Broadcasters, 1939.

Newcomb, Horace. *TV: The Most Popular Art.* New York: Anchor Books, 1974.

Nichols, Bill. *Introduction to Documentary.* Third edition. Bloomington: Indiana University Press, 2017.

Nochimson, Martha. *No End to Her: Soap Opera and the Female Subject.* Berkeley: University of California Press, 1992.

Norris, Renfro Cole. "A History of 'La Hora Nacional': Government Broadcasting via Privately Owned Radio Stations in Mexico." PhD diss., University of Michigan, 1963.

Orloff, Ann Shola. "The Political Origins of America's Belated Welfare State." In *The Politics of Social Policy in the United States,* edited by Margaret Weir, Ann Shola Orloff, and Theda Skocpol, 37–80. Princeton, NJ: Princeton University Press, 1988.

Ortiz Garza, José Luis. *México en Guerra.* Mexico City: Planeta, 1989.

Paget, Derek. *No Other Way to Tell It: Docudrama on Film and Television.* Second edition. Manchester: Manchester University Press, 2016.

Paget, Derek, and Steven N. Lipkin. "'Movie-of-the-Week' Docudrama, 'Historical-Event' Television, and the Steven Spielberg series Band of Brothers," *New Review of Film and Television Studies* 7, no. 1 (2009): 93–107.

Patterson, James T. *Congressional Conservatism and the New Deal: The Growth of the Conservative Coalition in Congress, 1933–1939.* Westport, CT: Greenwood Press, 1981 [1967].

Perkins, Frances. *The Roosevelt I Knew*. New York: Penguin, 2011 [1946].

Picciano, Anthony G., and Joel Spring. *The Great American Education-Industrial Complex: Ideology, Technology, and Profit*. London: Taylor & Francis Group, 2013.

Pickard, Victor. "Communication's Forgotten Narratives: The Lost History of Charles Siepmann and Critical Policy Research." *Critical Studies in Media Communication* 33, no. 4 (October 2016): 337–351.

Poole, Mary. *The Segregated Origins of Social Security: African Americans and the Welfare State*. Chapel Hill: University of North Carolina Press, 2006.

Rapping, Elaine. *The Movie of the Week: Private Stories, Public Events*. Minneapolis: University of Minnesota Press, 1992.

Ray, Angela G. *The Lyceum and Public Culture in the Nineteenth Century United States*. East Lansing: Michigan State University Press, 2005.

Razlogova, Elena. *The Listener's Voice: Early Radio and the American Public*. Philadelphia: University of Pennsylvania Press, 2011.

Reiman, Richard A. *The New Deal and American Youth: Ideas and Ideals in a Depression Decade*. Athens: University of Georgia Press, 1992.

Revermann, Martin. "Brechtian Chorality." In *Choruses, Ancient and Modern* edited by Joshua Billings, Felix Budelmann, and Fiona Macintosh, 151–169. Oxford: Oxford University Press, 2013.

Ribuffo, Leo P. *The Old Christian Right: The Protestant Far Right from the Great Depression to the Cold War*. Philadelphia: Temple University Press, 1983.

Robles, Sonia. "Shaping Mexico Lindo: Radio, Music, and Gender in Greater Mexico, 1923–1946." PhD diss., Michigan State University, 2012.

Rogers, Holly, ed. *Music and Sound in Documentary Film*. New York: Routledge, 2015.

Rosenberg, Emily. *Spreading the American Dream: American Economic and Cultural Expansion, 1890–1945*. New York: Macmillan, 1982.

Rosenberg, Jan. *Intercultural Education, Folklore, and the Pedagogical Thought of Rachel Davis Dubois*. Cham, Switzerland: Palgrave Macmillan, 2019.

Rowland, Allison L., and Peter Simonson. "The Founding Mothers of Communication Research: Toward a History of a Gendered Assemblage." *Critical Studies in Media Communication* 31, no. 1 (2014): 3–26.

Rugg, Harold. *Our Country and Our People: An Introduction to American Civilization*. Boston: Ginn and Company, 1938.

Russo, Alexander. *Points on the Dial: Golden Age Radio beyond the Networks*. Durham, NC: Duke University Press, 2010.

Rydell, Robert W. "Introduction." In *Designing Tomorrow: America's World's Fairs of the 1930s*, edited by Robert W. Rydell and Laura Burd Schiavo, 1–20. New Haven, CT: Yale University Press, 2010.

Sargent, James E. "Woodrum's Economy Bloc: The Attack on Roosevelt's WPA, 1937–1939." *Virginia Magazine of History and Biography* 93, no. 2 (1985): 175–207.

Savage, Barbara Dianne. *Broadcasting Freedom: Radio, War, and the Politics of Race, 1938–1948*. Chapel Hill: University of North Carolina Press, 1999.

Sayre, Jeanette. *An Analysis of the Radiobroadcasting Activities of Federal Agencies*. Cambridge, MA: Littauer Center, Harvard University, 1941.

Scannell, Paddy. "Radio Documentary from Profession to Apparatus." *Prix Italia: The Quest for Radio Quality: The Documentary* (1996): 33–40.

———. "'The Stuff of Radio': Developments in Radio Features and Documentaries before the War." In *Documentary and the Mass Media*, edited by John Corner, 1–26. London: Edward Arnold, 1986.

Scharf, Lois. *To Work and to Wed: Female Employment, Feminism, and the Great Depression*. Westport, CT: Greenwood Press, 1980.

Schlossman, Steven. "Perils of Popularization: The Founding of Parents' Magazine." *Monographs of the Society for Research in Child Development* 50, no. 4–5 (1986): 65–77.

Schoenwald, Jonathan M. "Brunauer, Esther (1901–1959), international affairs specialist and State Department official." In *American National Biography*. February 1, 2000. Accessed May 9 2021, https://doi.org/10.1093/anb/9780198606697.article.0700039

Schwoch, James. *The American Radio Industry and Its Latin American Activities, 1900–1939*. Urbana, University of Illinois Press, 1990.

Seeber, Frances M. "Eleanor Roosevelt and Women in the New Deal: A Network of Friends." *Presidential Studies Quarterly* 20, no. 4 (1990): 707–717.

Selig, Diana. *Americans All: The Cultural Gifts Movement*. Cambridge, MA: Harvard University Press, 2008.

Shepperd, Josh. "Infrastructure in the Air: The Office of Education and the Development of Public Broadcasting in the United States, 1934–1944." *Critical Studies in Media Communication* 31, no. 3 (2014): 230–243.

Siepmann, Charles A. "Can Radio Educate?" *Journal of Educational Sociology* 14, no. 6 (1941): 346–357.

Singhal, Arvind, Michael J. Cody, Everett M. Rogers, and Miguel Sabido, eds. *Entertainment-Education and Social Change: History, Research, and Practice*. New York: Routledge, 2003.

Singhal, Arvind, Rafael Obregon, and Everett M. Rogers. "Reconstructing the Story of *Simplemente Maria*, the Most Popular Telenovela in Latin America of All Time." *International Communication Gazette* 54, no. 1 (1995): 1–15.

Slotten, Hugh Richard. *Radio's Hidden Voice: The Origins of Public Broadcasting in the United States*. Urbana: University of Illinois Press, 2009.

Sneed, Edgar P. "Inman, Samuel Guy." In *Handbook of Texas Online*. November 9, 2020. Accessed October 12, 2021, https://tshaonline.org/handbook/entries/inman-samuel-guy.

Sobers, Kira M. "Preserving 'The World is Yours'." Smithsonian Institution Archives (blog), January 23, 2020. Accessed 25 October 2021, https://siarchives.si.edu/blog/preserving-%E2%80%9C-world-yours%E2%80%9D.

Sood, Suruchi, Tiffany Menard, and Kim Witte. "The Theory Behind Entertainment-Education." In *Entertainment-Education and Social Change: History, Research, and Practice*, edited by Arvind Singhal, Michael J. Cody, Everett M. Rogers, and Miguel Sabido, 117–145. Mahwah, N.J.: Lawrence Erlbaum Associates, 2004.

Spellacy, Amy. "Mapping the Metaphor of the Good Neighbor: Geography, Globalism, and Pan-Americanism during the 1940s." *American Studies* 47, no. 2 (2006): 39–66.

Spigel, Lynn. *Make Room for TV: Television and the Family Ideal in Postwar America*. Chicago: University of Chicago Press, 1992.

Staiger, Janet, and Horace Newcomb. "Docudrama." In *Encyclopedia of Television*, edited by Horace Newcomb, 514–517. Second edition. Chicago: Fitzroy Dearborn, 2004.

Stott, William. *Documentary Expression and Thirties America*. Chicago: University of Chicago Press, 1986 [1973].

Swain, Martha H. "The Harrison Education Bills, 1936–1941." *Mississippi Quarterly* 31, no. 1 (1977): 119–131.

Tapia, John E. *Circuit Chautauqua: From Rural Education to Popular Entertainment in Early Twentieth Century America.* Jefferson, NC: McFarland, 1997.

Taylor, Ella. *Prime-Time Families: Television Culture in Postwar America.* Berkeley: University of California Press, 1989.

Tyrrell, Ian. *Historians in Public: The Practice of American History, 1890–1970.* Chicago: University of Chicago Press, 2005.

United States Department of State. *Inter-American Cultural Relations.* Washington, DC: GPO, 1939.

United States Department of the Interior, Office of Education. *Americans All, Immigrants All.* Washington DC: Office of Education, 1939. Accessed 25 October 2021, https://archive.org/details/americansallimmi00unit/mode/2up.

Verma, Neil. "Radio's 'Oblong Blur': Notes on the Corwinesque." *Sounding Out!* (blog), June 25, 2012. http://soundstudiesblog.com/2012/06/25/6606/.

———. *Theater of the Mind: Imagination, Aesthetics, and American Radio Drama.* Chicago: University of Chicago Press, 2012.

Wandersee, Winifred D. *Women's Work and Family Values, 1920–1940.* Cambridge, MA: Harvard University Press, 1981.

Weckbecker, Lars. "Re-Forming Vision: On the Governmentality of Griersonian Documentary Film," *Studies in Documentary Film* 9, no. 2 (2015): 172–185.

Westkaemper, Emily. *Selling Women's History: Packaging Feminism in Twentieth-Century American Popular Culture.* New Brunswick, NJ: Rutgers University Press, 2017.

Whitehead, Kate. *The Third Programme: A Literary History.* Oxford: Clarendon Press, 1988.

Widener, Nathan. "Perón's Political Radio Melodrama: Peronism and Radio Culture: 1920–1955." MA diss., Appalachian State University, 2014.

Williams, Mary Wilhelmine. "The College Course in Hispanic American History." *Hispanic American Historical Review* (1919): 415–418.

Willis, Edgar E. "The Relative Effectiveness of Three Forms of Radio Presentation in Influencing Attitudes." *Speech Monographs* 7, no. 1 (December 1940): 41–47.

Winston, Brian. *Claiming the Real: The Griersonian Documentary and Its Legitimations.* London: British Film Institute, 1995.

Wood, Bryce. *The Making of the Good Neighbor Policy.* New York: Columbia University Press, 1961.

"Work of Office of Education Division Is Expanded by Additional WPA Grant." *Broadcasting, Broadcast Advertising* 15, no. 7 (1938): 34.

Index

About the Authors

DAVID GOODMAN is professor of history at the University of Melbourne in Australia. He is the author of *Gold Seeking: Victoria and California in the 1850s* and *Radio's Civic Ambition: American Broadcasting and Democracy in the 1930s*.

JOY ELIZABETH HAYES is associate professor of communication studies at the University of Iowa. She is the author of *Radio Nation: Communication, Popular Culture, and Nationalism in Mexico, 1920–1950* and coeditor of *War of the Worlds to Social Media: Mediated Communication in Times of Crisis*.

Printed and bound by CPI Group (UK) Ltd, Croydon, CR0 4YY

09/06/2025

14685727-0001